Jason R. Dunn
Digital media expert

Microsoft®

T3-ANT-325

Faster Smarter

Digital Video

Take charge of digital video technologies—
faster, smarter, *better*!

PUBLISHED BY
Microsoft Press
A Division of Microsoft Corporation
One Microsoft Way
Redmond, Washington 98052-6399

Library of Congress Cataloging-in-Publication Data
Dunn, Jason R.
        Faster Smarter Digital Video / Jason R. Dunn.
            p. cm.
        Includes bibliographical references and index.
        ISBN 0-7356-1873-9
            1. Digital cinematography--Handbooks, manuals, etc.   2. Digital
        video--Editing--Handbooks, manuals, etc.   I. Title.

        TR860 .D86   2002
        778.5'3--dc21   2002033728

Printed and bound in the United States of America.

1 2 3 4 5 6 7 8 9   QWE   8 7 6 5 4 3

Distributed in Canada by H.B. Fenn and Company Ltd.

A CIP catalogue record for this book is available from the British Library.

Microsoft Press books are available through booksellers and distributors worldwide. For further information about international editions, contact your local Microsoft Corporation office or contact Microsoft Press International directly at fax (425) 936-7329. Visit our Web site at www.microsoft.com/mspress. Send comments to *mspinput@microsoft.com*.

Acquisitions Editor: Hilary Long
Project Editor: Aileen Wrothwell
Series Editor: Kristen Weatherby

Body Part No. X08-99934

I dedicate this book to my wife, Ashley. Her patience, grace and support made the impossible deadlines seem possible. Without her encouragement, this book would not have been finished in time—thanks for the inspiration, Ash! I also dedicate this book to you, the reader—the world of digital video is an exciting one, and it's my dearest wish that this book will be a helpful guide as you jump in and start creating, capturing, and sharing all the precious memories life has to offer.

Table of Contents

Part I: Getting Started

You say you don't know anything about digital video? No problem! In the first section, I'll walk you through the basics: what digital video is all about, how it's used today, what kinds of tools Windows XP gives you to work with it, and what all that confusing terminology means. I'll also cover how to pick the right digital video camera for your needs—whether you're a beginner looking for your first camera or an intermediate user looking for a high-end camera, I'll show you what to look for.

Part II: Capturing

Once you have your digital video camera, it's time to start using it! This section covers getting familiar with the functions on your camera and having a plan for getting great footage. I also cover what
kind of computer hardware you need in order to have a painless video editing experience, what to
look for when you're shopping, and what the best solutions are. And once you have that footage, I'll
teach you how to transfer it onto your computer so you can begin to craft your masterpiece.

Part III: Editing

What's another word for unedited video? "Boring." In this section I'll cover both basic and advanced video-editing software suites, with a few detailed step-by-step walkthroughs to get you on the right path. Want to rip a song from an audio CD and make it a part of your video? I'll show you how. This section also looks at some of the newest software on the market and how it will help you to make your imagination a reality.

Part IV: Sharing

Now that you have your final product, how do you share it with others? In the final section, I'll cover methods to share your video digitally: using e-mail, uploading it to a Web site, or sending it over an instant messaging application. Want a keepsake you can share with others? Burning your project to a CD or DVD is covered, including a step-by-step procedure for making your own professional-quality DVD with a menu system. Confused about the difference between DVD-R and DVD+R? It's all covered in this section.

Acknowledgments

Many people helped this project come together. Hilary, thank you for having faith in me and believing in my ability to write this book. You were a great sounding board for ideas and concepts, and I appreciated your encouragement and patience. Aileen, you're a great editor, and your guidance and motivation helped me get it all finished in time. Alex, we're going to do a book together someday!

To all the great vendors who sent me products on short deadlines and answered my many questions: Canon, Sony, Panasonic, Adaptec, Apple, Pioneer Electronics, Henry's, Pinnacle, D-Link, Iogear, Tiffen, Sonic Solutions, Orange Micro, Maxtor, Intervideo, ADS Technologies, PoGo!, Roxio, Western Digital, Crucial Technology, Adobe, Intel, ACD Systems, DivX Networks, VFXPlug, Powerquest, muvee Technologies, Kingston, Sonic Desktop, Main Concept, Voodoo Computers, Boris FX, Pegasys Inc., Ahead Software, ScenaLyzer, Sonic Foundry, Logitech, and Ulead Systems.

Special thanks to the people at some of the above companies who went above and beyond the call of duty to assist me: Andy and Linda at Pinnacle, Shelly at Crucial Technology, Timo and Steve at nVidia, Christina at ADS Technologies, Fiona and Jeff at Intel, Philip & the team at muvee Technologies, Joanne at ACD Systems, Mandi and Wayne at Canon, Allison at Panasonic, Steve at Sonic Foundry, and Susan at Logitech.

To the Windows Media Team guys: Seth McEvoy, Matt Calder, and Mark Galiotio—thanks for the tech support!

To my team at Pocket PC Thoughts – Ed Hansberry, Brad Adrian, Marlof Bregonje, Andy Sjostrom, and Steven Cedrone. Thanks for picking up the slack on the Web site while I focused on the book. The site wouldn't be the same without you! To all Thoughts readers, thanks for sharing me with this book project—I hope the new site was worth the wait!

Thanks to the digital-video loving people in the public newsgroups. Jerry Jones, thanks for the fast answers to my questions. PapaJohn, RGBaker, FLY135—I learned a lot from your great responses in the newsgroup. Thanks for sharing your knowledge.

The support of my friends and family were important to me during this project—I lost count of how many family and church events I lugged my laptop to in order to meet the deadlines on this book, and I thank each and every one of them for being gracious with my obsession to get this book exactly right.

Finally, and most importantly, thank you to the Creator who gives me strength and passion to strive for great things. VIRTUTIS GLORIA MERCES.

Introduction

In this book I've only scratched the surface of what's possible, but it's my sincere wish that as you read, your imagination will be fired up to try new things and explore what you find interesting. What makes me excited about working on this book is the current state of the computer industry: we've finally reached the point where fast CPUs and huge hard drives are available in almost every machine sold. The tools for working with digital video are finally affordable—a digital video camera can be had for under a thousand dollars, and as long as you have a fairly recent computer, you probably have everything you need to get started.

Another factor worth getting excited about is the way in which various technologies have come together to create powerful but easy to use solutions. I can't think of a better example than a product called the Bungee DVD (*www.pinnaclesys.com*). The Bungee DVD is an unassuming blue box that lets you do some incredible things. For a relatively small amount, you can buy this product, connect it to your computer, watch TV on your PC, record that signal to your hard drive, and then burn it to a DVD or CD. What if the phone rings while you're watching your favorite TV show? Pause live television and watch it later—you won't miss a beat. It also offers scheduling software, turning your PC into a true digital VCR. Have some old VHS tapes with family movies you'd like to preserve? Connect your VCR to the Bungee DVD and create digital copies of those tapes. Impressive, isn't it? Various technologies have finally become affordable enough to allow tools like this to exist.

This Book Could Be For You

Even if you've never picked up a digital video camera, and don't know an MPEG from your left leg, don't worry—this book is for you. I've designed this book to be a true end-to-end solution, walking you through the important elements of digital video. It will take you through the basics of digital video terminology, which will give you the grounding to understand the later chapters. I'll cover the things you need to know when buying a new DV camera, give you tips on capturing great footage with it, and explain how to transfer that video footage to your computer. Once the footage is on your computer, I'll show you some of the great things you can do with it: edit it, add special effects, and then share it with others over the Internet or by burning it to a DVD or CD.

In order to fully take advantage of this book, you should be familiar with the basic operations on your computer, such as how to launch programs, install new software, and use the basic elements of Windows. I'm going to show you how to do everything on the Windows platform—all using Microsoft Windows XP—and that doing digital video on the Windows XP platform is equal to, if not better than, any other platform available.

As you read through this book, you'll see different elements in the text to make it easier for you to find the information you need.

- **Tip**   Snippets of useful information are presented as Tips—bite-sized bits of knowledge that are easy to understand at a glance.

- **Note**   Longer background information will be presented as Notes. This is the stuff you'll appreciate if you want a more technical explanation of things.

- **Lingo**   The digital video world is full of jargon, so word definitions will appear in the text as Lingo.

- **Caution**   Cautions to make you aware of the important things you should be cautious of—pay attention to these!

- **Try This!**   For the adventurous among you, there are elements called Try This! that give you suggestions about the kinds of things you can try on your own.

It's worth noting here that the focus of this book is firmly on the hobbyist digital video realm—if I say something isn't possible, or isn't available, I'm talking about the general consumer market. That certain something may very well be possible with an expensive piece of equipment from the professional video world, but unless it's something the average person can afford, I don't include it here as a realistic option.

System Requirements

Since this book covers so much ground in the digital video world, there are no true system requirements. You can learn a lot from this book even if you don't have a new computer capable of doing everything in it—in Chapter 5 I'll tell you how the various parts of your computer impact working with digital video. This will help you decide if you need to upgrade and whether or not you need a new system.

If you want to maximize your learning, however, ideally here's what you'll have:

- A fairly powerful computer (no more than two years old) running Windows XP Home or Professional.

- A digital video camera that uses MiniDV tapes.

- A high-speed Internet connection to download software demos, visit the Web sites I recommend, and connect to online digital video communities.

If you don't have everything on this list, don't worry—as you read this book you'll gain the knowledge you need to make purchasing decisions.

Lights, Camera, Action!

Digital video is all about possibilities: With the right tools, you can create memories, share ideas, or preserve the past. Communicating with others is a fundamental human need, and digital video allows you to share with others in ways that simply weren't possible a decade ago. Digital video opens up your world, and I hope this book will have a small part in that. I'd also encourage you to visit *www.fastersmarter.com* regularly to keep up on new developments in the digital media world—it will cover digital video, digital photography, and digital audio. And if you have any questions about the things I've covered in the book, send an e-mail to author@fastersmarter.com—I'll do what I can to help you.

Since you're holding this book in your hands, it's time to jump into Chapter 1 and get started on your journey to becoming a digital video expert. Let's go!

Support

Every effort has been made to ensure the accuracy of this book. Microsoft Press provides corrections for books at the following address:

http://mspress.microsoft.com/support/

If you have comments, questions, or ideas regarding this book, please send them to Microsoft Press via e-mail to:

mspinput@microsoft.com

or via postal mail to:

Microsoft Press
Attn: Faster Smarter Series Editor
One Microsoft Way
Redmond, WA 98052-6399

You can also contact the author directly at *author@fastersmarter.com* with any comments or suggestions.

Please note that product support is not offered through the above addresses.

Part I

Getting Started

Before grabbing a digital video camera and becoming the next Oliver Stone, there are some things you need to know about digital video. My goal in this book is to give you highly practical knowledge, with as little theoretical information as possible. The digital video world is vast, and there's an unbelievable amount of information out there—which I discovered when I started researching for this book. This first section focuses on the things I think you'll need when getting started: a basic understanding of digital video, how it's used, and what sort of things you should be looking for in a digital video camera. Even if you already know a little about digital video and own a DV camera, I'd encourage you to read this first section—you might learn a thing or two.

Chapter 1

Welcome to the World of Digital Video

Buckle your seat belt, because I'm going to take you on a journey into a realm where you probably have yet to tread. Just like that *Twilight Zone* intro, it's a journey beyond sight and sound—digital video is about a lot more than just pointing a camera at someone and hitting the Record button. Remember that feeling you got when your friend said, "We have this great two-hour vacation video that you're going to love…"? Don't be one of those people who inflict hours of boring video on his friends. Instead, by using this book, and making a small investment in new hardware and software, you'll create videos so cool you'll have people begging *you* to put on *your* vacation videos. How's that for a change? Let's go…

It's Not Just for the Digital Elite Any More…

In the world of technology, digital video has traditionally been considered a "power user" feat. Only the people with the most powerful systems, the most expensive equipment, and the most esoteric skills could possibly master the complexity of manipulating video digitally. Years ago, that was undoubtedly true. I remember my first foray into the dark realm of digital video—the year was 1997, and though it was only five short years ago, that's an eternity in the computer industry. It all started with a video card I bought for my new computer. The video card was a Matrox Mystique, a powerful card in its day, with four whole megabytes of random access memory (RAM). The card had the ability to accept an add-on card called the Matrox Rainbow Runner, which would give me the ability to capture video and edit it. I was thrilled beyond belief when I first purchased it—it was one of the first "affordable" digital video editing solutions in the consumer market. I say affordable, but it cost me a pretty penny.

The thing that was special about this setup was that unlike other video cards on the market, the Rainbow Runner would let me capture video that was high enough quality to manipulate and transfer back out to VHS tape—something that until that time was reserved only for the pros and their $10,000 computer rigs. It was nothing short of revolutionary! The problem was that, like all first-generation technology products, it was difficult to use, and the hardware available at the time simply wasn't powerful enough. Video editing was a slow and painful process, with every preview taking upwards of five minutes just to preview the effect. Every minute of video would take over an hour to work on, even with the most simple of digital effects. The seemingly spacious 9.1 gigabyte (GB) hard drive proved to be frustratingly tiny for the larger projects, and when it came time to render the video, it was a process that took upwards of 20 hours. That rendering time stretched into days if the computer crashed while rendering (which was an all-too-common occurrence). It was an exciting but frustrating time to be using digital video, and after wading through dozens of scenarios like the one described above, I gave up and left the world of digital video. I sold the software and hardware and promised myself that I'd return in a few years. Earlier this year, I did just that, and I've been wowed ever since—I'm actually having fun this time!

Today, things are very different than in 1997—we have incredibly powerful computers, huge hard drives, and sophisticated hardware and software that help us to create wonderful videos in a surprisingly short period of time. Digital video has truly come to the masses—it's now easy and affordable to capture digital video, edit it, and share it with your friends and family. Welcome to the revolution!

Digital Video in Your Daily Life

Digital video is in more places than you might realize—the ability to make fast copies of digital video, without any degradation of quality, has made it popular in a variety of scenarios. Here are just a few of the ways that you might have seen digital video being used.

On the Web

Surfing the Internet has become as common as watching TV—a few years ago if you told someone about a Web page that you found, you were probably met with a blank stare. Today, Web jargon like "URL" and "hyperlink" is quite common. Thankfully, so are high-speed Internet connections, commonly referred to as "broadband." Available in forms like cable modems, Digital Subscriber Line (DSL) modems, and even wireless satellite access, broadband is exploding in popularity. It's not quite as common as "they" said it was going to be several years ago, but it's growing in popularity.

> **Note**   What exactly is "digital video"? The easiest way to understand digital video is to understand how it's different from traditional video. When you go to a movie, you're seeing still images flashed up on the screen (usually around 29 images per second). Those still images come so quickly that your eye perceives them as moving. Remember making those little flip-books as a kid, where every page had a drawing in a slightly different position, and when you flipped through the pages quickly it seemed like they were moving? Same principle. Traditional video images are stored on a physical tape in magnetic format. Digital video, on the other hand, is a series of code (zeros and ones) that a computer interprets and displays on the screen. They remain a series of still images, just like regular video—the concept is the same, but the way in which that video is stored and played back is very different. Entire rooms of videotapes can fit on a single hard drive, and digital video will not degrade over time like regular video. Those are just some of the reasons why digital video is the format of the future!

Why is broadband so important? Without it, digital video over the Internet just doesn't work. Sure, it's technically possible to download a movie trailer on a 56K modem, but in order to view a good-quality clip (bigger than a postage stamp) of any significant length, it will take over an hour to download. Who has time for that? Broadband Internet access blows open the doors to new types of content and offers an immediacy that digital video has never before enjoyed. One thing that I still find mildly frustrating is the video resolution (size)—often even the "high-speed" clips will look quite small on a high-resolution (1280 x 1024) monitor. Hopefully, video technologies like Microsoft's 9 Series (discussed later in this chapter) will give us bigger, better-looking video. I have to give the nod to Apple for providing 320 x 240 movie trailers—when you view them in full-screen mode they look great!

Some of the places we're seeing digital video on the Web today include:

- **Movie trailers**   My wife and I are big movie fans, and when we're visiting our local movie Web site (*www.calgarymovies.com*) we frequently check out the trailers to help us decide which movie to go to. And with some sites offering Pocket PC optimized trailers (*www.pocketmovies.net*), I can carry them with me on my Pocket PC and show them to anyone who is curious about a movie. I had great fun showing off the *Star Trek: Nemesis* trailer on my Pocket PC.

- **Product and technology demonstrations**   In researching this book, I encountered several *streaming video* product demonstrations. It was a great way to learn more about the product in a more entertaining way than reading dry specification sheets. One in particular stands out: ADS Technologies (*www.adstech.com*) has a product called the USB Instant DVD. The product video told the story of a guy in a rock band who needed to make a DVD but didn't know how—the video explained the features of the product while weaving in characters and humor, making it a video that I actually wanted to watch through until the end. That's digital video that works!

Lingo   *Streaming Video.* This term is used to describe any sort of video which will start playing before it fully downloads. So rather than waiting for that large 10 MB video to completely download before you can watch it, if the file is set up to stream, you can start viewing it after only a few seconds. The video file continues to download in the background, so while you're watching the first ten seconds, it's downloading the next ten seconds.

- **News and weather**   Some news sites (*www.msnbc.com*, for example) offer top news stories and weather updates in streaming video. It's a great way to get caught up on the news that you missed from the previous night, and it's easy to listen to and work on e-mail at the same time.

■ **Sports**   Just like news, if you like sports, there are sites out there (such as *www.espn.com*) that will deliver sports news in video format. In looking around the Web, sports video news wasn't as common as I thought it would be.

■ **Educational and instructional**   Video is a wonderful medium for teaching and training. The immersive quality, the ability to pause and rewind, and being able to return later for another viewing all make digital video on the Web a winner. The Discovery Channel Web site (*www.discovery.com*) has some wonderful educational videos on a variety of topics.

■ **Movies**   Entire movies are available for download or viewing off the Web today. If you enjoy independent films and anime (sometimes called "Japanimation"), *www.sputnik7.com* is a great Web site to visit. We're not quite at the point where Hollywood feature films can be legally purchased and downloaded to our computers, but there are many companies working on solutions to that very problem. Who wants to watch entire movies on their computer? Not that many people, but it's relatively simple to connect your PC to your TV with the proper hardware. Digital video, big-screen TV—the perfect match!

■ **Webcast keynotes and meetings**   Corporations are putting keynote speeches, annual meetings, and other events up on their Web sites in video format. Missed the stockholder meeting? They might have it in digital video format.

■ **Web cam and conferencing**   Grab a couple of Web cams, some friends or family, and interact! We'll be covering Web cams in Chapter 3, "Choosing the Right Video Camera," and with the right software you can be up and running in minutes. Digital video streaming over the Internet can drastically cut down the cost of staying in touch over long distances.

Marketing and Presentations

Digital video is a great way to present information and ideas, so it's often used for marketing purposes. Many years ago during my school years, I worked at Blockbuster Video (hey, I've always loved movies!) and we'd play VHS tapes that were full of movie previews. Day in, day out—nothing but previews. After only a week or so, there would be a noticeable drop in the video playback quality. Tapes that were several months old had very poor video and audio—the tapes degraded from constant use. The same thing will happen to your home videos once they are viewed too many times. Digital video, on the other hand, remains as perfect as the original even after being played thousands of times. In a scenario like the one I described, where video is played over and over, the advantages of digital video become crystal clear.

Home Entertainment

Perhaps the most common use of digital video that you'd recognize, DVD (Digital Versatile Disc) players are now outselling VCRs. I've seen DVD players at discount stores like Costco for the same price as VCRs, so there's no excuse not to own one nowadays if you love watching movies. The quality of a DVD surpasses VHS by a wide margin, but some people won't understand the difference until they've been watching DVDs for months and go back to VHS—it then becomes obvious. Digital video is also used in some console games (Microsoft Xbox, Sony PlayStation 2) for playing back cut scenes, and of course by using this book you'll be able to create your own digital video in various forms.

Time-Shifted TV (PVRs)

This is technically "home entertainment," but time-shifted TV is so interesting that I wanted to talk about it a little more. There are different terms for this entire concept, like "PVR" (personal video recorder) and "hard disk recorder," but it all boils down to the same thing: Instead of recording a TV signal to a VCR and storing it on analog tape, a PVR records it to a hard disk in digital format (usually MPEG2 video). PVRs on the market today include Tivo, Microsoft Ultimate TV, and the Axis Communications Digital Video Recorder. PVRs are often combined with slick software that will learn which programs you like to watch and record them for you. The "time shifting" element simply means that you get to watch shows when you want, not when they are actually on. Most PVRs also have the ability to pause live TV—you hit pause, it starts to record the show, and when you unpause it, the show continues to play. I truly believe PVRs will play a pivotal role in shaping the next decade of digital video in the home, but they have a long way to go until they're in every living room.

On Your Windows XP Computer

Microsoft Windows XP is the best operating system (OS) for digital media on the PC today. Microsoft added several new features to the OS to make it very digital media–friendly. The Windows Media Player supports a wide variety of digital audio and video formats, and the OS makes it simple to view your photos as thumbnails, as a slideshow, to print multiple digital photos to a page, and a lot more. We'll discuss this in detail in the next chapter, but if you're using anything else other than Windows XP, put down this book (I know how hard that is) and go to a local store to buy the upgrade. Trust me, you'll thank me for it.

An Overview of Current Digital Video Technology

A few years ago, if you were lucky enough to find a video clip online, and you had the patience to download it, you'd likely be treated to a grainy, postage-stamp-sized image with poor sound. Digital video was a novelty, but it was almost useless for conveying any real information or entertainment value. Most of the first video online was created by individuals hooking up their VCRs to their computers equipped with low-end video capture cards. It wasn't a pretty sight, but it was exciting, even in that crude form. Thankfully, things have evolved.

Size Matters When It Comes to Digital Video

Pop quiz: Which is more enjoyable to watch movies on, a 60" big screen TV or a 4" portable TV? The bigger screen of course! The same principle holds true for digital video on the Internet. When I find a movie trailer that I'm excited about and they only offer it in ¼ VGA resolution (160 x 120 pixels), it's frustrating to squint at something so small. Smaller video means smaller file size, which is a requirement for the majority of Internet users who are still on dial-up modem connections. Those of us with cable or DSL modems want the good stuff, though! The minimum resolution I want to watch a movie trailer at is 320 x 240, and most sites offer a "high bandwidth" version around that size. Some sites, like Apple's *www.quicktime.com*, offer a larger video resolution of 480 x 272. I've even seen trailers at 640 x 480 resolution, a gloriously large size—but they were limited to people who owned Apple's QuickTime Pro software. It's a pity that a movie studio would restrict access to a trailer based on which video player someone was using. Size is also linked to the bandwidth used by the server offering the file—if you have a movie trailer that is 1 megabyte (MB) in size, you can serve it faster than a 5 MB trailer. And since bandwidth costs money, there are fiscal reasons for keeping the trailers small. We'll talk about how this affects you later in the book when we get to sharing video.

Home-Brewed Video on a CD-R Using VCD and SVCD

Creating digital video on your computer and watching it there is great—but the real fun is when you're able to pop your creation into a VCR or a DVD player and watch it on a big screen with your friends and family. Digital video is meant to be shared! When DVD burners were announced a few years ago, everyone thought that digital nirvana had arrived—we'd have the ability to take video from our computers, burn it to a DVD, and we'd be done. It didn't quite work out that way—today, a few years after DVD burners were first made available for consumers, we're stuck in the middle of two warring standards with sky-high media costs. There are some good solutions on the market that we'll discuss later in the book, but DVD burners are cost-prohibitive for some people. The Asian markets seem to have seen this problem coming first, so they created several methods of burning video using a standard CD-R drive that would play back on most DVD players. The quality isn't nearly as good as a DVD, but in most cases it's a little better than VHS and very cheap to create on CD-R. In Chapter 10, "Sharing Your Video with Others – Using a Physical Medium," you'll learn how to create your own *VCD* and *SVCD* discs to share with others.

Lingo   *VCD* and *SVCD*. Short for "Video Compact Disc" and "Super Video Compact Disc," these two formats were created to allow digital video to be stored on standard CDs rather than the more expensive DVDs. They offer lower quality video than a DVD, but it's much cheaper to buy a blank CD than a blank DVD.

DVD for Video and Data Storage

Despite some of the issues I mentioned above with DVD burners, they're a very real technology, and several companies make them. Apple has been shipping their DVD-R "SuperDrives" for over a year now, and Compaq was quick to follow suit with its own solution. At the time of this writing, on a new Dell computer you can have a DVD+RW drive included at a fairly affordable price. DVD capacity varies with the type of format you chose, but you can store 4.3 GB of data on the smallest format—which means 90 minutes of ultra high-quality video or thousands of data files. In the right format, the DVDs you create will work on almost any DVD player, making it easy to play your videos on a friend's DVD player. The two biggest problems facing users who want to go with a DVD burner are which format to choose (DVD-R or DVD+R) and the cost of the media. DVD burners are the future of sharing digital video, but it will be a while until one standard emerges as the victor. More on this later.

Microsoft 9 Series

A new development that has just been released in beta form as I write this chapter, Microsoft's 9 Series multimedia solution was code-named "Corona" for quite some time. Did they name it after the "luminous irregular envelope of highly ionized gas outside the chromosphere of the sun" (*www.dictionary.com*) or the Mexican beer? You decide. No matter what it's called, the enhancements that 9 Series will bring to the world of digital video can't be underestimated. Although all the details aren't public at this time, 9 Series will be a leap forward for streaming digital video. The days of waiting for a video to *buffer* before playing will be long gone—9 Series streaming video will start playing almost instantly, and, while it's playing, the video will still download in the background. This means that if you lose your Internet connection, the video won't stop playing right away—you'll have as much video as you were able to download. The caveat here is that it depends on the server—if they're not using the Windows Media Server technology, you'll still see buffering in your 9 Series player. The 9 Series multimedia solution will include new players, encoders, and server technology—it will be something worth keeping an eye on (*www.microsoft.com/windowsmedia*).

Lingo   *Buffer*. Before a streaming video can start playing, it needs to download the first few seconds of the video. This initial download is called "buffering" and depending on the server you're connecting to and the speed of your Internet connection, the buffering can be almost instantaneous, or it can be painfully long.

Using Digital Video in Everyday Life

So far, we've talked about how others use digital video, but what about the things that you can do with it today, using only the knowledge gleaned from this tome? The ideas below are just a handful of the many ways you can use digital video in your life.

Sharing Events with Friends and Family

By far, the most popular use of digital video is capturing special moments in life and sharing them with others. Whether that's your child's first steps, a grandson's graduation, or a cruise to Norway, recording those unique moments in life can bring tremendous joy when shared or viewed years later. Unlike the old analog camcorders that forced you to manually edit and dub tapes for every person that wanted to get a copy, digital video makes sharing much easier than you'd think. Throughout this book we'll teach you how to capture video with a digital camcorder, edit that video to let it tell a story, and share that video with others by means of e-mail, the Web, or physical mediums like CD-R and DVDs. It's much easier than you think!

Educational Purposes

Whether you're a teacher, a trainer, or just someone who has a passion for sharing knowledge with others, digital video has powerful applications in the world of education. As a teacher, imagine going to the local zoo with a class of children, taking video footage of the things they see and do, and then creating a video for them to take home and learn from. Enthusiasm for learning is perhaps the best gift anyone can give a child, and digital video can help create that enthusiasm. Some of the video editing programs we'll discuss later are so simple that with the proper supervision, a school-age child could easily sit down and produce his or her own video. Imagine the delight and joy they'd feel showing off their very own movies to their friends! Achievement is a huge motivator for learners of all ages, and creating fun projects with digital video has never been easier.

Independent Filmmaking

Digital video has broken down the cost barrier for independent (indy) filmmaking. For a fairly small investment you can get a new computer, a digital video camera, and the software you need to make a movie. You still need talent and commitment to make a movie, but money is no longer the deciding factor like it once was. Twenty years ago, you'd need thousands of dollars just for the film—never mind the editing suite time you'd need to make anything from it. You probably won't get Al Pacino to star in your indy movie or make a lot of money from it, but anything is possible. The Blair Witch Project was filmed on an analog Hi-8 format and transferred to a computer for digital editing with a complete budget of US $31,000. The result? A $200 million blockbuster that sent Hollywood scrambling for indy scripts and directors while redefining the essence of modern horror movies. There's a great story online that gives you more background if you're interested (*www.apple.com/hotnews/features/blair*).

Virtual Presence

I was asking my friend Chris Pirillo (of *www.lockergnome.com* and TechTV fame) for ways in which he could use digital video, and he came up with a great concept that never occurred to me. You see, I've lived in the same city for most of my life. When it came time to go house hunting, my wife and I hopped in the car and went looking. For people being transferred to a new city across the country, house hunting is a major issue. How can you minimize the time and money you spend investigating the houses? How can you get a good look at a potential house without actually being there? Digital video, of course! Bring a digital video camera with you, take a whole bunch of footage, and, using the tools and techniques discussed in this book, create a short movie of the potential new home. E-mail that to your significant other at home, and see what that person thinks. Have a digital video-savvy friend in the city you want to move to? Ask him or her to take some footage for you and get it through e-mail or the Web before you even come looking for the house. Some realtors are experimenting with digital video of homes that are for sale, making it available over the Web. It's almost like being there—true virtual presence.

Insurance Purposes

One of the frustrating things about home insurance is that, in most cases, you have to prove that you owned a certain item before the insurance company will replace it for you. It makes sense, of course, but the thought of looking for a five-year-old receipt for a TV set is daunting—and sometimes impossible if there was a fire or other damage to your records. Most insurance companies will accept video footage of items as sufficient proof of ownership, so an easy way to keep a home inventory is to grab your digital video camera and walk around the house, taking video footage of all your valuables. Burn that video to a CD or DVD, then give it to a friend to hold on to—you never know when it might come in handy.

Archiving Old Home Movies

One of the reasons I got interested in digital video again after a few years' hiatus was the desire to take old home movies and archive them digitally. I found an old VHS tape that contained footage from the very first time I picked up a video camera. The tape was over 15 years old, so I had some grave concerns about it someday degrading to the point of not working in a VCR. There were also nearly six hours of footage on the tape, and it was almost all unedited. There's only so much footage of "walking around the house holding the video camera" that I can look at, so editing this monster down to something more manageable was a big job (in fact, it's something I'm still working on). My younger brother saw some footage of himself 15 years ago, and it brought a big smile to his face. There's something almost magical about memories captured on video—it takes us back to that time in a way that no other medium can. Old photos are nice, but there's no substitute for seeing the faces and hearing the voices of people from your past. Archiving old videos is probably one of the strongest market forces driving digital video right now, and several of the hardware and software packages we're looking at will help you do just that. Of all the possible uses for digital video, this one is most likely to put a smile on your face! I'll show you how to archive your old VHS and camcorder tapes to a digital format in Chapter 6, "Capturing Your Video."

Key Points

- Digital video has evolved tremendously over the past few years.
- Broadband Internet access allows for a rich video experience.
- VCD, SVCD, and DVD are popular formats for sharing digital video.
- Microsoft 9 Series digital media technology is an important evolution.
- Independent filmmaking has grown with digital video technologies.
- Archiving home movies to digital format is a good way to preserve them.

Chapter 2

Windows XP and Digital Video: The Perfect Partnership

Microsoft Windows 95 and Windows 98 brought a new level of multimedia power to the Windows platform, and Windows NT and Windows 2000 were rock-solid platforms for business computing. It wasn't until the arrival of Windows XP that we were given the combination of stability and multimedia flexibility. And, not coincidentally, it's the first operating system that my mother can use to check her e-mail—it's far less intimidating than previous efforts from Microsoft. And that's a good thing! If you're using Windows 95, Windows 98, or Windows Millennium Edition, do yourself a favor and upgrade to Windows XP. There's nothing worse than working on a video editing project for hours and then having the application or entire operating system crash, potentially losing your work. Windows 2000 and Windows XP share the same stable code, but Windows XP adds more multimedia flavor to the mix.

Note   As far as multimedia features go, there is absolutely no difference between the Home and Professional versions of Windows. For essentially all of what we discuss in this book, either flavor of Windows XP is fine. The one exception to this is that if you have a dual central processing unit (CPU) system (a computer with two processors), you'll need Windows XP Professional to take advantage of them—Windows XP Home supports a single processor only. If you're looking to upgrade to Windows XP, for most people the Home version is just fine (and less expensive than the Professional version). For my needs, though, I prefer the Professional version because I like to use the Remote Desktop feature to log on to my home computer when I'm on the road and remotely check e-mail and work on projects. It also works nicely when I'm sitting upstairs on the couch with my laptop and using Remote Desktop to work on this book. Want to know more about which version of Windows XP to choose? Check out this Web site: *http://www.microsoft.com/windowsxp/whichxp.asp/*.

Tools Inside Windows XP for Digital Video

Right out of the box, Windows XP Home and Windows XP Professional come with some great features for the multimedia-hungry among us. These features are so well integrated, in fact, that most people overlook them entirely. The first category of tools involves the way your video files are displayed inside folders, and the second category deals with digital video applications included with Windows XP.

Thumbnail Folder View

Most people figure out the Thumbnail Preview mode (in any folder, click the View menu, then Thumbnails) in their My Pictures directory pretty quickly, but did you also know the Thumbnail mode works for most video files as well? It's easy not to realize this because it can take several seconds for your computer to decode the video files and give you a preview; so if you're on a slower computer it may look like nothing is happening. If the video file starts by displaying a solid color (many do), your thumbnail preview will be an uninspiring black icon. Figure 2-1 shows a video folder that I have, and the icons are all the first frame of my video. This makes it easy to browse through a folder and pick out the right video because in most cases you'll recognize the video by looking at the first frame. I use the Thumbnail view most of the time because I'm a visual learner and I find it easy to look at a folder and quickly see what files are in it.

Note   The thumbnails can only be created for video files that the Microsoft Windows Media Player can open and view. This includes Moving Pictures Experts Group (MPEG), Windows Media Video (WMV), and most Audio Video Interleaved (AVI) files. If you have a QuickTime video file in your folder, an AVI file created with a nonstandard codec or any other sort of unsupported video file, you will get a generic Windows icon instead of a preview of your video file.

Figure 2-1 The Thumbnail view is displayed.

Detail View

The Detail view, illustrated in Figure 2-2, has unique features when selected in a folder containing video files. In addition to the standard columns like Name, Size, Type, and Date Modified, there are columns for the duration of the video (measured in hours, minutes, and seconds) and the dimensions of the video. This can be quite useful if you're looking at a large folder of video files and you need to find short clips to use as transitions in your video or combine clips based on their resolution. The Type is also useful to sort by—if it simply says "Video Clip," it's a video file in AVI format (explained later in this chapter). MPEG files are denoted as such, as are Windows Media Video (WMV) and Windows Media Audio (WMA) files. Unsupported video formats, like QuickTime, do not have duration or resolution information displayed.

Name	Size	Type	Date Modified	Duration	Dimensions
Wedding Video	13,050,800 KB	Video Clip	7/7/2002 2:53 PM	0:58:47	720 x 480
Family Memories - Cinema	1,294,200 KB	Video Clip	6/15/2002 11:13 PM	0:05:49	720 x 480
Family Memories - Chaplain...	950,946 KB	Video Clip	6/16/2002 6:09 PM	0:04:29	
UIST 2002 - fishcal	54,243 KB	Movie File (MPEG)	7/30/2002 10:13 AM		
Funny clip	17,677 KB	Windows Media Audio/Video file	5/23/2002 12:21 PM	0:10:29	320 x 240
Fancy Countdown	15,378 KB	Video Clip	9/23/2000 3:17 PM	0:00:10	720 x 480
movie trailer	3,937 KB	Movie File (MPEG)	5/10/2002 2:14 PM		
Pretty	3,430 KB	Movie File (MPEG)	7/26/2002 9:12 AM		
TV static	2,031 KB	Video Clip	9/23/2000 3:17 PM	0:00:01	352 x 240
CHCC Baptism	1,983 KB	Windows Media Audio/Video file	6/14/2002 4:40 PM	0:01:50	208 x 160
Drumroll please...	947 KB	Video Clip	9/23/2000 3:17 PM	0:00:03	320 x 240
Movie Maker Slide Show	531 KB	Windows Media Audio/Video file	7/25/2002 9:01 AM	0:00:20	320 x 240

Figure 2-2 The Detail view is displayed.

Task Pane Information

Task panes like the one seen in Figure 2-3 give context-sensitive shortcuts based on what options the user has with that sort of data.

Figure 2-3 Task panes are an important part of Windows XP.

When you click a video file, you have the following task pane options:

- **Play All**   This option starts up the Windows Media Player, puts every video file that's inside that folder on a playlist, and begins to play them all based on the order in which they were sorted in the folder (name, size, length, etc.) You might use a function like this if you had prepared several videos and, before burning them to CD or DVD, you wanted one last viewing.

- **Copy To CD**   This function will copy the files to a temporary folder, and if you don't have a blank disc in your CD-R drive, Windows XP will give you a notification message that there are files waiting to be written to a CD (if you have a CD in the drive, it will start up the wizard for CD burning). From the file window that appears, you can burn them to a CD, add more files, or delete those temporary files without affecting your original files. Remember that a blank CD can store between 650 and 700 MB of data, so in many cases it won't be big enough for raw video footage. After you've finished your product, it just might fit—we'll talk about this in Chapter 10.

Note   You can make a selection of several files in order to confine the Video Tasks to just those files. For example, if you only want to copy 5 of your 10 video files to a CD for storage, you'd select those 5, and then Copy All Items To CD Video task would now read Copy To CD. Play All becomes Play Selection. This is a good way to use the feature while still being selective.

- **Rename This File**   Functionally the same as hitting F2, this allows you to rename your file. If your files have less-than-descriptive names, consider renaming them to add shooting date information, location, etc.

- **Move This File**   A quick way to move a file or files to a new directory or drive. I tend to use Control+X (Cut) and Control+V (paste) to move files around.

- **Copy This File**   This function will make a copy of the file in whatever folder you specify in the window that pops up.

- **Publish This File To The Web**   This command will start up the Web Publishing Wizard. This easy-to-use wizard will step you through creating a Web folder and uploading your video to that folder. There's a 1 MB limit per file, however, and a 3 MB overall size limit (unless you upgrade from the free service), so this service isn't for larger video projects.

- **E-Mail This File**   Click this task to open up a new message from your default e-mail client and attach the video file to it. We'll discuss issues of e-mailing video files to others in Chapter 9.

- **Delete This File**   Pretty self-explanatory. The file is deleted and sent to your Recycling Bin, unless the video file is larger than your Recycling Bin can accept, in which case it will ask you if you want to permanently delete the file. Be careful—if you say yes, it's impossible to recover that file without a third-party tool, and even then it may be damaged if data is written over the spot on the hard drive where it used to be.

- **Details Pane**   This area contains a lot of useful information. If you're in any other View mode than Thumbnails, you'll see a small version of your video. It will only show the first frame, not your video (this feature existed in Windows 2000, but was removed in Windows XP). You'll also see much of the same information you'd get in the Detail view—video file type, date last modified, file size—and it adds author information if that is embedded in the metadata of the file.

The task pane is very useful, but I hope that someday third-party companies and end users will be able to add to the list of Video Tasks at the top. It would be useful to have commands for Edit Video, Convert Video, etc., in the Video task pane.

File Properties

If the information provided in the Details view isn't enough for your needs, right-click the video file you want to investigate and select Properties. The General tab tells us very little, but the Summary tab shown in Figure 2-4—now there's the good stuff! The unique information here includes the bit rate (explained below in the terminology section), the audio sample size, the format of the audio, the frame rate of the video, the data rate of the video, the video sample size, and the video compression. Some of this information is useful to us, some of it isn't. You'll learn what most of these terms mean below, but the lesson to take away here is that when you need to know the details about your video file, checking out the properties is the best way to find them.

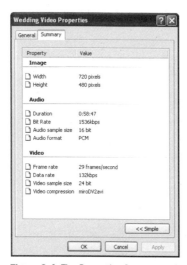

Figure 2-4 The Properties Summary tab tells you a lot about your video file.

Note   Different video clips will display varying amounts of information. In a folder where I have various video clips, one AVI file displays all the above-mentioned information, while the other AVI file shows nothing more than the duration. And the strange part is that the same software created both files! Most of this information is created at the time of encoding, so the amount and type of information present will vary greatly depending on which video encoder is used. One video format seems to have more flexibility than the others when it comes to field data: Windows Media Video.

Windows Media Video (WMV) formatted files have two fields that Windows XP can access and update that other video formats do not: Title and Comments. If you have a WMV file, view the properties by right-clicking the file, left-clicking Properties, then selecting the Summary tab. You'll see both Title and Comments fields as Figure 2-5 shows, and more than likely they'll be blank (I've entered some information about the tool I used and the date the images were shot). To enter your own information, simply left-click the blank space and you'll get a blinking cursor. Start typing! You can enter whatever sort of information you want, but be aware that it's just for your own reference—as far as I've been able to determine, this information doesn't show up in Windows Media Player when playing the video nor can any tool on the market index or search it. It's basically just for your reference.

Figure 2-5 You can update Title and Comments fields with useful information.

Windows Media Player

Recently released in beta at the time of this writing, the 9 Series Windows Media Player shown in Figure 2-6 is a significant upgrade to the Windows Media Player that came with Windows XP. It offers enhanced playback features, support for third-party plug-ins, variable bit-rate audio encoding (this gives you greater sound quality with smaller file sizes), and a host of other improvements. The Media Library functionality has also been greatly improved, so it's easier to work with your media and build playlists. Unfortunately, many of the same issues still exist from the last player—playing the video and audio clips in the Media Guide cause a confusing series of Web browsers to pop up instead of playing the content inside the player. And even with the improvements in how video is streamed, every video clip I tried to watch after installing the beta software sputtered and paused continuously—this is no fault of the player, however. Movie studios and Web sites with multimedia content aren't providing adequate bandwidth for their visitors.

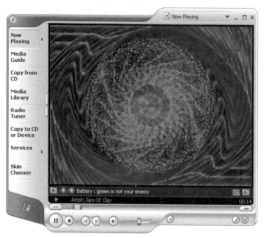

Figure 2-6 This figure shows the 9 Series Windows Media Player.

Windows Movie Maker

Windows Movie Maker, shown in Figure 2-7, is a tool we'll discuss in Chapter 7 when we delve into the basics of video editing. As a video-editing tool, it looks very basic, lacking even a single transition (an effect that allows you to move from one clip to another—like fading to black, etc.), but it's a perfect place for beginners to start and has some surprisingly useful features. It allows you to record video and audio signals from a variety of sources, offers scene detection (where it splits up video clips based on scenes), and has a variety of preset output templates. I have to admit, I wasn't very impressed when I first fired it up, but for simple projects where quality isn't paramount (e-mail and Web sharing), it's quite a useful little application. And did I mention it was free with every copy of Windows XP?

Figure 2-7 Windows Movie Maker is perfect for simple projects.

Third-Party Digital Video Tools

Although technically not a "part" of Windows XP, the compatibility that Windows XP has with video tools created by third parties is impressive. Unlike the Macintosh or Linux platforms, a huge number of companies are creating digital video hardware and software solutions. Pinnacle, Ulead, muvee Technologies, Adobe, ADS, Maxtor, Western Digital, Sony, Adaptec, Sonic, Panasonic, Canon, Roxio, Sonic Desktop—these are just a handful of the many companies offering products for the digital video market. The sheer variety of choices that you have with Windows XP is refreshing—I wouldn't want to be limited to only a couple of choices, and neither would you. We'll discuss third-party video tools throughout the rest of the book, but for consumer-level video editing, Windows XP is my platform of choice. Don't believe people who say, "You need a Mac to do digital video." Hand them a copy of this book and they'll learn the truth.

Digital Video Compression Explained

You'll see the term "compression" used throughout this book, so I thought it was important to explain what it is and why it's important. The term "compression" simply means "to make smaller." The most common form of digital compression that you're likely familiar with are the ubiquitous Zip files—Zip files are everywhere, and Windows XP has built-in support for opening them (but not creating them—you need WinZip from *www.winzip.com* for that). The easiest way to understand compression is to think of an object like a hamburger (work with me here). A hamburger is usually composed of different kinds of food, like lettuce, tomatoes, beef, and a bun. Most of us make homemade hamburgers that are bigger than our mouths can fit, so it's common to see someone squish the burger down before taking a bite—one could say the burger goes through premastication compression. With me so far? The materials become smaller in different ways—the bun has a lot of air in it, so it gets smaller very easily. The beef, on the other hand, would only compress a little bit because it's already condensed into a hamburger patty. You end up with a smaller hamburger overall, but some of the elements compress more than others.

Now, believe it or not, the same logic applies to compression on your computer. Things like text files are full of "spaces" that can be compressed very tightly—a text file can be made at least 90 percent smaller, resulting in a great compression ratio (the ratio of compressed data to uncompressed data). Other file types, like MPEG video or JPEG photos, hardly compress at all—that's because they're in a file format that's already compressed. Why is this important to understand? Keep reading.

Why Is Digital Video Compressed?

As odd as this sounds, one reason digital video is compressed is that our senses don't know any better. Researchers have charted the limits of the human sensory systems over the years, and we know that humans can hear sounds ranging from 20 hertz (Hz) to 20,000 Hz. We also know that although mathematically there are billions upon billions of colors, as humans we can perceive roughly 1024 shades of the same color. That's a huge range of possible colors, but if every one of those colors takes up space in a digital file, does it make sense to have them all in a picture if we can't tell the subtle difference between one color and the next? There's also the matter of redundant images—if, in every second of a 60-second video, there's a chair in the same spot, why save the data of that chair in every frame of the video?

Another reason compression exists is to cut back on the amount of space needed to store digital video. How big would digital video be if it weren't compressed in some way? It would take up a staggering amount of room! I found this interesting formula on *www.adobe.com*:

Frame size K = (*[Pixel Width* x *Pixel Height* x *Bit Depth*] / 8) / 1024
Frame size K = ([720 x 480 x 24] / 8) / 1024 = 1012.5 KB

That tells us that one frame of raw, uncompressed video footage at standard digital video (DV) resolution (720 x 480) would take up roughly 1 MB. And since video is usually around 30 frames per second, we're looking at 30 megabytes per second (MBps) of video! A short, five-minute video would require 9000 MB, or 9 gigabytes (GB), of storage. And if you were shooting a 60-minute video? That's 108 GB—and remember, that's just for the video. It gets even bigger when you add audio. In addition to the tremendous storage you'd need to work with uncompressed video, there's the issue of having a computer fast enough to handle it. Throwing around a digital signal at a sustained rate of 30 MBps is almost impossible for most computers to keep up with—the FireWire hard drive from Maxtor that I tested could only write around 9.1 MB per second. That's quite fast for an external hard drive, but not fast enough to work with uncompressed video. In order to make video easier to work with, we compress it.

By throwing away the data that we can't perceive, we get compressed video. Standard DV cameras compress video at a ratio of 5 to 1, which allows them to store more information per tape. Different video formats offer various options for compression—some allow you to compress the video up to 100 times smaller than the original. Too much compression, however, can be a bad thing. Remember that the more you compress a video, the more data you're throwing away. Throw away a lot of data, and the changes become noticeable. Throw away even more data by using heavy compression, and you'll get a video that you can hardly recognize!

Tip   When you're compressing your video, always try several compression settings (start with a high amount of compression). The goal is to compress as much as you possibly can, until the data loss becomes noticeable. Then notch the compression back a little and you'll have the right balance between small file size and quality. And remember that every video is different—some videos will still look great highly compressed, others will not. You'll have to experiment with each project to get the best results.

Bit Rate Explained

I was talking about how much data uncompressed video would take and referring to it in terms of MBps. *Bit rate* is the common term used to describe how much data exists, per second, in a given stream of data. You might have seen audio files referred to as "128-Kbps MP3" or "64-Kbps WMA." Kbps stands for "kilobits per second," and the higher the number preceding Kbps, the higher the amount of the data. The 128-Kbps MP3 audio file contains twice the data of the 64-Kbps WMA file and would be twice the file size. However, some file formats can use their data more effectively than others, so the 64-Kbps WMA file would sound just as good as the 128-Kbps MP3 file. It's a little confusing, but I'll explain how this works in the next section. The important thing to understand here is that the higher the bit rate, the more information there is, and thus the more effort it takes to decode that information. Selecting the proper bit rate for your projects depends on the playback target: if you're making a VCD for playback on a DVD player, the video needs to be exactly 1150 Kbps and the audio 224 Kbps. A typical Pocket PC running at 206 megahertz (MHz) can work with MPEG video up to 400 Kbps—anything above that will cause it to sputter during playback. Later in the book, when I get into the details of creating appropriate output formats, this will make more sense.

Psychoacoustic Audio Compression

Psychoacoustic looks like a complicated word, but it simply means "the way your sense of hearing and brain interpret the sounds you hear." I mentioned above that a 64-Kbps WMA file would sound just as good as a 128-Kbps MP3 file. But if the MP3 file has twice as much data per second as the WMA file, how can it possibly sound better, you ask? Simple: The WMA format packs more of the good sound and gets rid of the stuff that you can't hear anyway. The digital audio on a music CD is compressed to 1411 Kbps, and few would argue with the quality of a CD. MP3, WMA, and any other form of compressed audio are based on powerful mathematical algorithms that discard audio information that we can't hear. Here's an example: If I shout at the top of my lungs and also lightly tap my foot, you'll hear my voice above everything else. Will you hear my foot tapping? Likely not. Yet in the strictest sense, that foot-tapping noise is still present, and in a digital world that would represent data. By getting rid of that foot tapping, we'd end up with less information and therefore a smaller file size. The MP3 psychoacoustic model was created way back in 1987, so when Microsoft introduced the WMA model in the late 1990s, it simply had a better model that was able to produce better-sounding audio in less space.

Psychovisual Video Compression

This term is very similar to its audio counterpart, so I won't repeat the same explanation. Instead of discarding audio that we can't hear, however, psychovisual models discard things that we can't see. For instance, an uncompressed video shot of a wall that is painted black would have a black pixel for every spot on that wall. But if it's just black pixels over and over, why not store one pixel that simply replicates itself to fill up the space? This type of compression is called "statistical data redundancy," which simply means to discard data that's repeated. This, and other mathematical tricks, allows video formats like WMV and MPEG to be highly compressed while still retaining good quality.

Lossless Compression

The term *lossless* means "no loss of data." When a file is compressed in a lossless fashion, it means that 100 percent of the data is still there. If you zip a Microsoft Word document, it will get smaller, but all the letters of your document are still present when you unzip it. You can also save lossless video over and over without any loss of data—any compression applied simply squeezes that data into a smaller format and does so in the same way every time. In the video world, lossless compression would be achieved by using an AVI file. Lossless compression typically results in only minor compression (3:1) because you can compress only so much data without discarding it. Other forms of lossless data include WAV and bitmap (BMP) files.

Lossy Compression

Lossy compression formats include WMV, WMA, MP3, MPEG, and any other form of compression that discards data in order to achieve a lower bit rate (this includes image formats like JPEG). Using the psychoacoustic and psychovisual rules described above, you'll end up with a much smaller file size but less of the original source data. And although this would seem to defy logic, every time you save your file in a lossy file format, it discards more of the data—even if you're saving it in the same format. A good rule of thumb is to move to a lossy format only as the very final step in your project. We'll talk more about this in Chapter 7 when we delve into editing your video.

Terminology You Need to Know

Unless you're the kind of person who curls up in bed with a dictionary instead of a good book like this one, the word "terminology" probably makes you yawn. I won't bore you with detailed histories of each term, but understanding what words mean is important to getting you on the digital video fast track.

Codec

A *codec* (short for compressor/decompressor) is a type of translator for video and audio data. If that translator (codec) isn't present on the computer trying to play the audio or video file, it won't play back properly, if at all. Have you ever downloaded a video file and, when trying to play it back, you get audio but no video? That usually means you're missing the right video codec, but you have the correct codec for audio. Conversely, if you get video but no audio, you might be missing an audio codec (this is much rarer than a missing video codec). One of the problems with sharing video online today is with users creating videos using codecs that not everyone has. It's important to encode your video using codecs that your users will have. If you do want to use a special codec, make sure you indicate which codec is needed to view the video and where people can get it. I've noticed that codec problems are more frequent with AVI files—it's rare to get an MPEG or WMV file that won't play.

Digital Artifacts

Have you ever looked at a JPEG photo that's "blocky"? Parts of the images look pixilated and very "digital." Or have you looked at a video file and seen squares making up the edge of someone's face instead of a smooth line? Those are all examples of something called *digital artifacting*. When an image or video is highly compressed, the loss of data becomes noticeable to the viewer, usually in the form of visible areas of discoloration or the partial destruction of a shape (like a smooth line). In Figure 2-8 I took a high-quality JPEG image directly from my digital camera (a Canon Powershot S110) and applied a 90 percent JPEG compression to it. The original image is on the left, and no digital artifacts are visible. The ultra-compressed image is on the right, and although the file size of this image would be much smaller than that of the image on the right, you can see many examples of digital artifacting. The color on the wall isn't uniform, her jacket looks blotchy, and the overall quality of the image is poor. I overdid the compression on this image to make the effect obvious, and thankfully it's unlikely you'll ever see an image quite this badly compressed on the Internet. You will, however, run across video like this; because video files are so large and bandwidth is so expensive for people with Web sites, they'll overcompress the video past the point of good quality.

Figure 2-8 On the left, a standard JPEG image with minimal compression. On the right, a highly compressed image showing extreme digital artifacting.

Note   Whenever you save your video in a compressed format you'll have to make trade-offs between quality and size. If you're posting your video on a Web site, do you want visitors to be able to download it quickly over a common 56K modem? If so, you'll have to highly compress your video and the quality will likely be poor. Or do you want to offer it at maximum quality and restrict it to people with the rarer broadband connections? These are the questions you'll have to ask yourself—there are compromises with both methods.

FireWire

Also known as IEEE (Institute of Electrical and Electronics Engineers) 1394 and iLink (the Sony name for it), FireWire was invented in 1995 and although largely a Mac-based technology for several years, the digital video industry has accepted it as the de facto standard for connecting DV cams to computers. To keep things simple, I'll be using the term FireWire throughout the book, but if you hear someone refer to iLink or IEEE 1394, you'll know it's the same thing. FireWire goes far beyond video cameras, including a host of external devices from Web cams to hard drives. FireWire offers blistering performance—up to 400 megabits per second (Mbps), making it perfect for high-bandwidth data— things like video. I'll talk about FireWire hardware later, but I have a Maxtor 3000XT external 160-GB FireWire hard drive, and I was extremely impressed with how fast it is and how easy it was to connect. Items connecting through FireWire can be "hot swapped," which means that you can connect a hard drive to your computer without powering it down first, and it will appear in your My Computer folder within seconds and be ready to use. FireWire devices require a FireWire port, which can be added easily using an Adaptec or ADS PCI card that plugs into your motherboard. Many new computers are shipping with FireWire ports, so be sure to check your computer manual to see if you have one.

USB 1.1 and 2.0

USB stands for "Universal Serial Bus," and it's a technology that allows external devices like floppy drives, printers, mice, keyboards, and dozens of other devices to be connected to a PC. USB devices are "hot swappable," which means that you can connect and disconnect them while the computer is running. USB 1.1 offered a meager 12 Mbps of bandwidth, which was enough for a mouse but not for high-performance external hard drives. USB 2.0 kicks the spec into overdrive, offering 480 Mbps of bandwidth and full backward compatibility with USB 1.1 devices. The older USB 1.1 devices don't perform at USB 2.0 speeds, but they work in the USB 2.0 hubs and ports. Some newer computers are starting to offer USB 2.0 ports, but it's easy enough to add them by installing a PCI card into your computer. Adaptec (*www.getadaptec.com*) makes a product called the DuoConnect, and it offers three USB 2.0 ports and two FireWire ports. I'll talk more about USB hardware later, but my tests with a Maxtor 3000LE USB 2.0 hard disc were very encouraging—I was able to move huge video files quickly, with sustained write speeds of 6.6 MBps and read speeds of 8.0 MBps.

Digital Audio File Types

A critical part of any video is the audio—unless your goal is to create a panto-
mime masterpiece, you'd be wise to pay attention to your audio track. Working
with audio requires a basic knowledge of the file formats that you may encounter, so listed below are the most important ones.

- **WAV**   A lossless file format, WAV files tend to be quite large (a typical
  song in WAV format will be 40+ MB in size), but they're very high quality and can be saved over and over without any data loss. WAV files are
  easy to work with in audio programs like Sonic Foundry's Sound Forge
  6.0 (*www.sonicfoundry.com*), and all video-editing applications should
  accept WAV files as valid audio track sources.

- **Windows Media Audio (WMA)**   A revolutionary file format from the
  Windows Media Team at Microsoft, WMA is a powerful format for digital audio. It offers MP3 quality in half the file size and bit rate. I take
  exception to the statement by Microsoft that they can offer "CD-quality
  sound" at 64 Kbps (it comes close at 96 Kbps), but there's no arguing
  that WMA is the superior format for low-bit rate audio. Unfortunately,
  many digital video programs can't accept WMA files as input, so you
  may need to have your original CDs on hand to get the song you need.

- **MP3**   Short for MPEG Layer 3, the granddaddy of all lossy audio compression formats, MP3 has been around since 1987, but it wasn't until
  almost 10 years later that it became popular with the advent of peer-to-
  peer file sharing services. MP3s offer reasonable quality sound at 128
  Kbps in one-tenth the size of a similar WAV file, and that size savings
  is what makes it popular. Early MP3 files actually sounded horrible, but
  going from a 40 MB WAV file down to a 4 MB MP3 file was so amazing
  that people put up with it. Today, nearly every video-editing package
  can accept MP3 files as an audio track.

- **MP3Pro**   A newer format, MP3Pro was created as an enhancement to
  MP3. It offers a superior psychoacoustic model, very similar to WMA.
  There doesn't appear to be much industry support for this format,
  however—the only encoder and player (*www.mp3prozone.com*) is still
  a demo limited to 64 Kbps, just as it was nearly a year ago. I haven't
  seen a video-editing program that can accept MP3Pro files, so I'd avoid
  this format completely.

■ **Ogg Vorbis** Despite the strange name, this format offers a lot for the future of digital audio. Unlike any of the other compressed formats, it's completely free, open, and not patented (which is highly unusual in the technology industry). It's more interesting to developers than end users—if you have software that creates MP3s, you need to pay a royalty fee to Fraunhofer (the creators of the MP3 format). I'm not aware of any video-editing programs that accept Ogg Vorbis files as input, so this format is best to avoid for now. Over the next few years, however, it will be interesting to see how this evolves (*www.vorbis.com*).

■ **RealAudio** Once the king of the streaming digital audio world, RealAudio isn't as popular as it once was. RealAudio is a good format for streaming audio, but for a high-quality audio track you'd be better served by going with another format. Most video-editing programs will not accept RealAudio as an input format. Avoid this format.

Digital Video File Types

Digital video has existed in various forms for over a decade now, so it's not surprising that multiple formats have popped up. It's not necessary to know a great deal about each format, but having a basic grasp of what each one is good for will help you when we discuss sharing your video in the latter part of the book.

■ **AVI** Short-form for Audio Video Interleaved, this is the most common, and oldest, form of digital video on the PC platform. AVI files are essentially "containers" for video. Most AVI format videos are compressed with a codec. In most cases, unless an unusual codec is used, AVI files will play in the Windows Media Player without any problems. Unless you're using a powerful codec for compression (like the DivX coded from *www.divx.com*), your video files will tend to be quite large. AVI is a good format to archive your videos in—if my video projects aren't too large, I try to burn a copy of my source footage to a CD for keeping. With most standard codecs, saving to an AVI format is a lossless form of compression.

■ **Windows Media Video (WMV)** A brother to the WMA format, WMV is a highly compressed video format that has taken the Web world by storm since being released in 2000. The WMV format uses special psychovisual codecs to discard data, resulting in a high-quality video in a surprisingly small file size. How small? I had a full DV-resolution AVI file (720 x 480) that was 408 MB in size. While maintaining a similar resolution (640 x 480), I was able to crunch that huge file size down into 19.8 MB! Unless I zoomed the video to 200 percent of normal size, I couldn't tell the difference between the two. The video data rate was 1506 Kbps, so it's certainly not meant for streaming, but a 20 MB download would go fairly quickly with a cable modem and give people a high-quality video to watch. As you can tell, I'm a big fan of the WMV format. We'll discuss how to create and share WMV format video files in Chapter 9. WMV is a lossy compression format.

- **ASF**   A Microsoft format that was only around for a couple of years, Active Streaming Format (ASF) was designed primarily to be streamed over the Internet. ASF files will play in the Windows Media Player but you likely won't see them around very often—WMV has replaced ASF in almost every way.

- **MPEG**   Short for Moving Picture Experts Group, MPEG has been around for a long time and is still the basis for many of the video formats on the market today. MPEG was the first format on the PC that allowed huge AVI files to be compressed to a much smaller size while still retaining decent quality, having been optimized for video playback from a CD-ROM at about 1.5 Mbps. MPEG video files can be viewed in the Windows Media Player, and most video-editing packages will output in some variation of MPEG. MPEG is a lossy compression format, and a good cross-platform way to share your video over the Internet.

- **MPEG2**   A variation on the original MPEG specification, this is a newer version that supports a new compression scheme, allowing for better-quality video. It was created to address the need for higher-quality digital video, specifically in the 4 to 9 Mbps range. DVDs use a form of MPEG2 video, as do some digital video cameras. MPEG2 files are saved using lossy compression and often have a .m2v file name extension. Most should play fine in Windows Media Player.

- **MPEG4**   Yet another offshoot of the original MPEG specification, MPEG4 was originally created specifically to target video at low bit rates. It has since evolved into a replacement for the original MPEG video format by targeting video from 64 Kbps and lower up to 4 Mbps. It won't replace the high-quality video on a DVD, but it offers some interesting options for storing and sharing video. Most of the video-editing packages on the market today don't support MPEG4 video, but there are stand-alone programs to create MPEG4-based content. Now here's where it gets a little confusing: Many of the video formats on the market today are MPEG4-based. QuickTime and RealVideo are both based on MPEG4 codecs. Each format simply "wraps" them up differently. It doesn't have much relevance to you as an end user, so I won't try to explain how they all relate to MPEG4. It's simply important to understand that MPEG4 technology is core to much of the streaming video that is happening right now.

■ **RealVideo**   Once the king of video streaming, RealVideo is still quite popular, but Windows Media and QuickTime formats have caught up and surpassed it in most ways. To play back RealVideo content you need the RealOne player from *www.real.com*, which makes it a poor choice for sharing video with others (because they have to download a special player to see your video). Most of the video-editing applications can't work with RealVideo content, and there are better formats for archiving. Although several applications I tested will output files in RealVideo format, I don't recommend you use this format at all.

■ **QuickTime**   QuickTime, the video format championed by Apple, has quite a few supporters in the industry. It's particularly popular with movie studios for releasing trailers on the Web. QuickTime video quality is outstanding, and it streams well over the Web. The biggest problem I have with QuickTime is the fact that their "free" player, upon loading, will frequently pop up an advertisement for QuickTime Pro, the professional version of QuickTime. A truly free player should not hassle the user to upgrade. That aside, QuickTime import and export is supported by several video-editing packages currently on the market. Because native QuickTime support is not included in Windows XP, if you e-mail someone an MOV file (the file format for QuickTime), that person might not be able to open it without downloading QuickTime from Apple (*www.quicktime.com*). Something to keep in mind!

■ **DivX**   The DivX format is a relatively new one, and it's technically not a video format unto itself: It's an MPEG4-based codec for the AVI format that creates highly compressed video while still retaining superb quality. There's a lot to like about DivX, including great quality and small file sizes, and the tools to create and watch DivX are free

(*www.divx.com*). DivX claims over 60 million people are using their
software, and it's quite popular for sharing movies (though, I should
note, not legal). So what's not to like? Unfortunately, if you send people a DivX-format AVI file by e-mail or through the Web, when they try
to play it with the Windows Media Player, they'll hear the audio but get
no video (as I mentioned above when talking about codecs). When it's
missing a codec that it needs, Windows Media Player has the ability to
connect to the Internet and download the missing codec. For whatever
reason, Microsoft doesn't offer the DivX codec, so whoever is viewing
your video will have to go to *www.divx.com* and download their free
software. Not difficult, but a hassle.

- **VCD**   Short for VideoCD, this format emerged from the Asian markets,
  which didn't want to pay royalties to the DVD consortium for the ability to play back video on a DVD player. The format is based on MPEG1
  video and supports 74 to 80 minutes of video on a standard 650/700
  MB CD-R. VCDs are limited to 1150 Kbps for video at 352 x 240 pixels
  and 224 Kbps for audio. The quality of a VCD is roughly comparable to
  VHS tape—not bad, but not great, either. VCDs work on the vast
  majority of DVD players on the market today, and every new DVD
  player I've seen supports the format. If you don't have a DVD burner,
  VCDs are a great way to share your video with others. There's an offshoot of VCD called XVCD with a higher bit rate of 2500 Kbps, but it's
  an unofficial format and should be avoided for now. We'll go into how
  to create VCDs in Chapter 10, and with more and more software packages supporting VCD creation, it's extremely easy. A great source for
  learning about VCDs is *www.vcdhelp.com*.

- **SVCD**   Short for Super VideoCD, this MPEG2-based format has a lot in
  common with VCDs. Support for SVCDs is increasing, but it's not quite
  as broad as VCDs when it comes to DVD playback. Still, if your DVD
  player can support it, this 2500 Kbps video format will give you excellent
  quality video. SVCD video is 480 x 480 pixels, so when you play it back
  on your computer it might look "squished." SVCD is an excellent and
  inexpensive format for sharing short videos. Several software packages
  support the creation of SVCDs, so we'll discuss how to make them in
  Chapter 10 when we get into how to share your videos using discs.

■ **DVD**   Perhaps the best-known term in the digital video world, DVD stands for Digital Versatile Disc, not Digital Video Disc as some believe. DVD players are becoming common in the average home, and the sales of DVD players are growing faster than VCRs ever did. The 9800 Kbps video bit rate and 720 x 480 resolution ensure extremely high-quality video, and the audio can support up to eight tracks containing Digital Theatre Sound (DTS), Dolby Digital, or regular Pulse Code Modulation (PCM) audio. A standard DVD can hold roughly 2 hours of digital video, but that number can change depending on the video's quality. Until recently, it was an expensive undertaking to create a DVD and out of reach for most consumers and small businesses. That has changed in the past few years, but there are two warring standards for DVD burning, which creates confusion and slows down the adoption of DVD burning as a solution. Things have gotten better in the past year, but I still find it frustrating that the computer industry can't unite behind a single format.

■ **DVD-R and DVD-RW**   DVD-R offers the greatest compatibility with stand-alone DVD players. It's the only format officially sanctioned by the DVD Forum, a collection of hardware and software manufacturers that are involved in creating standards for the DVD format (Hitachi, Pioneer, Sony, Toshiba, and others). DVD-RW is simply a rewriteable version of this format. DVD-R drives can support up to 4.7 GB capacities, and this type of DVD burner comes standard in many computers from Apple and Compaq. Look for Pioneer to release a 4X speed burner, twice as fast as their current drive, in the winter this year (2002).

■ **DVD+R and DVD+RW**   Although this format offers some advantages over DVD-R, it's slightly less compatible with stand-alone DVD players (for now at least). It does have the backing of electronics giant Philips, however, and DVD+R products are included in some of today's top-end PCs. DVD+RW is a rewriteable version of this format. DVD+R supports up to 4.7 GB of data on a single disc.

Note   In September 2002, Sony released a DVD burner that will read and write in both DVD+R and DVD-R formats (and their RW counterparts). This is a brilliant move by Sony, because it effectively offers consumers a solution to the warring standards—why chose one over the other when you can have a drive that does both? I couldn't find any pricing information at the time of this writing, but assuming the price is comparable to other DVD burners, this is a great solution.

■ **DVD-RAM**   This format was created to allow DVDs to be used like a
hard drive, specifically for data storage. DVD-RAM discs aren't compatible with stand-alone DVD players. The DVD Forum also supports this
format. Current DVD-RAM drives can support up to 9.4 GB on double-
sided discs.

There are other formats of digital video, including DVD-VCD and DVD-
SVCD, but until they become more common they're not worth considering as
viable choices for storing and sharing your video.

Digital Image File Types

Some of the video-editing packages I'll be talking about include support for
image files, so it's important to understand what each image format offers.

■ **JPEG**   Sometimes referred to as JPG files, this format is what most digital cameras use for storing images. Offering 24-bit color and lossy file
compression, JPEG files offer a good balance between quality and file
size. Every time you save an image in JPEG format, you'll lose more
data; so when you're editing JPEG images, make sure to save them
only once and keep your original. Most video-editing packages support importing JPEG images to include in your video presentation. Videos with integrated still photos can be very interesting!

■ **BMP**   The bitmap file format is as old as Windows itself (perhaps
older). It supports 24-bit color and offers no compression format, making it a good format for multiple saves but a poor choice for saving
space. Most video-editing applications support BMP files, but you
likely won't be using them very often.

■ **GIF**   The GIF format stands for Graphics Interchange Format and is
limited to 256 colors, making it a very poor choice for photographs.
You won't likely work with GIF images during video editing.

■ **TIFF**   Short for Tagged Image File Format, this format is still popular
in the printing industry but fairly rare outside of it. TIFF images support
a lossless compression scheme, but they still tend to be quite large.
Supporting 24-bit color, the TIFF format is a high-quality image format,
but it's unlikely to be used much in the video-editing packages we'll be
looking at.

▪ **PNG**   This 24-bit color format stands for Portable Network Graphics, and although it's technically very superior in what it offers (24-bit color, transparency, lossless compression), adoption of this format has been slow. Some editing packages support the PNG format, but in most cases you won't be using this file format.

Key Points

▪ Windows XP includes several tools for digital video users.

▪ Digital video is compressed to conserve space.

▪ There are two types of digital compression: lossy and lossless.

▪ FireWire and USB 2.0 are high-speed data transfer protocols important to digital video.

▪ DVD-R and DVD+R are the two main standards fighting for dominance.

▪ JPEG images are the most common images you'll work with in digital video.

Chapter 3

Choosing the Right Video Camera

I need to make one very important statement before you read any further: there is no perfect DV camera. What's advanced enough for one user is confusing to another, and every camera involves trade-offs in the battle between features and price. There is no perfect DV camera. If you can accept that, you're ready to educate yourself on what sort of features are available on modern DV cameras, how they affect your use of the DV camera, and whether they're worth the extra money you'll spend to get them.

Digital (DV) vs. Analog (HI-8, SVHS)

Although this should go without saying in a book called *Faster Smarter Digital Video*, digital video cameras are truly the only way to go today for the kinds of things that you and I will do with them. However, not everyone would agree with me, so it's important to understand exactly *why* they're the best choice today for the average person. I was at a celebration recently, and a gentleman overheard me talking about digital video and the book I was working on. Just as I was leaving, he came up and asked a few questions about digital video. He had an analog HI-8 camera and wanted to shoot and edit several lengthy videos on it. I politely suggested that between the costs of getting an analog video capture board and the time it would take to capture the footage manually, it would be cheaper for him to get a DV camera—and he'd have much higher quality footage to boot. Much to my surprise, he said that he "heard" digital video cameras produced inferior quality video to HI-8. I assured him that this wasn't the case and rattled off some advantages of digital video. He seemed surprised and said he'd look into getting a DV camera.

So how can someone think that analog video cameras are still the way to go? In my experience, there are two types of people who will express an opinion like this:

- They've been into video for years, are early adopters of technology, and have tried a first-generation digital video product. Anything digital that tries to duplicate something in the analog world usually does a very poor job in the first generation. The advantage of digital, though, is that it can improve in quality very rapidly. If someone hasn't looked at a modern DV camera lately, they shouldn't be opening their mouth on the subject of quality.

- They're die-hard traditionalists who refuse to believe that anything digital can surpass the quality of analog. They usually have expensive Betacam SP equipment and exist on a different plane of reality when it comes to price vs. performance comparisons. You can't compare the image quality of a $1,000 DV camera with a $15,000 Betacam SP using a $20,000 lens.

In either case, DV cameras represent the best choice for affordable, easy-to-use, high-quality video (for the price). If anyone tells you different, lend him or her your copy of this book (better yet, suggest they buy their own copy—my publisher and I thank you!). Don't let anyone dissuade you from buying a DV camera in favor of an analog one.

DV Cams Are the Only Way to Go

Some of the key advantages of digital video include:

- **Resolution** Video quality is typically measured in "lines of resolution." The more lines, the better the video will look. VHS has 240 lines of resolution, 8mm camcorders have 220 lines, S-VHS camcorders have 400 lines, and DV cameras have 500 lines.

- **Easy connection to a PC** Modern DV cameras were designed to talk to a computer. All DV cameras support *FireWire*, which allows an easy Plug and Play connection between your PC and DV camera. Windows XP will recognize the camera, and even if you have no other software installed, you can use Windows Movie Maker to transfer the video.

- **Zero quality loss** When you transfer video from your DV camera to your computer, there's no loss of quality. The video on your PC is an exact duplicate of what the camera recorded. Contrast that to digitizing analog content, where the quality will vary wildly based on what hardware you use, and the digital advantage is clear.

- **Small size of cameras** Because digital video is compressed, the tapes and recording mechanisms can be made smaller than comparative analog technologies. DV cameras will be smaller, lighter, and have better battery life than most analog video cameras.

Lingo A standard developed in the early 1990s for high-speed data transfer, *FireWire* was adopted by the consumer electronics industry as a way to allow camcorders to communicate with desktop PCs. FireWire supports speeds up to 400 megabits per second (Mbps). For comparison purposes, Universal Serial Bus (USB) 1.1 is 11 Mbps.

Buy the Best You Can Afford

When you're shopping for a DV camera, you'll no doubt have a budget in mind. By the time you're done, you'll likely end up with the DV camera itself, accessories for it, tapes, software for your computer, and perhaps a few hardware upgrades (like a FireWire card). Although it's easy to get carried away when starting out, I'd encourage you to put the bulk of your money into the camera itself. You can purchase new software packages later, and computer hardware is relatively simple to upgrade. Your DV camera, however, is a one-time investment that you won't be able to upgrade or enhance later (with rare exceptions).

For this reason, I suggest you spend the bulk of your investment on the camera—buy the best camera you can afford, focusing on features that you'll use today and those you may grow into down the road.

The Features You Don't Need

Although this may not endear me to all the DV camera manufacturers out there, I think this is something that needs to be said: some features offered on today's cameras are things that you simply don't need. Most cameras, especially some of the high-end cameras, include certain features that are designed for people who will never connect the camera to their computer to edit the footage. Since you've bought this book, you're not one of those people, right? There are three main classes that these features fall into.

Tonal Shooting Modes

Some cameras offer the ability to record footage in black and white, sepia (a yellowish tone that makes the movie look aged), mosaic, mirror, trail, and any number of other effects. The reality is, all these effects can be easily achieved in any video-editing package on the market today. And what happens if you want to use that footage for something that requires color, like part of a larger video montage? You can't. Ignore all the special shooting options on the camera—take your footage in "normal" mode and get creative with it later in *post-production*.

Lingo   *Post-production* is used to describe anything that occurs after the video has been shot. Editing, rendering, and outputting to DVD would all be considered post-production steps.

Gee-Whiz Effects

In an effort to make video footage more exciting, certain camera makers have implemented what I like to call "gee-whiz" effects. Typically these will be effects the salesperson will be very excited about—"differentiators" that make this one camera "better" than all the others. They'll be things like putting a static image "frame" around your video (like a window or a picture frame). This has the same net effect as the tonal shooting modes above—if you capture all your footage with a cute window around it, what happens when you want to use that footage a few years from now for another project? Your footage is ruined by an effect that's cute only the first time you see it. Don't consider the gee-whiz features to be a deciding factor in choosing a camera.

Communications

Some cameras today are starting to ship with built-in wireless communications, typically based on Bluetooth. The theory is, if you have a Bluetooth phone (like the Sony Ericsson T68i), you'll be able to wirelessly e-mail photos taken with the camera through the modem on the phone. Sounds great, right? In theory, yes. But in reality, there's not enough bandwidth using Bluetooth to e-mail any high-quality video. And in experimenting a little with the cameras that offer this feature, the technology is still very immature and difficult to use. That's not to say the concept is a bad one: imagine having a camera with built-in high-speed wireless, something fast enough to send a live video stream up to a Web site while simultaneously recording the high-quality DV footage for later. You'd have a live, mobile Web cam! I'm convinced that someone will figure out a way to implement this in a clever fashion—the technology is available today to create this.

> **Note** The one exception to the above rules is the "cinema" mode that some cameras have. This mode is similar to the wide-screen effect you see on a DVD, with black lines running horizontally across the screen, confining your video to a more central position. This gives a professional, sharp look to your footage. Although it's possible to add this later using a video editor, as long as you leave your camera in this mode and shoot all your footage this way, you're unlikely to run into any trouble.

Things to Look For on Your DV Camera

When you go shopping for a shiny new DV camera, you'll be faced with a great many choices: seven major home electronics companies sell DV cameras (Sony, JVC, Panasonic, Canon, Sharp, RCA, Samsung), each with multiple cameras. There are easily over 30 different DV cameras on the market to choose from today, so it's important to identify what your needs are and what features will meet those needs. Make up a checklist before going into a camera store—decide what's important to you and what isn't, so when you're faced with that smooth-talking salesperson you won't be talked into getting something you don't want.

Video Storage Format

The first question you have to ask yourself is this: What video format do I want my DV camera to record onto? Although the vast majority will record onto MiniDV, there are other formats on the market today that you may run into. Figure 3-1 shows the tremendous difference in size between the VHS format and the two digital video formats, MiniDV and MicroMV.

Figure 3-1 Shown is VHS tape size compared to MicroMV and MiniDV (left to right).

When you go shopping for a camera, you'll encounter three DV camera recording formats:

■ **MiniDV**   A standard created by an industry-wide agreement on a format for digital video, MiniDV is the most common form of video storage in today's DV cameras. MiniDV cameras connect using FireWire, and they're universally compatible with any brand of FireWire card and any software designed to work over FireWire. Standard MiniDV tapes will hold 60 minutes (15 gigabytes [GB]) worth of footage, or 90 minutes at Long Play (LP). MiniDV cameras are the most flexible of the three formats.

■ **MicroMV**   Invented by Sony, the incredibly tiny MicroMV tapes store video, up to 60 minutes per tape, in a special MPEG-2 format that can be accessed only by another Sony MicroMV camera or Sony's MovieShaker software. While this is an impressive feat of engineering, the FireWire on any Sony MicroMV camera isn't standard, so you won't be able to connect the MicroMV camera to your video-editing software. Although the MicroMV format is extremely small and has allowed Sony to create some incredibly tiny cameras, I strongly urge you to avoid any camera that uses this format until Sony creates MicroMV cameras that will function over a standard FireWire connection, or until all the video-editing software on the market supports MicroMV. You need to make too many compromises with this format.

■ **DVD**   The rarest of recording formats, some cameras starting to emerge on the market record video directly to a DVD-R (DVD-recordable) or DVD-RAM (DVD-random access memory) disc in MPEG-2 format. It's an interesting concept—in some ways, it's like the old cameras that took VHS tapes. You record onto the final format that you would put into your display device (VCR, DVD player, etc.). In practice, this storage method is fraught with problems. Although I haven't tested a camcorder that uses this storage medium, I believe it's problematic on several levels: the MPEG format will be compressed, and when you edit that video and export it again, you'll be compressing the video twice—this will result in an overall lower quality. Few DVD-ROM (DVD–read only memory) drives on the market today support reading DVD-RAM discs, and the cost of using write-once DVD-R discs would be prohibitive. In a few years we all may be using this format, but it will have to mature a little first. I suggest avoiding cameras that use this format.

At this point in time, I feel MiniDV is the only viable choice—MicroMV and DVD recording mediums require too many sacrifices for little gain. Stick with MiniDV and you won't go wrong.

Tip   If you're shooting an important event, use a brand-new tape. Most tapes can be used at least half-a-dozen times before you'll see any drop in recording quality, but if you want to maximize the quality, pick up a new tape. There are no hard and fast rules for how many times a tape can be reused, but, to start, I'd recommend getting three MiniDV tapes and alternating among them from event to event.

Tip   If you have several MiniDV tapes and you're not going to immediately transfer them to your PC, you may want to create labels for the MiniDV cassettes that are more legible than your own handwriting. Check out this freeware application: *http://www.rodus.com/videomatica/*.

The Lens

The lens is an extremely important part of the camera. When considering the lens on the camera you're looking at, here are some issues to consider:

■ **The importance of optical zoom**   Repeat after me: there is no zoom but optical zoom. Optical zoom is accomplished with real glass lenses, resulting in a high-quality image. The level of optical zoom will typically be printed on the side of the camera or lens. Most cameras will have 10x optical zoom, but some (like the Canon ZR50) have 22x zoom. Most cameras will print the digital zoom in large letters because it looks like a more impressive number: 120x, 400x, even 700x! Ignore these numbers and look for the optical zoom value—this is the true measure of the cameras zoom capabilities. Decide how much zoom you need—will you be shooting video footage relatively close to the subject, like people at birthday parties? Or will you be far away from the action, like sporting events or an African safari? For most scenarios, 10x zoom is just fine. If you want to get close to the action without physically being there, however, look for something in the 20x and higher realm.

Tip   Remember, however, that the more you zoom in, the steadier you'll need to keep the camera—even with the stabilization features of modern DV cameras, shooting hand-held at 20x zoom is extremely hard to keep jitter-free. Remember to get a tripod if this is the type of shooting scenarios you see yourself in.

■ **Ignore the digital zoom**   As I mentioned above, camera manufacturers like to tout enormous digital zoom numbers, but they rarely mean anything. What does one do with a 700x zoom anyway? Digital zoom is accomplished by the camcorder's onboard image processor taking the digital image and enlarging the *pixels* that make it up. The result is that every pixel is bigger, and therefore the image is bigger, but at the cost of quality. You end up with a jagged, blocky-looking image that can't be fixed through video editing. Completely ignore the digital zoom feature when shopping for a camera. In fact, it would seem that on some level the camera manufacturers agree with me— from the cameras I tried, nearly all of them had digital zoom turned off by default.

Lingo   A *pixel* is the smallest part of a digital image, and when you're working at a computer, everything you see is made up of pixels. Pixels are either red, blue, or green, and when they're arranged close together, you get all the colors in the spectrum. Pixels are also tied to resolution—when I say that digital video is 720 x 480, that means every frame in that video is 720 pixels wide by 480 pixels high.

Note   The same rules about optical vs. digital zoom apply to the digital still photography world. Always focus on the optical zoom for maximum quality!

■   **How does the zoom control feel?**   If possible, pick up the camera
and see how the zoom control feels. Do the buttons feel natural and
easy to access? Does the zoom control allow subtle, smooth motions?
Or is the zoom jerky and too fast? Try to get a feel for how the zoom
control works—next to actually pressing the Record button, zooming
in and out will be the most common task you'll perform on the camera.

Inputs and Outputs

Getting maximum value from your DV camera involves taking the footage and
then getting it off the camera to work with. Although all DV cameras will have
a FireWire port, you may need other ports depending on what tasks you want to
perform with the camera.

■   **A/V outputs for connecting to devices**   Every camera I tested had
the basic composite RCA connectors: yellow (video), red and white
(for stereo audio). You can easily connect to a TV for playback or VCR
for recording using these connections. All cameras that have a photo
capture mode with a memory card (discussed later in this chapter) will
also have a USB cable and port to connect to a computer. Some of the
higher-end cameras also have an S-Video (Super-Video) cable, which
offers a higher-quality video signal when recording to a VHS. Ultimately though, since you'll be transferring the video to your computer,
none of these ports are as important as the FireWire port.

■   **A/V inputs for accepting connections**   There are only a few cases
where incoming connections will be useful. Although it's technically
possible to connect one camera to another for transfer, it's an unlikely
scenario. One scenario that's quite plausible is connecting a VHS or old
camcorder to the DV camera. Some DV cameras have the ability to
accept incoming composite (RCA) video and audio signals, which
allows you to transfer the video from the old format onto a MiniDV
tape. In addition to being a good way to save old footage from dis-
appearing off decaying tapes, this is also a great way to avoid having
to get an analog video capture card (discussed more in Chapter 5).
Once you transfer the video to the MiniDV tape, you can then transfer
the video to your computer over FireWire. This saves time and will
result in your getting the best-quality video that you can.

Caution   Remember that MiniDV tapes can only hold 60 to 90 minutes of footage, so if you have an old VHS tape with six hours of footage on it, you'll need to monitor the transfer process manually and stop the video to swap in a new tape at the appropriate time.

Image Stabilization

Even if you have the steady hands of a surgeon, the "camera jitters" will likely show up in your video footage at some point or another. Whether it's the wind jostling you, or just the subtle rhythm of your breathing, you will move the camera when filming. It's a problem that plagued home video users a decade ago, resulting in motion sickness-inducing vacation videos, and modern DV cameras have technology that helps make this problem a little easier to manage. Every camera will implement this feature differently, and, as you might expect, some solutions are more effective than others.

There's no true way to measure the effectiveness of a camera's image stabilization other than to try it. When you're trying out the DV camera, first zoom all the way out and move the camera side to side—does the image in the LCD (liquid crystal display) viewfinder seem to "float" slightly as you move it? That's the image stabilizer at work. Ask the salesperson to turn off the image stabilizer and try the same movement again—see the difference? Now try the same thing at maximum zoom—see what the results are. Also try keeping the camera as steady as possible while at maximum zoom. You'll likely see some camera jitter, but it's important to know how well the image stabilizer on the camera you're looking at can compensate for your movements. You should also ask if the image stabilization is optical or electronic/digital—optical will provide the best image quality but is usually only found on the higher-end cameras.

If you find that you have a lot of problems keeping the camera steady at a medium zoom length, you may want to put a lot of weight on the importance of this feature. Still, keep in mind that it's better to have a great-quality camera on a tripod than one that has poor video capturing abilities but great stabilization.

Caution   Using Image Stabilization can cut down on the light sensitivity your camera has. If you're shooting in low-light environments, turn off the image stabilization to get the best image—but have that tripod handy if you don't have steady hands.

Tip   To learn more about Image Stabilization, check out this excellent Web resource: *http://www.adamwilt.com/DV-FAQ-etc.html*.

Still Photo Capabilities

One of the recent developments in the DV camera world is the addition of dedicated memory cards for photo storage. It's an attempt to bridge the gap between motion and still photography, and every modern DV camera will include a photo function. Some will even include built-in flashes for taking shots in low-light conditions. Seems like a great idea, right? Well, before you throw away your digital camera, take a close look at Figure 3-2, especially the wall to the upper left of the woman. See all those "speckles"? In the photography world, that's called "noise"—it represents visual data (pixels) that the camera sensor can't quite interpret properly. The end result is a substandard image that's worse than a cheap digital camera would produce. Figure 3-2 was photographed with an expensive high-end, three-sensor camera. None of the cameras I tested, from the entry-level cameras up to the superb Canon GL-2, took images that I would ever use for printing.

Figure 3-2 This is a sample photo taken with a high-end DV camera.

Since all DV cameras have this feature now, even if it's not something you use often, it's a good idea to understand the basics.

- **Resolution**   The size, in pixels, of the image taken. Usually measured in "megapixels," most cameras have around 1 to 1.7 megapixels. This has no impact on the quality of the image, however—the 1.7-megapixel images had just as much noise in them as the 1-megapixel images.

■   **Quality**   There are usually quality settings for taking photos. They allow for varying levels of JPEG compression—the higher the compression, the smaller the file size and the lower quality the image. In my tests, however, I found that even when set to maximum quality, the overall image produced was unacceptable.

■   **Memory card format**   You'll encounter three main memory formats when looking at DV cameras, and two of them are essentially the same in terms of compatibility.

● MultiMediaCards (MMC): These cards are very small, around the size of a postage stamp. Only 1 mm thick, they are very light yet surprisingly strong. MMC cards are currently available in capacities of up to 128 MB. Every brand of camera I looked at, save Sony, used MMC or SD cards. Both MMC and SD cards are useable in a wide variety of devices from digital cameras to Personal Digital Assistants (PDAs) to MP3 players.

● Secure Digital (SD): Very similar to MMC, SD cards are 2.1 mm thick. They are currently available in capacities of up to 512 MB. Most DV cameras on the market today accept SD cards.

● Memory Stick: A proprietary Sony standard only useable with Sony DV cameras, a Memory Stick is about the size of a stick of gum. It's quite thin and is longer than it is wide. Available in capacities of up to 128 MB, Memory Sticks are also used in Sony digital cameras and Sony laptops.

Note   One factor that may influence your decision of which memory card format to use is what type of devices you use to view the images. Do you have a PDA or laptop that takes SD cards? Look at a camera with an SD card slot. Do you use a Sony PDA that uses Memory Sticks? Unsurprisingly, look to the Sony DV cameras for a compatible format.

As you can tell, I'm not all that thrilled with the quality of current still picture technology in today's DV cameras. I would urge you to not let this be a deciding factor when shopping for a camera. You'd be far better off getting a low-end digital camera to take pictures with and only using the still picture capture in a pinch. Hopefully, as the technology matures we'll see better-quality images—with a massive 20x zoom lens, a DV camera that took high-quality pictures would be a dream come true for someone like me!

Low-Light Performance

The quality of your video image often depends on the amount of illumination. Too much light, and your video will be washed-out-looking. Too little light, and your video will look "muddy." All DV cameras will have a function called "auto exposure"—the camera will adjust itself for the amount of light and attempt to achieve an optimal image. Cameras have an iris, much like our own, that will close to reduce the light flooding in in bright situations or open up all the way to maximize the light available in low-light shoots. There are two modes that will help enhance the low-light performance of a DV camera:

- **Low-light mode**   Most cameras will have a low-light mode as an autoexposure preset that you can select. The camera will maximize the iris to get as much light as possible, but it's usually at the expense of image fluidity—the camera will usually shift into a lower shutter rate where it can capture more light per frame of the image, but the result is a blurred image if the subject moves very much. The low-light mode is good for capturing subjects that don't move, but if you're filming fast action in the dark, you might as well save your battery and put the camera away. Unless your camera supports Night mode, that is!

- **Night mode**   Sony is one of the few, if not the only, brand names that offer this feature. Using a special infrared "spotlight," the Sony is able to capture images in complete darkness. Video footage captured in this manner will be in "black and green" (two-tone), but the results are truly amazing (and I've seen only Sony cameras that can do it). If you're planning on doing a lot of night shooting and don't mind the greenish hue, a camera that supports true "night vision" is a big plus. Please note that not all "Night modes" are created equal—some cameras will have a true Night mode like the Sony, while others will simply have an enhanced "low-light" mode and call it "Night" mode. Be sure to test the Night mode in the store before buying the camera (yes, it will still work with the lights on).

Try This! When you're in the store, find a darker area (perhaps in a corner) and zoom in on it and allow the camera to adjust to an optimal light level. Now quickly pan the camera over to a bright area and watch how long it takes to adjust the image. Some cameras are quick to adjust, while others are painfully slow. Try to select a camera that adjusts rapidly—it's common to be shooting indoors and, when panning to follow a subject, that person will step in front of a sunny window. That change in light levels will throw off any camera, but the faster the camera can adjust, the more useable footage you'll get.

Note Some cameras have an optional light attachment that functions like a miniature spotlight. It's good only for throwing light a few feet, but it will do in a pinch. The light is usually attached to the top of the camera where a standard flash or microphone would go.

Battery Life

Like all electronic devices, a DV camera depends on electricity to function. If you have a dead battery, you have a dead DV camera. You don't want to go through the frustration of having a useless camera while a great moment is passing you by, so here are the things you should consider when selecting your camera.

- **Recording time**   Every camera will have a stated recording time— the good news is, most camera batteries will outlast a single 60-minute tape. The battery life you see on the sticker isn't going to be what you get in day-to-day operation. Ask to see the manual for the camera and look up the actual battery life. You'll typically find something like this: 2 hours maximum recording time in controlled tests, 1 hour of recording in "real life" using the eyepiece viewfinder, and 55 minutes using the LCD screen. The maximum recording time is based on pressing Record and letting it record with no pausing or zooming—as you can imagine, you'll likely never record under those conditions, so always assume a battery life less than what you're promised.

- **Optional batteries**   Most cameras have batteries that you can purchase as accessories—a very good idea if you're planning on using the camera in an environment away from electricity (like a camping trip). Picking up an extra battery is generally a good idea, and you may also have the option of buying an extended-life battery. These are batteries that are larger and heavier than the included battery but have massively increased runtime. The Canon GL2, for example, has a maximum recording time of two hours with the standard battery, but an impressive seven hours with the largest battery pack (BP-945). Consider your uses and buy the best battery pack for the job.

Tip   If you think you're going to be recording long events near an electrical jack, look for a camera that offers an AC pass-through. This is essentially a special battery pack that allows you to plug into an electrical outlet for unlimited shooting time (or until you run out of tapes).

Ergonomics

The way a camera fits in your hand is one of the most critical elements in picking the right camera for your needs. If you find the camera awkward, you're less likely to use it, and your investment becomes a paperweight. Just like clothing, one size does not fit all—there are several key factors to consider when it comes to camera ergonomics.

- **Weight**   How heavy is the camera? If it's too heavy, you won't want to use it for very long. Some cameras are too light and feel almost flimsy. What about the balance and the weight? Does the camera sit evenly in your hand, or does it tend to tip forward? Imagine struggling with that every few seconds for 30 minutes, and you'll see why a well-balanced camera is a must.

- **Size**   Is smaller always better? Not necessarily—it depends on what you need from your camera. Is portability the most important thing to you? Then pick the smallest camera you can find (like a Sony DCR-IP5J) and live with the limitations (usually awkward button placement and short battery life). Or do you think you'll be shooting from a tripod most of the time and having a larger, well-balanced camera will be most beneficial? Pick a larger camera with a little more "heft"—something you can use comfortably for hours at a time (like the Canon GL2).

- **Buttons**   One of the most critical ergonomic elements, button placement is something you should pay close attention to. It might sound a little silly, but poor button placement can make or break a camera.

When you hold the camera, how easily do your fingers reach the Record/Pause button and zoom controls? Do you have to twist your fingers at an uncomfortable angle to reach them? Reaching the most often-used buttons should feel very natural. I've found with some cameras, like the tiny MicroMV models by Sony, that the cameras seem to be designed for people with very small hands—I'm 6'2" and found the buttons a little awkward to use, yet a woman of 5'5" may find it perfectly comfortable. Try out the camera to get a feel for the button placements before buying.

- **LCD Screen**   The size of the LCD view screens varies widely among cameras. The size you'll need depends on factors like your vision (larger screens are easier to see) and the battery life you're looking for (smaller screens use less power). Will the LCD screen be easy to see outdoors? How does it look—is the resolution sufficient for crisp images? Do you have to use a button to control the menus, or is it a touch screen? Weigh all these factors when considering what type of LCD screen works best for you.

- **Upright vs. Standard**   There are two basic body designs for cameras on the market today. The camera is either the standard body type, with it being longer than it is tall. The upright body design reverses that: the camera is taller vertically than horizontally. Each camera design has pros and cons, so it's important to pick the design that works best for you. I personally find the standard design easier to use and less awkward, but you may find the vertical body type easier to use.

Interval Timers

Have you ever seen video footage that is shot over a period of several hours where a flower goes from being closed to blooming? This is typically done with an interval timer—some DV cameras have the ability to shoot a predefined amount of video every certain number of minutes. You could point your camera at a plant and film it for 5 seconds every 5 minutes and watch it turn toward the sun. Shooting video like this can give you some very interesting results, but it requires a great deal of patience to get the perfect shot.

Caution   If you're going to be shooting video using an interval timer over more than an hour or so, consider an external power supply or running an extension cable to the camera. The last thing you want is your battery dying just before the final stage of your event occurs!

One CCD vs. Three CCD Cameras

Digital video cameras capture images through something called a "charged coupling device," or CCD for short. Without getting too technical, the CCD is a highly sensitive photon detector—it "sees" light and captures the image, recording every part of the image as a pixel that is red, blue, or green in color (RBG). As you shop for a camera you'll see some cameras being advertised as "Three chip" or "3CCD" cameras—unlike most low to mid-range cameras that capture the RBG images using a single CCD, the 3CCD cameras have a dedicated CCD for each color: one for red, one for blue, one for green. This allows greater clarity of color and rich tones—which means a much better overall image. Cameras with three CCDs are much more expensive than single CCD cameras, so you'll have to decide if the image quality is worth the gain. In my nonscientific tests, however, I found that although most of the three CCD cameras had superb video quality, some of the single CCD cameras (like the Canon ZR50) had image quality that came very close to the more expensive cameras. Is the improvement in image quality worth the extra cost? You'll have to decide that for yourself.

Note   One of the newer selling points with DV cameras now is the term "Megapixel camera." DV is 720 x 480 in resolution, which means there are 345,600 pixels in a single frame of DV. A "megapixel" is 1 million pixels, and the concept is that the more pixels you have, the higher the quality of the image. But if 345,600 pixels are the maximum, why go up to 1 million? Megapixel cameras use up their extra pixels for digital image stabilization and other forms of digital processing, giving you the "best" 345,600 pixels possible. However, in all my searches I couldn't find a good description of "Megapixel technology" or exactly how the technology worked to create better images. I have a feeling that that although there are some technical reasons why megapixel cameras will produce better images, for now this feature is mostly marketing hype.

Classes of DV Cameras

Four main classes of DV cameras are on the market today: entry-level consumer, mid-range consumer, high-end consumer, and high-end Prosumer. There are no hard and fast rules about how to decide what category each camera fits in, but here's how I would define each category—see which one comes closest to matching your needs.

Entry-Level Consumer Camera

The camera for someone with simple needs who is just starting out in the DV world. Entry-level cameras offer few features, adequate picture quality, and a low price tag. They're a good starting point if you're unsure how much you'll be using the camera and don't want to sink too much money into the investment.

Mid-range Consumer Camera

Cameras in this range offer a higher price tag than the entry-level cameras and more expansive features to boot—enhanced zoom functions, higher-quality video capture, and features like a flash for still photos. Most people buying cameras in this category have an idea of what they want in a camera and will get good use out of the product.

High-End Consumer Camera

Reserved for the more serious buyers, or those who like having the best of everything, high-end consumer cameras will typically offer excellent performance, small size, and superb image quality. They'll often have a plethora of special shooting modes and some of the other features I mentioned earlier that you don't particularly need. They're not all gloss, though—cameras in this price range are almost always excellent performers.

High-End Prosumer Camera

The pinnacle of the consumer buying market, the Prosumer is typically for someone who will buy a product for both professional and personal use. Part-time videographers who film weddings on the weekend would fall into this category—they're willing to spend the money to get the top-tier consumer products but aren't quite at the level where they'd invest in the camera and gear to make a full-time career out of it. These will be the cameras with the 20x optical zoom, three CCDs, and jaw-dropping image quality.

A Look at Today's Camera Market

So what sort of cameras are on the market today? It would be beyond the scope of this book to give you detailed reviews of every camera, but I wanted to give you brief overviews of at least a few of the cameras that you might see when you go shopping for one. I contacted Canon, Sony, and Panasonic, and asked them to lend me an entry-level camera, a mid-range camera, and high-end consumer or high-end Prosumer camera. Here's a snapshot of what you can expect to see when you go camera shopping.

Entry-Level Digital Video Cameras

Canon ZR50

Canon has been a powerful presence in the consumer electronics market for a long time now, specifically in the camera and video realms, so it's no surprise that their DV cameras are solid contenders for your money. The ZR50 shown in Figure 3-3 is a great entry-level camera that offers solid features and surprisingly good image quality. The 22x zoom is fantastic for filming subjects from far away—even their high-end GL2 tops out at 20x. With options for adding a directional microphone and buttons that light up in the dark for easy use, this is a well-rounded camera that feels great in your hand. The button placement is well thought-out, and everything is easy to access. The video quality is excellent, with strong color saturation—and it also handles reds quite well (a common weakness among entry-level cameras). The LCD screen is of average size but is difficult to see outside in direct sunlight (switching to using the viewfinder negates this problem, however). If you're interested in a lower-priced model, the ZR40 is the little brother to the ZR50. It has less zoom (18x optical) and a bit fewer features.

Figure 3-3 The Canon ZR50 is great for filming subjects from far away.

Panasonic PVDV102K

At the time of this writing, Panasonic has 14 different DV camera models on the market. They're aiming for all the market segments and have produced some solid contenders. The PVDC102K (who names these cameras anyway?) shown in Figure 3-4 is a good entry-level choice with a lot of value for your money. It was the least expensive camera that I looked at, but it still offers a 10x optical zoom, a great Leica Dicomar lens, and the ability to also function as a Web cam while connected to a computer. The video it captured was of good quality. I was surprised how small the LCD screen is, considering that the flip-out panel that holds it is quite large. LCD screens are among the most expensive components on a camera, so this is understandable—look to the higher-end Panasonic cameras if you want a large LCD viewscreen. If you're looking for the lowest entry-level camera possible, look at the Panasonic PV-DV52—it is very similar to the PVDC102K.

Figure 3-4 The Panasonic PVDC102K offers a good value for your money.

Sony DCR-TRV25

Sony is well known for high-quality consumer products, and the DCR-TRV25 shown in Figure 3-5 is no exception. Sony is an elite brand name, and the price tag reflects that—their entry-level cameras cost as much as some of the mid-range products from other vendors, but they also offer features to match. This model offers a 10x optical zoom, the superb night vision I mentioned earlier, digital image stabilization, and the ability to take both digital still photos and MPEG video clips to the small Memory Stick. The LCD screen was easier to see outdoors in direct sunlight than most other cameras I tried. Sony also offers the DCR-TRV18, a slightly less expensive version that is very similar to the DCR-TRV25.

Figure 3-5 The Sony DCR-TRV25 offers superb night vision.

Note   For more information on Sony digital video cameras, you can visit their Web site at *www.sonystyle.com*.

Mid-Range Digital Video Cameras

Canon Optura 100 MC/200 MC

Canon has several mid-range cameras, and the Optura series is a vertical-styled camera with solid features. The Optura DV cameras can be expanded with a detachable boom microphone for enhanced audio and a directional video light for low-light situations. The pop-up flash makes digital still photos easier, and the optical image stabilization helps balance out the video with the 10x optical zoom. The Optura 200 MC camera adds a "Super Night Mode" where the camera actually emits a bright LED light to add supplemental light to a shot. I haven't tested this, so I'm unsure of how well this feature works and how it compares to the Sony night vision. Both the Optura 100 MC and 200 MC have SD card slots for still photos. I found the Optura 100 MC shown in Figure 3-6 a little awkward to hold (I prefer the standard body designs to the vertical body designs), but the video quality and color saturation were very strong. Button placement was a little clumsy for my taste, and although the zoom was smooth, it wasn't very fast. Still, minor quibbles aside, the Optura is a strong mid-range camera.

Figure 3-6 The Canon Optura 100 MC offers good video quality.

Panasonic PVDV702K

The mid-range Panasonic PVDV702K shown in Figure 3-7 offers features quite standard for cameras in this range at a reasonable price. The LCD screen is very large in comparison to other cameras on the market, but I found it somewhat difficult to see outdoors (many cameras have this problem). The camera is very lightweight and well balanced, and it offers a strong digital image stabilization feature. The 10x optical zoom works well, and if you're interested in taking digital still photos, images are stored on an SD card. All the Panasonic cameras I tested had great zoom features—subtle pressure allows you to zoom slowly in and out, and increased pressure gives you a rapid zoom.

Figure 3-7 The Panasonic PVDV702K offers standard features at a reasonable price.

Sony DCR-PC101

Sony's mid-range DCR-PC101 has a standard body design with good balance and weight. The 10x optical zoom was smooth at slow zooms and very responsive at faster zooms. The image stabilization Sony uses is quite effective and appears to be digital in nature—it made the shots taken at 10x zoom much smoother. The DCRPC101 offers features similar to the DRC-TRV25, including an MPEG movie mode that stores video on the Memory Stick, a still picture mode, and the superb Sony NightShot mode that allows you to film in complete darkness. As Figure 3-8 indicates, the DCR-PC101 is a vertical-body design and has some of the awkwardness that comes with that approach in terms of button placement and balance. The DCR-PC101 is very small compared to other cameras—it would fit easily into a purse or small bag, so it's a good choice for people who want to carry a camera with them without being inconvenienced by the size or weight of a larger camera.

Figure 3-8 The Sony DCR-PC101 is a good choice for people looking for a smaller camera.

High-End Consumer/Prosumer Digital Video Cameras

Panasonic PVDV952

Panasonic's top-end camera, the PVDV952 shown in Figure 3-9 is a three-CCD design aimed at the high-end consumer. This camera is for the serious amateur videographer. Offering high-end features like a manual focus ring, very strong digital image stabilization, and 10x optical zoom, this is a solid camera. Ergonomically, it's brilliant—the camera is fairly large in comparison to most other cameras, but it felt great in my hands. Excellent balance and superb button placement make this a delight to shoot with. Zoom was smooth but quick, and the enormous LCD screen helps make shooting even easier. Colors seemed a little on the pale side to me, but this may be something that can be fixed with some tweaking.

Figure 3-9 The Panasonic PVDV952 is a solid camera with high-end features.

Sony DCR-IP55

Part of Sony's new MicroMV line, the DCR-IP55 shown below in Figure 3-10 is an amazing feat of engineering. Weighing in at a featherweight 15 ounces (435 grams) (without a tape or battery), and only 2 $\frac{3}{8}$ in x 2 $\frac{7}{8}$ in x 5 $\frac{1}{8}$ in (60 mm x 73 mm x 128.5 mm) in size, this camera is the smallest one I've ever used. It may be small, but it's packed with some impressive features: a Carl Zeiss Vario Sonnar lens with 10x optical zoom, a single 1.07-megapixel CCD, superb Sony NightVision, integrated Bluetooth, a pop-up flash, and an LCD screen that looks equally superb indoors and outdoors (the only one I examined with this type of LCD screen). The battery is actually in a swing-down handle that makes for easy hand-held shooting. Color saturation was superb, with rich, vibrant tones. There are some caveats, though, in getting the camera to be so small: I found the buttons to be too small and tightly packed together for me to manipulate comfortably. The Record button is very close to the Photo button, so I found myself snapping pictures instead of recording video a few too many times.

Figure 3-10 The Sony DCR-IP55 is a small camera with impressive features.

Although I found myself enamored with the hardware and tiny size, unfortunately this camera has one fatal flaw that, for the moment, means you shouldn't buy it if you're planning on transferring the video to your computer for editing. Because Sony uses a special version of MPEG2 to record the video, this camera can't be connected to your PC like normal FireWire cameras can. This means that you can't connect it to your favorite video-editing program—you have to use Sony's MovieShaker application. When I tried to export the video to standard Audio Video Interleaved (AVI) for editing in another application, for some reason it limited me to 9 minutes of video footage (2 GB). This 2 GB limit was obliterated years ago, so I don't understand why the application limits the export. I captured some footage from a wedding on this camera, only to find out that I wasn't able to access this footage in any other application other than MovieShaker. And since I don't find MovieShaker to be a good choice for video editing, I effectively lost that footage. If Sony can find a way to make the MicroMV work in other applications as easily as other FireWire cameras can, they'll have a real winner on their hands.

Canon GL2

Canon's GL2 falls firmly into the Prosumer range, and as such it offers features no other camera in this line-up has—including a hefty price tag. Still, there is no other camera that I tested with its unique blend of quality and functionality. The GL2 shown below in Figure 3-11 is large in comparison to other cameras I looked at—this is not a camera you can easily slip into your coat pocket. If you can accept that, you'll be in for a treat: ergonomically, this camera is utterly brilliant. When you slip your hand under the strap, your fingers naturally slide into position with the buttons: Record, Zoom, Standby, Lock, Photo, and even the tape eject mechanism. Canon put a lot of thought into the way this camera looks and feels. Although the camera is fairly large, it's very well balanced and can be comfortably used for long periods of shooting. The LCD screen is moderately sized and somewhat difficult to see outdoors, but it's high-resolution and offers very accurate playback when viewing your footage.

Figure 3-11 The Canon GL2 offers a unique blend of quality and functionality.

The GL2 boasts a three-CCD design, and I can't state this strongly enough: the quality of the video and color accuracy is unmatched in any camera I looked at. My jaw hit the floor when I saw the footage—it was simply stunning. The boom microphone and adjustable levels allow you to tweak your audio recordings, something few other cameras offer. The Fluorite lens offers a 20x optical zoom, and with an optically based image stabilization system, your shots will never look so smooth. The camera allows for slow or fast zooms, and Canon did something very innovative: they added a handle on the top with integrated Zoom and Record buttons. This allows you to film by holding the camera by the top to get some unique angles on things. It's quite challenging to do, but it offers some unique opportunities. The GL2 has a horseshoe slot on top that allows you to add on another microphone or a small light, and immediately below that you can flip up the handle for access to all the playback buttons. The camera also has a feature that will display "zebra lines" on areas of the scene that are over-exposed. This allows you to lower the exposure and correct for the problem before you even hit Record. This is a real lifesaver in some situations!

As you can tell, I really enjoyed using this camera. If you're a serious videographer interested in pro-quality results, this camera is well worth the investment. I wouldn't recommend it for first-time buyers, but if you're willing to learn and grow into your camera, it's a good tool to use. The XL1S is an even higher-end version of the GL2 with more features.

Getting the Proper Accessories

You thought it ended with picking out the DV camera? Not quite—any good DV camera owner should have a few accessories. Although you'd think that the camera you're spending hundreds (or thousands) on would include everything you need, that's never the case. Here are some of the more popular accessories to consider to round out your DV camera purchase.

FireWire Cables

I was more than a little surprised when I discovered that of all the cameras I was sent to evaluate, none of them had FireWire cables included for me to transfer the digital video to my computer. I imagine this is because not everyone will be connecting the DV camera to his or her computer, but you can count on having to purchase one cable before you leave the store. The salesperson might not even ask if you need a cable, so be sure to pick one up before you leave. There are two types of connections: 4-pin and 6-pin. The larger 6-pin connections are typical for desktop computers with FireWire cards, and every camera I've seen has used a 4-port connection. So in almost every case, you should buy a 4-pin/6-pin cable. The exception to this is if you have a laptop: most laptops (specifically Sony and Dell laptops) have a 4-pin connector. This means you'll need to get a 4-pin/4-pin cable. FireWire cables vary in price, depending on brand and length. The cable should be long enough to reach from the FireWire ports on the back (or front) of your computer up to your camera without it being awkward.

Tapes

Even starting out, you should have two or three MiniDV tapes. Although tapes are fairly sturdy, accidents do happen: tapes break, get lost, or are eaten by the family dog. The last thing you want is not to have a tape when you need it. Tapes are fairly cheap, so stock up on a few. Especially for unpredictable events where you're not quite sure how long it will last (like weddings), an extra tape is a must.

Spare Battery

Running out of battery power at the wrong moment can be very frustrating, and if you're going to be filming long events (over an hour), you'll almost certainly exhaust your battery. Consider purchasing a second battery, and if the camera has an option for a high-capacity battery, buy one and keep your standard battery as a backup. The cost of spare batteries will vary depending on capacity and brand.

Tripod

A tripod is one of the most important purchases you can make (Figure 3-12). If I could sum up the problems that plague most home videos, I would use two words: motion sickness. Even with advanced image stabilization technologies, it can be difficult to keep your shots jitter-free. Learning to perform smooth zooms will help mitigate this problem, but even with steady hands you'll have a hard time keeping things steady at extreme zoom. Tripods are the single-most valuable tools for getting great shots, and learning to use one can take a bit of practice. Learning to combine the camera zoom with the horizontal pan of the tripod is a skill you'll pick up fairly quickly, and it can really enhance your shots.

Figure 3-12 A Tiffen tripod (*www.tiffen.com*) will help keep your shots jitter-free.

Note   For a compromise between stability and mobility, look into getting a monopod. Instead of having three legs that intersect, a monopod is essentially a single pole that attaches to the bottom of the camera. It offers vertical stability when you plant it on the ground but not the horizontal stability of a tripod, so you have to keep the horizontal plane reasonably steady on your own.

Tip   If you're looking for a wider selection of tripods, look at your local camera store. Most tripods have the same attachment points as cameras, so you can often find a tripod that will work for both your digital video camera and your digital still camera. Double-duty means one less thing to carry.

Lens Filters

If you're looking to subtly alter the look of your video footage, filters like the one in Figure 3-13 are a great way to do this. Because lens sizes vary from camera to camera, you need to make sure that you get the right type. In some cases the size of the lens will be printed on the lens ring (usually measured in mm), but when in doubt check your manual. So what do lens filters "do"? DV cameras are so accurate that they often pick up more detail than we want them to—there's a reason why movie stars look better on the big screen than in real life. Filters help remove the sometimes harsh colors of DV footage. Lens filters can be anything from a clear filter to help protect your expensive lens from dirt and dust to a warmth filter which removes ultraviolet light, giving you warmer skin tones and less harsh blue tones. Filters can also soften skin by giving it a diffused look, erasing skin blemishes and wrinkles, or tone down excessive image sharpness. Tiffen is the leading maker of lens filters and offers several kits—learn more at *www.tiffen.com*.

Figure 3-13 Tiffen lens filters (*www.tiffen.com*) can subtly alter the look of your video footage.

Steadicam

The Steadicam was an invention, brought to the videography world by Garrett Brown, that revolutionized the film industry. A Steadicam is a specially balanced camera platform that a cameraman uses, and it allows for some amazing shots. I haven't used one myself, but by all accounts it will eliminate camera jitters in a way nothing else can. You can turn, move up and down, rock back and forth—and the Steadicam will remain fluid and smooth. A relatively inexpensive add-on for what it allows you to do, the Steadicam JR shown in Figure 3-14 is offered by Tiffen (*www.tiffen.com*).

Figure 3-14 The Tiffen Steadicam JR is a specially balanced camera platform.

> **Tip**   If you're interested in learning more about the Steadicam JR from an enthusiast just like
> you, check out this great Web site: *http://www.geocities.com/Hollywood/Lot/7385/.*

Where to Buy Your Camera

So now that you're equipped with the knowledge you need to pick the perfect
camera for your needs, the question quickly becomes "Where do I look"? Online
shopping vs. the "bricks and mortar" stores of the real world—each offer advantages and disadvantages. Let's look at them.

Shopping Online vs. Going to a Local Store

The classic conundrum: buy locally or buy online? There's no perfect answer to
this question, because it depends on many factors. A big factor is how experienced you are—intermediate and expert users who know exactly what they

want will usually prefer online purchases, while beginners will prefer the hand-holding of a local store. Here are some of the things you should consider:

- **Hands-on time**   Because DV cameras are devices that demand physical inspection, local stores will likely be your only opportunity to examine the cameras and get an idea of how they differ in features and feel. There's no substitute for testing a camera before purchasing it, and this is something an online store can't offer. Some of the smaller stores may even let you take a DV camera home for the evening and try it out before making your purchase. If you already know what camera you want to purchase, this may not be an issue.

- **Selection**   Local stores will carry products based on local supply and demand, whereas online stores can sell anything the manufacturer makes. This broad selection can be very useful when you're seeking a specific camera or accessory. If you live in a small town, your local store may not carry a high end DV camera like the Canon GL2—ordering it online may be your only choice. However, be sure to ask the local store if they can special-order products—if they carry one Canon DV camera, they may be able to get any of them.

- **Price**   The big advantage that online stores have is usually in the realm of price. With less overhead, they can afford to charge smaller margins on the products. Some local stores will price-match against online stores, so you can sometimes get the best of both worlds (it's rare though). Remember to factor in all the "hidden" costs of buying online, however: shipping, handling, sales tax, duty, and tariffs (if you're ordering from another country). Sometimes that cheaper price can end up costing you extra! Do all the calculations up front before placing your order. It may even be a good idea to call in your order to an online store to make sure you're not going to be surprised.

- **Service**   Purchasing your camera at a local store means having a resource you can turn to for help if you need it. They won't teach you how to use it, but they can often answer basic questions over the phone. Local service also means being able to return the camera more easily if it's not what you want—but make sure to clarify what their return policy is before buying the camera! You may find the 15 percent restocking fee difficult to swallow if it's not the DV camera you thought it was.

■ **Warranty**   Most DV cameras on the market come with a one-year warranty, and if the camera needs repair work you may be without it for days (if not weeks). One advantage that a local store can offer is in the area of warranty: most larger chain stores offer enhanced warranties that cover everything from breakdowns to damage. If your camera stops working, you can go back to the store and swap it out for a new one—even if it's six months after the fact. Considering the environments in which DV cameras are often used, warranty coverage like this can be quite advantageous. I haven't seen an online store that offers anything like this before, so score another point for the local store.

Tip   You can always combine the two by shopping locally for a camera to get a feel for which one you want and then making the purchase online to get a better price. Remember, though, that stores are trying to earn a living, too: if you spend hours at a store trying out various cameras, quizzing the staff on features and functions, you should probably buy it there to support them.

Beware the Gray Market

"Gray market" is a term used to describe goods that are being sold outside their geographically allowed locations. Manufacturers make goods according to the specifications and laws in each country and, due to differences in economy and currency, will often sell the goods for less in one market than another. The gray market occurs when a vendor from one country buys the products meant for another market and illegally imports them. A sad truth of buying online is that if the price seems to good to be true, it usually is. If you see most vendors offering a DV camera for $900 to $1,000 US, and one vendor offers the "same" camera for $600 US, it's likely a gray market camera.

So what happens if you buy a gray market camera? As far as I know, there's no law against it—but you can lose warranty support, technical support, and, in some cases, your DV camera may not be compatible with the accessories sold in your local store. Getting stuck with a product that you can't get repaired isn't worth saving a few bucks.

Tip   There's no 100 percent surefire way to spot a gray market DV camera, but signs to look for include having a manual that includes no English section, the packaging or other printed material having no English, and power adaptors that don't match up with the rest of the hardware—because power voltages are different all over the world, gray market sellers will sometimes jury-rig power adaptors to get a working solution. One more reason to avoid gray market cameras!

Caution   Always check the feedback ratings for online vendors. If you use a service like PriceGrabber (*www.pricegrabber.com*), you can see buyer feedback. Read through the comments to get a feel for how trustworthy the vendor is—if the vendor is selling gray market hardware, people who have been stung will often mention that fact. Be aware, however, that some vendors are being accused of making false entries to boost their low ratings—if you see a vendor that has a lot of very low ratings and an equally high number of perfect ratings they're likely engaging in this practice. In general, most vendors aren't bipolar—a company with poor service will deliver poor results consistently, so look for consistency in the ratings. I can virtually guarantee that the company with the lowest price will also have the worst vendor rating—it seems to be a sad truth of buying online. You should also try doing a Google search for the vendor's name to see if any other buyers out there have been talking about that vendor on Web sites or online forums. You'd be surprised what you can find!

Alternate Digital Video Capture Devices

Although we've focused strictly on DV cameras so far, many other devices are capable of capturing digital video. None are as capable at capturing video in a way that matches MiniDV quality, but each offers something unique—and you may just find that you enjoy digital video so much you'll want to work with it on different devices.

Digital Still Cameras with Video Modes

Every modern digital camera on the market that I've seen offers a movie mode. Instead of capturing a single picture at a large 2-megapixel to 5-megapixel size, the camera captures much smaller images (320 x 240 resolution in most cases) and most include support for audio. I have a Canon G2 that I bought earlier this year (Figure 3-15), and, while on a vacation in Cancún, Mexico, I used it to shoot some short video clips (I didn't have a DV camera with me—for shame!).

Figure 3-15 The Canon Powershot G2 can shoot short video clips.

The results were definitely nowhere near as good as a DV camera, but I will say that I was more impressed with the video abilities of my digital camera than I was with the still-photo abilities of the DV cameras I tested. Clips are usually limited to 30 seconds and under (though some cameras limit it only to storage card size), and since most cameras have 4x and under zoom, they're only good for shooting video clips of something close by. The video files the camera will generate should be in AVI format, which will allow you to pull the clips into a video-editing program for manipulation. This can be a good way to get your feet wet with a video-editing program—experiment with your digital camera before taking the plunge and buying a DV camera.

FireWire and USB Web Cameras

Web cameras have been around for several years now—Logitech (*www.logitech.com*) was one of the pioneers in this field, and it was able to accomplish impressive things considering the meager 11 Mbps bandwidth of USB 1.1. Now that FireWire and USB 2.0 have hit mainstream, Web cams suddenly have a great deal more bandwidth to use, and that means higher-quality digital video (but don't discount the excellent video Logitech is still able to capture at USB 1.1). The most popular use of a Web cam is for video chatting with other people (videoconferencing). If you have a friend or relative who lives far away, video Web chats are a great way to keep in touch. The chief limitations to doing this successfully are twofold: what type of Internet connection each person has and what type of Web cam you're each using. In order to get a decent experience out of a videoconference, both parties should have high-speed connections (DSL or cable modem) and one of the newer breed of Web cams like the two shown below in Figures 3-16 and 3-17.

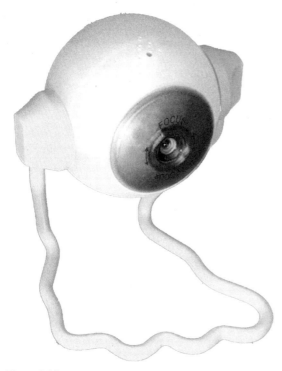

Figure 3-16 The Orange Micro iBot is available in USB 2.0 and FireWire flavors.

The Orange Micro iBot Web cam is a strange-looking creature, but it's an excellent Web cam. Both the FireWire and USB 2.0 speeds allow for an unprecedented 30 frames per second (fps) at 640 x 480 in 24-bit color. In short: excellent-quality video. I found that the FireWire version seemed to be a little smoother when the video preview was larger, but either camera would be a good choice for videoconferencing. Neither camera has a built-in microphone, so you'll need to buy a microphone separately. Both cameras can be purchased from *www.orangemicro.com* (they offer various bundles—some include microphones).

Figure 3-17 The ADS Pyro 1394 is a FireWire-based Web cam.

The ADS Pyro 1394 WebCam is, as you might expect, a FireWire-based Web cam. With the broad 400 Mbps bandwidth that FireWire offers, this camera is capable of a sustained 30 fps at 640 x 480 resolution. The video stream is uncompressed and uses a quality Sony CCD for good-quality video. The camera has a wide vertical rotation angle (over 180 degrees), a translucent blue shell, and a manual focus ring. You can get more information by visiting *www.adstechnologies.com.*

Note   I evaluated one of the new Logitech Quickcam Pro 4000 Web Cams just as this book was finishing up, and I wanted to mention it here. This camera was extremely impressive, especially considering it's a USB 1.1 camera. Video was superb, with rich colors and great quality, and the camera includes a built-in microphone with a good software bundle. I highly recommend this Web cam!

Note   You can use Web cameras for far more than just chatting. Although they are tied to a computer and don't have the freedom of movement that a regular DV camera has, you can still do a lot with them: Record personal greetings to e-mail to relatives, make a narrative-type film, record product demonstrations of items you're selling on eBay, or even attach the camera to a laptop for a mobile video camera.

Tip   Did you know that you can use your DV camera as a Web cam? Learn how in Chapter 6, "Capturing Your Video."

Wireless Cameras

One of the more unique devices that I tried out was the D-Link DCS-1000W 2.4 Ghz Wireless Internet Camera (*www.dlink.com*) shown in Figure 3-18.

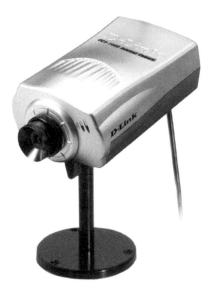

Figure 3-18 The D-Link DCS-1000W is a Wireless Internet Camera with a built-in server.

This camera has built-in 802.11b wireless communications, as well as a built-in server. What does that mean? Well, once you plug the camera in, you can access the camera and the video it records from any place in the world that has a Web browser. The camera needs only power, although if you have a hardwired Ethernet cable you can plug it in if you don't want to use the 802.11b wireless connection. The camera can be set to record video in various resolutions, triggered only by motion or set for continual recording, and it can even e-mail you photos of what it sees! The applications for this are endless: set it up at your front door to see who's there before answering, put it in the baby's bedroom while you're working, use it at the office for security, or even put it in your family room to watch the kids (and the babysitter) while you're out on the town (using a wireless Pocket PC). The video it captures can be stored, manipulated, and used for many things. Like most Web cam devices, the video isn't very high quality when compared to a DV camera—you won't be making home movies with the DCS-1000W, but if you're creative you can find many uses for it.

Key Points

■   DV cameras are the best investment for consumer-level video work.

■   MiniDV is the most viable recording format for a DV camera today.

■   The lens, zoom, image stabilization, battery life, ergonomics and low-light performance are all factors you should consider when choosing a DV camera.

■   The proper accessories are a must for a good DV camera experience.

■   There are pros and cons to buying online vs. at a local store.

■   Other devices, like digital cameras, Web cams, and wireless cameras, are all capable of capturing digital video.

Part 2

Capturing

Once you have your camera, it's time to start using it. Where do you start? It's easy enough to point the camera at someone and press the Record button, but getting the most effective video footage takes a bit more planning and effort than that. In this section of the book I'll be covering methods for shooting video footage, things to keep in mind to get the best shots possible, what sort of hardware you'll need in your computer to work with the digital video, and finally, the actual process of transferring the video from your DV camera (or a VHS tape) to your computer.

Chapter 4

Ready, Set, Film!

Get To Know Your Camera

Now that you have your camera and a deadly arsenal of digital video knowledge from the previous chapters, it's time to grab your camera and get to know it a whole lot better. I'm not a big fan of reading manuals, usually because most are poorly written (and utterly boring), but spending some time with your DV camera manual is always helpful. Although you can learn some features intuitively (with a well-designed DV camera that is), others take more time to absorb, and manuals are a good way to learn this. I should note, however, that one of my criteria for judging a good DV camera is how easy it is to pick up and use immediately—I was at a wedding recently and had two evaluation cameras with me: a Sony IP-55 and a Panasonic PV-DV952D (Figure 4-1). It was interesting to watch my friends pick up each camera and see how quickly they could figure it out. Between the two, the Panasonic seemed easier for them to figure out, although not by a wide margin.

Figure 4-1 This is a standard digital video camera.

For this reason, and the reasons mentioned in the previous chapter, I've chosen to use the PV-DV952D as the camera for the first part of this chapter. Ergonomically, it's a great camera, and the buttons are easy to manipulate. Every digital camera is slightly different, but most have the same basic functions. I'm using the Panasonic for the first part of this chapter, but your camera should have similar features. Pick up your digital camera as you're reading through this first section and find the corresponding feature—knowing what each button does will help you get that great footage when it comes along. The last thing you want to be doing is trying to figure out how to activate a certain function on your camera while a unique moment is passing you by!

Power, Record, and Mode Selection

The Power, Record, and Mode buttons are usually located very close together, within easy reach of your fingers when you pick the camera up. The idea here is to keep the three functions that you'll use most grouped tightly. Thankfully, the concept works quite well—unfortunately, not all camera manufacturers do it that way. The power function is self-explanatory—off and on. Most cameras don't have a "standby" state like computers do because cameras require almost no time to go from off to being ready to shoot (the exception here is the Canon GL2, which does have a Standby mode). In Figure 4-2 you can see that the power function is a simple up/down affair. Panasonic was clever in that it used the upper portion of the dial to switch modes.

Figure 4-2 The Power, Record, and Mode buttons are usually located near each other.

Modes on a DV cam are usually Camera (for recording), VCR (for playback of video currently on the tape), and usually a third mode. On the Panasonic, the third mode is "Card Playback." This is a mode designed to display the photographs stored on the Secure Digital (SD) memory card. On the Sony IP-55, the third mode is called "Network," and it puts the camera in a special mode to communicate through Bluetooth. Not all cameras have a third mode, but most will have an easy way to switch between them.

Viewfinder

Coming quickly on the heels of what you'd want to do after powering it on, the viewfinder is one of two interfaces by which you see what your camera sees. The viewfinder (Figure 4-3) helps you aim the camera and focus in on your subject. Having a viewfinder that has a vertical range of motion is helpful—if you're tall and the viewfinder doesn't raise at all, you'll be forced to have the camera at eye level and you'll be filming downward.

Figure 4-3 The viewfinder helps you focus in on your subject.

Every camera I've seen also includes an LCD (liquid crystal display) viewscreen (discussed below), but using the viewfinder helps to conserve battery power. When you've got the camera up to your face, however, you tend to miss out on what's going on outside the view of the camera lens. For this reason, the majority of users use the LCD viewscreen.

LCD Viewscreen

At one point, only the high-end cameras had LCD viewscreens, but even the entry-level DV cams I tested all had LCD viewscreens. The technology has become more affordable, which is a good thing—the LCD viewscreen greatly enhances the use of a camera. Although basically all DV cameras have an LCD viewscreen, the size and quality differ greatly. Less expensive cameras have smaller LCD viewscreens, with lower resolution and clarity, while more expensive cameras have larger LCD viewscreens with better resolution and image quality. The Panasonic shown in Figure 4-4 has a very large viewscreen—don't be surprised if your entry-level camera's LCD viewscreen is a little smaller.

Figure 4-4 LCD viewscreens vary in size and quality.

Most viewscreens will also rotate 360 degrees vertically and 90 degrees out from the body of the camera. This allows you to position the viewscreen in a location that you're comfortable with. And if you're doing any filming where you need to be in front of the camera, by rotating the viewscreen you'll be able to see what the camera does for accurate positioning.

Tip If you're buying a camera from the store, it's a good idea to ask them to power it up so you can see the LCD viewfinder—it's rare for LCDs to have flaws called "stuck pixels," but it does happen. A stuck pixel is a white or black pixel that stays that color instead of changing like the other pixels. This can be distracting when filming. Most camera makers have a certain tolerance level for those faults and won't let you return the camera unless there are a certain number of stuck pixels. If the camera in the store has a stuck pixel, ask to look at another one. You're investing your money in the camera, so there's no sense in having anything less than a perfect product without obvious flaws!

Tape Carrier

Known by several names, the tape carrier is simply the part of the camera that holds the tape. Every camera functions a little differently in this regard, but more often than not there's a panel you flip open and the camera brings up the tape carrier automatically, as shown in Figure 4-5.

Figure 4-5 The tape carrier is the part of the camera that holds the tape.

It's not like a VCR where the tape just slides in—due to the ever-demanding decreases in overall camera size, the tapes actually go into the body of the camera. Often there are instructions on the tape carrier itself on where to push—one of the things you don't want to do is push on the wrong part of the tape carrier. It could jam, or even break the device. Loading tapes is easy once you know how it works, but this is one skill you'd be wise to master early on.

Tip If you happen to get stuck with a tape carrier that won't close properly, and you haven't physically jammed it up, try removing the battery on your camera. Put the battery back on the camera, and then turn the camera off and on several times. The camera should recognize that the tape carrier isn't fully retracted, and it will try again. Assuming that no physical damage has occurred, it should return to its home position. You may need go through this process several times—the Sony IP-55 I was testing locked up in this manner, and it took removing the battery three times before it retracted properly. Never, ever force it back through—always take it to an authorized service center if it refuses to fully retract. Better to have a temporarily dysfunctional camera than a permanently broken one!

Lens

Perhaps one of the most critical elements of a DV camera, the lens is the digital eye of your camera. For this reason, you should protect it—always keep the lens cap on when you're not filming, and never touch the lens with your fingers. If you do get smudges on the lens, see if your camera came with a soft shammy cloth to clean it. Wipe in a gentle motion away from the center. And if you have to use a cleaner, pick one made for cameras—don't use household cleaners or anything abrasive. Once you damage the lens, even with a small scratch, everything you film will be marred by it. Thankfully, in most DV cameras and as shown in Figure 4-6, the lens is sunk, so it's fairly rare to get it dirty.

Figure 4-6 The lens is one of the most critical elements of your camera.

Printed around the edge of the lens will be information about the level of optical zoom, the sensitivity to light, and sometimes the brand of the lens (for those discerning buyers who come from a photography background where the lens brand is everything).

Zoom Control

Zooming in and out is one of the most critical, and most often abused, features on a DV camera. But let's get to know the zoom function first before getting into the rules on how to use it. Zoom controls are universal in the way they function and have their roots in traditional photography. "W" stands for "wide angle," and it means to zoom out or away from the object. "T" stands for "telephoto," and means to zoom in or toward an object. Zoom controls all look a little different—some are vertical and some horizontal—but in general they all have some sort of button or stick that will zoom in or zoom out. Figure 4-7 shows an example of a horizontal zoom control.

Figure 4-7 The zoom control offers wide angle and telephoto zooms.

Note   It's a good idea to practice zooming in and out—it sounds simplistic, but most zoom controls are quite sensitive, and knowing the exact amount of pressure it takes to make smooth zooms is important. Fast zooms can be extremely jarring to the viewer, so practice smooth zooming for the best video footage possible.

Input/Output Ports

Once you get all that great video footage into your camera, how do you get it out? And how do you connect external devices to the camera? The answer is the input/output port panel. Every camera is different, but you'll usually find the ports clustered together, as shown in Figure 4-8.

Figure 4-8 Input/Output ports are usually clustered together.

Which ports exist depends on the camera—more advanced cameras have more ports. The ports on the Panasonic that you'll likely see on your camera include:

■ **A/V In/Out Phones**   If you plug headphones into this jack, you'll be able to hear what the built-in microphone is picking up. You'd be surprised how sensitive the microphone is—if you're doing any sort of interviews where the speaker needs to be heard clearly, putting on the headphones to get an accurate sound level is important. Even if you can't adjust the volume level of your DV camera microphone (of all the cameras I tested, only the Canon GL2 had this feature), you'll know to move to a quieter area. The built-in speaker will usually be deactivated when you have headphones plugged in—perfect for those times when you want to privately review your footage without disturbing those around you. If you plug in an audio cable to connect it to an external audio source, it will activate the camcorder speaker.

- **To PC**   Any DV camera that has a memory card option for taking pictures will have a port for a special cable to connect through Universal Serial Bus (USB). This is strictly for transferring digital stills, not video. When the proper drivers are installed on your PC and the camera is connected, you'll have a Removable Drive listed in My Computer that you can browse and copy files from just like a normal hard drive.

- **S-Video In/Out**   You may have a dedicated port for video output. S-Video is a higher-quality signal than regular video over an RCA cable and will give you the best non-digital quality on a regular DV. This port can often be used for video input as well, allowing you to connect an S-Video signal and record it digitally to the MiniDV tape. Depending on the camera, you may not have an S-Video port—in order to save space some cameras offer a generic "output" port that carries audio and video signals and uses a cable with multiple connection points on it.

- **FireWire port**   Whenever you see the "iDV," it means "IEEE 1394" or "iLink"—both are alternate names for FireWire. In short, this is your port for connecting the camera to your computer. All DV cameras have the smaller 4-pin ports, and most desktop PCs have the larger 6-pin ports (some laptops use 4-pin ports). You'll want to make sure you have the right cable to make your connection, or you'll be unable to connect to your PC.

- **Microphone port**   Many cameras support the use of external microphones. If you're in a noisy environment and want to record someone speaking, using an external microphone is a must. It allows you to pick up audio that would otherwise be drowned out and can often save otherwise unusable footage. There are many types of microphones, from small clip-on types to larger hand-held microphones. Be sure

that the cable for the microphone will fit in your DV camera—
professional-level cameras will sometimes have XLR jacks for high-
quality microphones, but most consumer-level cameras have a 3.5 mm
jack (often called a "mini-jack" or "headphone jack").

Tape Playback Controls and Jog Dial

When your camera is in VCR mode and you're viewing your footage, you'll want
to control the playback. The controls are just like your normal VCR or DVD
player—play, pause, stop, fast forward, and reverse. The input mechanism differs from camera to camera. The Sony IP-55 has an innovative touch-screen control, which saves space on the body of the camera. The Panasonic pictured in
Figure 4-6 uses a small joystick that works well—once you get used to the
illogical nature of pressing away from yourself to rewind the tape.

Camera manufacturers often position another type of control in the same
area—usually one that allows for varying levels of adjustment. Figure 4-9 shows
a jog dial that could be rotated to adjust the shutter, iris, system volume, flip
through pictures, etc. Pressing the jog dial inward is like hitting the Enter key on
your computer. You'll have to read your manual in order to understand which
control is used for which feature. When I was first learning how to use the Panasonic camera, I was mystified as to why I couldn't advance through the photos
using the tape control joystick—it seemed perfectly logical to me, but the jog
dial was the control for advancing from photo to photo. Not very intuitive, but
that's why it's a good idea to have the manual with you for the first few weeks
of using the DV camera.

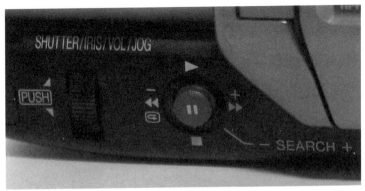

Figure 4-9 Tape playback controls and the jog dial allow you to adjust your camera.

Battery

Your new DV camera is no good without power, so the battery is an important part of the equation. All cameras come with a battery, and part of your first steps when unpacking the DV camera should have been to start the battery. Batteries come in all shapes and sizes—the one pictured in Figure 4-10 is a large Lithium Ion battery that will power the camera for quite some time.

Figure 4-10 The Lithium Ion battery pack powers cameras for a long time.

Generally, the smaller the battery, the less power it provides (there are some exceptions). There's not much to understand about the battery other than that it simply works.

Note   If you have an older DV camera that has undergone significant use over the years, and the battery simply isn't lasting as long as it used to, you may have exceeded the charge cycle of the battery. Every battery is rated for a certain number of charges/discharges. Once you go beyond that number, the battery has less capability to hold a charge. There's no solution other than buying a new battery—the good news is that it generally means you're getting your money's worth from your camera!

Flash

The addition of a flash is a relatively new development with DV cameras—the battery on a typical DV camera isn't powerful enough to support a sustained lighting system for long, but now that the cameras can take photos and store them on a memory card or on the tape itself, a flash became a necessity. The flash functions just like a standard camera flash—it can be set to fire off with every single photo, or be put in an autosensing mode in which it fires only when there's not enough light for a good photo. Because the flash isn't used all the time, on most cameras it is a pop-up flash that you trigger manually by pressing a button, as shown in Figure 4-11.

Figure 4-11 The pop-up flash for still photography works just like a standard camera flash.

Flashes on DV cameras are about as powerful as flashes on a digital camera—good enough for photos within a few feet, but not much more than that. Using the flash heavily will drain your battery quickly, so be careful of that.

Microphone

The microphone type, style, and placement differs from camera to camera.
Some have it below the lens, some have it above, some behind. In Figure 4-12,
the microphone is on the top of the camera, to the rear of the lens. The placement isn't quite as critical as the sensitivity, and I was quite surprised at how
sensitive the microphones were on the cameras I tested. If you have a habit of
muttering to yourself while filming, break that habit right now—even the slight-
est whisper by the cameraman is usually picked up. If the microphone doesn't
do what you need, consider getting an external microphone and connecting it to
the camera.

Figure 4-12 DV cameras have built-in microphones for audio.

Memory Card Slot

Now that most DV cameras can take digital photos (albeit not very good ones
in most cases), many have adopted the use of memory cards. Sony cameras use
its proprietary Memory Stick technology, and most other cameras use Secure
Digital (SD) and Multimediacards (MMCs). Figure 4-13 is a good example of a
memory card slot that uses an SD card.

Figure 4-13 This is a memory card slot with a 256 MB Secure Digital card inserted.

The slot is fairly basic—you insert the card, it will usually click, and to eject the card you either use a button or press gently on the card and it will eject itself. You can connect the DV camera to your computer through USB to transfer the photos or use an external memory card reader.

Speaker

The speaker (Figure 4-14) makes the sound during playback of your video. Nothing surprising there! The speaker is also responsible for producing the irritating "bing" sounds that always seem to come at the worst times. Sometimes the speaker is behind the LCD viewscreen, and sometimes it's on the back of the camera facing the operator (you).

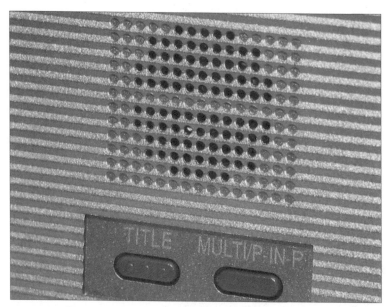

Figure 4-14 The audio playback speaker is responsible for producing the sound for your video.

Stabilizer, Focus, Menu, and White Balance Selection

Depending on your camera, there may be other buttons with important functions. Figure 4-15 shows the following buttons:

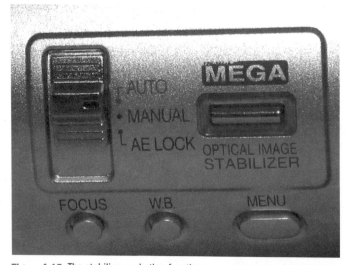

Figure 4-15 The stabilizer and other functions on a camera can help improve your shots.

■   **Optical Image Stabilizer**   This function often has different names, but it's essentially a digital method of eliminating the camera "jitters" that happen when you don't have a steady hand. Camera makers implement this feature differently—some cameras have a very effective image stabilizer, others don't. It's no substitute for using a tripod, however, so don't rely on this feature to completely compensate for your jittery hold on the camera.

■   **Auto and Manual Focus**   Auto focus is a given on all modern DV cameras, but not all cameras have a manual focus option. If your camera has this feature and you're in a situation where the auto focus simply can't get locked on your subject, you can switch to manual focus and use the Focus button to get a lock on your subject. Although there's a ring around the camera lens on the Panasonic I was using, it didn't act as a focus—it simply spun round and round. Some cameras, like the Canon GL2, have a manual focus ring.

■   **Auto Exposure (AE) Lock**   The term "exposure" relates to how the lens on the camera reacts to light. If you're in a very bright environment, the camera automatically adjusts the exposure to give you a natural-looking picture. If you're in a low-light environment, the camera boosts the exposure to make things as bright as possible. This is done automatically, and the exposure changes as you follow a moving subject around. If you were to move the camera away from the subject to a scene that had more or less light, the exposure would readjust itself. When you came back to the subject, it would take a few seconds to lock in again—for those few seconds, your subject might be practically invisible. If you want to keep the exposure locked, you would engage the auto exposure lock. The whole issue of exposure sounds more complicated than it is—you only need to understand that it will take your camera a few seconds to adjust itself.

■   **Menu**   This button brings up a menu on the LCD viewscreen. You can typically navigate through it using the VCR controls or the scroll/jog dial. Menu options vary, but it usually contains things like tape speed recording quality, audio recording quality, setting the time and date, and more. Some cameras have advanced features allowing you to add special effects, backgrounds, and more. Get to know your camera menu!

■ **W.B.** This typically stands for "white balance" on a camera, and adjusting the white balance helps you keep the colors more true-to-life. Colors look different based on the amount of light in the area, and the camera needs a baseline from which to judge. White is always white (you've never heard anyone mention "shades of white," have you?), so this is the benchmark cameras use. Using the White Balance feature is simple— you usually point the camera at something white that fills up the whole screen, and hold the White Balance button. Check your camera manual for the exact procedure. Some cameras have White Balance presets like Automatic, Fluorescent, Outdoor, and Indoor (incandescent lights). In most cases, the Automatic mode will do just fine. But if you're shooting a scene where you want the most accurate colors possible, adjust the white balance manually.

Tip   Not sure what to use for accurate white balance? A white paper napkin, a white t-shirt—anything will do, as long as it's pure white (not a tan or light gray). If you find yourself adjusting the white balance on your camera frequently, consider carrying around a piece of white paper or white cardboard.

Tripod Mount

Look on the bottom of your camera and you'll see a small hole with ridged edges—this is where you'll screw in a tripod attachment. We talked about tripods in the last chapter, but if for some reason the camera you're looking at doesn't have a tripod mount (which would be extremely rare), put it down and walk away. A tripod is critical for achieving stability with your video footage.

Other Buttons

Every camera design has different buttons (and only some of them will be truly useful to you). Typically, the entry-level cameras don't have as many buttons as the high-end cameras do, but here are some of the fairly common buttons you might encounter and what each does:

■ **Fade** Holding this button in will fade the picture to black, and letting it go will fade it back up again. Want to start faded to black? This will take some dexterity, but hold down the Fade button until the LCD viewscreen shows only black, press Record, and then let go of the Fade button. It will fade up to a normal shot. Because this can be somewhat awkward, don't worry too much about using it—remember that you can add all the fades you want later with your editing software.

■ **Card Mode**   If your DV camera supports a memory card, you'll often have the option of selecting what sort of data you want to store on it: photos, video, or voice recordings. In most cases you'll want to leave this on photo.

■ **Still**   The Still button freezes the image of what your camera is seeing.

■ **Special Recording Modes**   Some cameras have preset adjustments created for specific shooting environments like sports events, portrait mode, low light mode, spotlight mode, and even "surf and snow" modes that compensate for extremely bright light. Getting to know which modes your camera supports will help you when you're shooting in these scenarios.

Now that you understand what most of those buttons on your camera do, let's get to the good stuff: getting out there and capturing some great video!

Fail To Plan, Plan To Fail

Yes, that old adage your mother told you is true when it comes to getting great video footage. Although a certain amount of "winging it" is just fine, you'll be much further ahead if you spend a little bit of time coming up with a plan. Some events, like getting footage of your kids playing in the park, are purely spontaneous and "point, shoot, and edit later" will work well. Other events will have more structure, and being able to take advantage of that will allow you capture better video footage. Here's how.

Know the Event

If you're going to be filming a highly structured event (an awards ceremony, wedding, etc.) you'll want to know what the structure is going to be. If possible, contact the event organizers and get the schedule. Take it with you, and when you arrive, orient yourself to the timetable. Knowing what order the events are in will help you plan. For example, if you have a single battery, do your heavy shooting before a meal and recharge the battery while everyone is eating (most people don't like to be filmed while eating anyway). Is there an event like a dance that will be held in a darkened room? You may need to bring an external light source. Read event descriptions to understand what will be happening. It's also important to understand the rules around filming—will the event organizers allow you to bring your camera? Do they have rules about certain types of equipment like lights or microphones? It's always better to ask in advance than to show up and be disappointed (or asked to leave).

Tip   Sometimes, if the event has no official videographer, you can get special permission to shoot the event and more freedom to move around and get the shots you need. Often the only thing you'll need to provide in return is a single copy of your event tape.

Arrive in Advance

Even if you think you know what's going to happen at an event, arrive 30 minutes early to get oriented. I'm usually late for things, so I find this one particularly challenging, but it's extremely important. There's nothing worse than walking in carrying your camera bag only to see the event has already started. The action will pass you by while you're groping for the camera's "on" switch. One of the most important reasons for arriving early is getting a good seat! Unless you have special permission from the event organizer to move around during the event, it's a little rude to walk around filming and blocking people's view. Try to get a seat near the front that will allow you to capture the event, but not so close that you'll be filming "upward" when zooming in closer.

Tip   It's frustrating when someone sits in front of you who has, shall we say, "larger than average hair." Even if you're sitting in an aisle seat, you may want to "reserve" the seat directly in front of you to minimize the chance of having someone block your shooting angle.

What Are the Key Elements You Want to Capture?

If you're at an event that will last several hours, like a graduation ceremony, figure out exactly what you want to capture and prepare accordingly. Do you want to capture the entire event? You'll likely need several tapes and batteries (or a power jack). If it's a short event that will occur in different locations, scope out a spot to shoot from at each location.

Capture Based on Opportunity, Not Order of Events

This is a very important one, so pay attention: the reason they call it "nonlinear editing" is that by using digital tools, you can rearrange video footage with ease. This means that the order of the events on your tape doesn't matter—your final product will likely be very different from your original footage. So look for the shots that have impact regardless of when they occur. Here's an example: let's say you're filming a friend's wedding, and after the whole event is over you see the bride, still in her gown, looking thoughtfully out the window with the sunlight streaming in. What a great shot! It would be perfect for the beginning of the video, to go with the footage you took of the groom getting ready. When opportunity knocks, open the door and hit Record—capture high-impact footage whenever possible, and worry about fitting it in later.

Tip   If you're a Type A personality like me, you may have a slight tendency to want to "direct" people while you're filming. It's in our nature to want to control things around us. Unless you're making a corporate video with actors, or you're being paid to capture certain events, resist this urge strongly. There's nothing worse than trying to orchestrate something that is supposed to be spontaneous—let your kids play on the beach, let your friends have fun, and just hit Record and go with it. The best footage will often be the things you never expected to happen!

Get in Close to the Action

Bad video is like a bad photo—the subject is a small blur very far away from the person taking the photo. Unless the viewer can feel involved, you've failed in capturing the moment. So get in close! You have a great advantage over people with cameras at an event—most DV cameras have an optical zoom of 10x to 20x, which allows you to zoom up close without leaving your seat. Sometimes that zoom simply won't be enough, however, and you'll need to muster up your courage and get in close. It can be intimidating at first (being the only one standing and moving around while everyone else is seated), but if you want to get high-impact footage, you'll need to get in close. It's also worth noting that even with the stabilization technology, shooting at maximum zoom can be a very jarring experience for your viewer. Getting in close reduces the jitter effect of hand-held shooting because you don't have to shoot at such a high zoom (the higher the zoom, the more noticeable small movements are).

It's All About the Angles

There's nothing more boring than video of an event shot from a single angle.
Move around! Before you first start shooting, scope the room and look for
spaces where you can stand. Capture some video from that spot, wait for a
break in the action to pause the recording, then move to a new location and
start filming again. Even if you're filming the same thing (like someone speaking), by varying the angle you're giving the viewer a new perspective and
greatly adding value to your video. Angle is something you can't add later in the
editing software, so it's important to capture at least a few angles. It can be distracting for people at an event to have someone constantly moving around, so
look for opportunities to move discreetly (like when the audience is applauding,
for instance).

In addition to varying your shooting angle on the horizontal plane, consider
altering it on the vertical plane. Stand up on a chair to get a different angle, or
get down on your stomach to capture video of a baby crawling. Don't shoot the
entire video this way, though—alter the angle for variety.

Tip   If you're filming an event, especially weddings, avoid drawing attention to yourself or having
your subjects "wave at the camera." Filming an event is about capturing what's going on without
being a part of it and letting viewers feel like they're really there, seeing the action for themselves.
If the video is more personal in nature (like a going-away party, for instance), interacting with the
camera can add a fun element to your video.

Length of Shots Depends on Final Footage Use

Your video's final form will have a great impact on the type of video footage you
will want to take. For instance, if your goal is to tape an entire event for archival
purposes or for someone who couldn't be there, you're going to take very long
shots and capture the event completely. If your goal is to make a music video
from the footage, shorter clips are all you need. The software you use will also
have an impact here: muvee AutoProducer (described in Chapter 7), for example, works best with shorter (5-second to 10-second) clips. If you're planning on
editing the video yourself manually, but you still want to keep the overall video
short, focus on capturing 30-second clips of each major event. Remember that if
you're not recording the entire event, your goal is to re-create the important
moments of that event. You often don't need a lot of footage to do this!

Scripting Events

Scripting an event is when you sit down and plan out which shots you want to get and then direct people in order to achieve these shots. For obvious reasons, you wouldn't want to take this approach at a wedding, but if you were shooting a video for a realtor showing off the benefits of a home he's trying to sell, you'd want to carefully script the shots. Think of it this way: most of the time you're going to be capturing reality as it happens and archiving it for memories. Trying to communicate a specific concept requires planning and scripting—you'll need people in front of the camera to communicate the ideas (a spokesperson).

Scripting can be as simple as jotting down the major scenes you want to capture or as complex as doing a shot-by-shot storyboard where you draw out every scene you want to capture (this is how most feature-length movies begin). This is a topic that goes far beyond the scope of this book.

Where Will the Video Be Used?

Taking into account how people will be seeing your video will help you decide what kind of shots to get, and much of it boils down to the size of the screen. For example, filming someone from the torso up will look fine on a 30" television set—the person will be large enough to see, and facial expressions will be evident. But if you're streaming that video over the Internet at 160 x 120 resolution or putting it on a Pocket PC, you'd want to get "head and shoulder" shots to compensate for the smaller display size.

Do's and Don'ts with Your Camera

In addition to the things I've mentioned above for shooting techniques, there are some things you should and shouldn't do with your camera. This list is by no means comprehensive—as you use your DV camera more and more, you'll learn what works best for you. Here are some quick tips that relate to the camera itself.

Don't... Use Special Effects on Your Camera

Most cameras come with special effects like a black and white mode or sepia tone. Don't use them. It's easy to create these effects afterward in a video-editing program, and you don't want to be filming the memory of a lifetime in sepia only to find out later that your friend wanted it in color. Always film in standard color mode—effects are easy to add later!

Do... Experiment with the Footage Later

Once you have the video footage in a video-editing program, experiment to your heart's content! Try different colors, tones, filters, effects—go wild! We'll talk more about this in Chapter 7 and Chapter 8 when we discuss video editing.

Don't... Hit Record Too Quickly

If you hit Record before you have the camera in position, you end up with a few seconds of jarring motion where you try and find the subject and remove the lens cap.Get set up first, and then press Record.

Do... Allow an Exposure Lock Before Recording

Unless the shot is happening right before your eyes and you're missing it, take your time setting up the camera. Focus on your subject, wait a few seconds for the camera to adjust itself to the lighting (exposure lock), get into a comfortable and stable position, and hit Record. You'll find footage like this is much easier to edit later.

Do... Use Standard Play (SP) Recording Mode

Most DV cameras have two recording modes: Standard Play (SP) and Long Play (LP). A standard MiniDV tape will hold 60 minutes of footage in SP mode and 90 minutes in LP mode. LP mode records more footage, but at the expense of quality. With tapes being so affordable (under $10 US each), I strongly recommend that you capture footage in SP mode and carry a couple of extra tapes for longer events.

Do... Turn Off Those Beeps!

I was at a wedding recently, and just as the bride was coming down the aisle, with everyone in attendance holding their breath in anticipation, I pressed the wrong button on the DV camera I was using and it started beeping ferociously. How embarrassing! Learn from my mistake and, prior to the event, go into the set-up screens and turn off all audio. Unfortunately, on some cameras even after you turn off the audio certain functions will still beep. It's frustrating and I wish manufacturers would add a "mute" button on to the camera.

Don't... Forget About the Audio—Unless You Don't Need It

Regardless of how well you set up your shots, if you have poor audio, it can often ruin the shot. First, decide if you even need the audio at all. For example, when I'm at an event and I see there's an official-looking videographer with a high-end Canon XL1S, I know that my footage won't be able to compete with that. So instead I focus more on getting creative shots, knowing that I'll be mixing it with some music later. If you do need to get the audio, you'll want to position yourself fairly close to the subject—usually within 10 or 15 feet. If the subject is speaking into an amplified sound system, you have more flexibility with your positioning.

Do... Use An External Microphone If Needed

Even with the sensitive microphones on today's DV cameras, it can be a real challenge to get good, quality audio. I saw one professional cameraman do an interesting trick: he had a wireless receiver hooked up to the audio input ports on his camera, and he attached the wireless microphone to the groom's tuxedo for the wedding. This allowed him to get high-quality audio without having to get up close with a boom microphone.

Key Points

- Get to know the various functions on your camera.

- Plan ahead by getting to events early and finding a good location.

- Capturing spontaneous action results in more natural footage.

- Don't be afraid to get in close to the action.

- Don't use special shooting modes on the camera (like sepia tone).

- Experiment with your footage using video editing software.

Chapter 5

Examining Your Computer Setup

Although having the right camera is an important step in the digital video process, since this book is also about editing the digital video, having a fast and efficient editing platform (your computer) is critical. This chapter may seem a little technical, and in truth I'm a hardware geek at heart so I love this stuff, but even if you don't know ROM from RAM, you'll still learn quite a bit from this chapter. Let's dive in!

Having the Right Hardware for Maximum Performance

Your computer is a lot like your car—when you buy it you have certain ideas about what you want to do with it. You buy a car to get to and from work, run errands, and travel to other places. You buy a computer to write letters, check e-mail, browse the Web, and perhaps play games. But the analogy stops there—unlike your car, which is more or less the same from the day you bought it (exotic vehicle modifications aside), your computer can be enhanced and changed through hardware and software. As your needs grow, so will your computer. Since you're now holding this book, it's my dearest wish that you'll soon be editing digital video on your computer and having a lot of fun while doing so—and I guarantee that you'll have more fun than you do just writing e-mail! But just like you wouldn't take a little compact car 4x4 off-roading, your computer might not be up to the task of heavy video editing. Part of this chapter's goal is to help you look at the computer hardware you do have and help you decide how to upgrade or replace it. My goal in this chapter isn't to have you spend more money—on the contrary, if you're informed about what kind of upgrades you really need for video editing, you may be able to get away with a minor upgrade instead of buying a whole new system.

Balancing Cost vs. Performance

When deciding what to upgrade on your computer, always remember to balance the cost vs. performance gain. For example, at the time of this writing the 2.8 gigahertz (GHz) Pentium 4 from Intel is the fastest processor you can buy. It also carries a hefty price tag—yet the 2.53 GHz processor, at only a 10 percent slower clock speed, is more than 50 percent less in price! Buying on the cutting edge of technology is always costly, so you need to decide what the best use of your money is. That 10 percent gain in CPU power probably isn't worth the cost, especially when you can take the money you saved and put it into extra RAM or a faster hard drive. When looking at component prices, always look one level below the top tier and do the cost vs. performance comparison.

The Value of Your Time

If there's one thing that will bring a computer to its knees, it's video editing. Pushing around huge multi-GB video files will be a strain on any system, and when a computer is busy working away on something, that usually means that you, the user, will be staring at the screen waiting for it to catch up. The most arduous task in this process is the video's final *rendering time*—depending on how many effects you use in your video and your computer's speed, you could be looking at upward of an hour of rendering time per minute of video. That's right, *per minute*—and if your production is 30 minutes long, your computer will be rendering a very, very long time. This is an extreme case, but I've seen more than one *newsgroup* posting from someone with a computer several years old running at 300 MHz trying to do video editing and complaining about the 25-hour project rendering time. That's someone with a lot of time to spare!

Ultimately, that's the question you have to ask yourself as you start to edit your videos: what is your time worth? If you're doing intense effects to every video clip, your rendering time will go way up. If you have no problem leaving your computer churning away at a long video project for 24 hours, and you don't need to use it for anything else, you may be just fine with the hardware you currently have. For most of us, though, that's not the case. We need to use our computers, and having them inaccessible to us isn't an option. As we go through this chapter and discuss how each hardware element will affect your computer, decide if spending the money is worth saving you time. As you can probably guess, I personally believe that in order to have an enjoyable video-editing experience, free of frustration, a powerful computer is a must. Computers should wait for humans, not the other way around!

Note Computer hardware also has an impact on the speed of the video-editing application beyond just rendering. Previewing effects, applying filters, even moving clips around—they all take major computer horsepower, and an underpowered machine will slow your use of any video-editing application, turning a simple video edit into a 30-minute procedure of click, wait, click.

Lingo *Rendering Time.* The time it takes for video-editing effects to be applied to your video and output into the final form. The more changes you make to your video, the longer the rendering time will be (generally).

Lingo Also known as UseNet, *newsgroups* are one of the oldest portions of the Internet still active. Much like a bulletin board in an office, you can post messages, read what others have posted, and reply to posts. The knowledge within the newsgroups is amazing—odds are, if you're having a computer problem, someone else has had the same problem and has posted a message about it. There are newsgroups on every topic you can imagine—well over 100,000 newsgroups exist today (not all of them are active or useful, though). You need a newsreader like Microsoft Outlook Express to access the newsgroups, so odds are you already have everything you need. Your Internet service provider (ISP) should provide UseNet access, but if it doesn't, you'll need a third-party service like *www.athenanews.com*. A free alternative is to use Google.com's "Groups" search function—it will allow you to read UseNet posts and find some answers.

How Each Hardware Element Affects Working with Digital Video

Your computer is an amazing creation—hundreds of parts, all working in concert, to give you a powerful tool, capable of some impressive feats. Some pieces of hardware have a significant effect on video-editing performance, and others have very little. It's important to understand what each piece does and how it affects your digital video-editing experience so you know what sort of upgrades you may need. Before we get into that, however, let me show you how to figure out what assets you currently have on your computer—there's no sense in upgrading if you have sufficient power.

Taking Stock of Your Current Computer Assets

Three basic elements make up the core of your computer, and they're tightly related: the CPU (processor), RAM, and the hard drive. The CPU transfers information to and from the hard drive (permanent storage) and RAM (temporary storage for whatever you're currently working on). You may not remember exactly what is inside the computer, but there are some simple steps to discover what is inside your computer.

Try This!   Discovering RAM and CPU speed is a straightforward process that was greatly improved in Microsoft Windows XP. Prior to Windows XP, you'd have to reboot your computer to see how fast your CPU was—Microsoft has now integrated this into the operating system. Getting this information is simple if you're running Windows XP: click on the Start menu, click on My Computer, and in the top left task menu select View System Information. A new window will appear (like Figure 5-1), and in the bottom part of that window you'll find what you were looking for: the first line shows the type of processor, and in the case of some newer processors (like the Pentium 4) it shows the rated speed of that processor. The next line shows the processor's current speed, in MHz or GHz (remember 1 GHz = 1000 MHz).

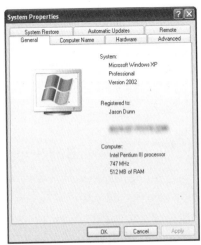

Figure 5-1 This window shows your CPU speed and RAM.

Why show the processor's rated speed and the current speed? Because processors don't always run the speed they're supposed to—in a computer I put together, the actual CPU speed was 1.9 GHz instead of the 2.54 GHz that the processor was capable of. Until I changed it by altering the *BIOS* settings, I was getting far less speed than I was supposed to. The last line shows the amount of RAM installed on the system. Unfortunately, this doesn't show the type of speed of the RAM. Write down the CPU type, CPU speed, and amount of RAM for later on.

Lingo   *BIOS*. Short for "Basic Input Output System," the BIOS is like a small operating system that controls the hardware on your computer without Windows XP getting involved. It controls the detection of hard drives, the CPU, and the RAM.

Try This!   Want to look around your BIOS? When you reboot your computer, watch the screen for a message that will tell you what key you need to press on your keyboard to enter the BIOS. It will usually be the Delete key, but sometimes it's a function key (F1 or F12). Don't change anything unless you know exactly what you're doing—changing the wrong setting could disable your computer completely and prevent it from booting. Some commercial computers have no BIOS that is accessible by the end user.

Next, you should check your storage situation. The best way to do this is to go into the Computer Management Console—this tool offers the easiest view of your drives and space situation, and it's easier to see it all in one place. The fastest way to get there is to click on the Start menu, click Run, and type **compmgmt.msc**—you should see a screen similar to Figure 5-2.

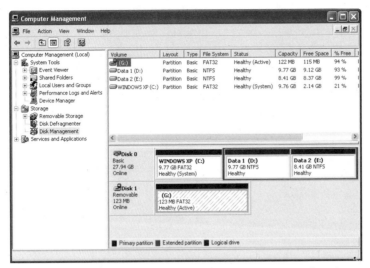

Figure 5-2 The storage drives displayed in the Computer Management Console.

The section we want to be in is Disk Management, found under the Storage heading. This view tells you a great deal about your hard drives and how they're divided. Your computer will be different from mine, but here's what we can learn by looking at Figure 5-2:

■ There's only one physical hard drive inside this computer, and it's 30 GB in size.

■ It's divided into three partitions: 10 GB, 10 GB, and 9 GB. All the partitions are NT file system (NTFS) format.

■ One removable hard drive is attached to the computer, and it has one *partition*, with 123 MB of space.

Note   The discrepancy in hard drive size above will be explained later in this chapter under "Hard Drive Partitions."

Lingo   *Partition.* A virtual divider set up to segment a single hard drive into multiple drives. Although there is physically one hard drive, Windows will see each partition as a separate hard drive and treat it as such.

From this view you should be able to see how many physical hard drives you have and how they're divided. This information will be important later.

Since having to type **compmgmt.msc** every time isn't very easy to remember, it's a good idea to add the Computer Management Console onto your Start menu for later use. You can accomplish this by doing the following:

1 Right-click the task bar at the bottom of your screen and select Properties.

2 Select the second tab, Start Menu. Click Customize.

3 A new window appears. Select the second tab, Advanced, and in the bottom window (Start Menu Items), scroll down until you see the option for System Administrator Tools. It should be at the very bottom of that list (Figure 5-3).

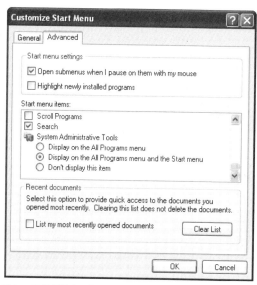

Figure 5-3 This is where to add the System AdministratorTools to the Start menu.

4 By default, this is set to "Don't Display This Item." Set this to "Display On The All Programs Menu And The Start Menu."

5 The Administrative Tools has now been added to your Start menu. Select the Computer Management icon to start up the Computer Management Console.

Try This! Want another way to access the System Administrator Tools? Click Start, then click on the Control Panel icon. Once that window loads, you should see an icon called Administrative Tools. Double-click on that icon and you'll have access to the same tools from the Start Menu. This allows you to have fast access to these tools without cluttering up your Start Menu.

Space Requirements for Digital Video Capture

If there's one factor that dominates digital video on a computer, it's the sheer space that the video takes up. Most computers today are shipping with 40 to 60 GB hard drives. Although spacious for most tasks, those drives can quickly become full when digital video enters into the picture. Why? Well, think of it like this: every frame of video is like a JPEG photo. There are usually 30 frames per second of video, so if you have a 5-minute video, that's like having 9000 JPEG photos on your hard drive! An hour of DV quality video will take up around 13 GB, and that's just for the capturing—you'll need that much space again if you're going to be outputting a final project without much trimming.

Video-editing software will often have options to minimize the storage space used—the most common is that it captures a low-quality version of the video, lets you work with and edit that video, and then during the final step it goes back and recaptures the relevant segments in high-resolution. This method is workable, but ultimately not all video-editing software packages support it, and it usually requires you to leave your camera on for the duration of the process (which requires a long-life battery or yet another power cable). Another method is to capture the video in MPEG format, but this takes extra time and results in lower overall quality. I prefer to capture the video in full resolution (we'll discuss how in Chapter 6) and put the camera away—this takes more storage space, but I find it's less hassle.

Tip   I'd say the minimum size of hard drive you'd want to have for digital video editing would be 40 GB. That would allow you to capture roughly two hours of video, and still have enough space to edit it down to 60 minutes and output that file to the same drive. You wouldn't have room for much else though!

Where to Store Your Digital Video

So now that we've talked about how much storage space digital video takes up, the next question becomes "So where do I put all this video while I'm working with it?" A lot of different storage options are on the market today, from hard drives to DVD burners to Iomega Zip drives. Here's my take on each of them as they relate to digital video and active project workspace:

- ■ **CD burners**   Almost every new computer ships with a CD burner, and adding one to your current computer can be done inexpensively. CD-Rs have a capacity of 650 or 700 MB. Although CDs are useful for archiving your smaller video files once the project is over, they're not useful for raw project data—once a file is burned to a CD-R, it becomes "read only" and can't be edited. It's technically possible to edit these files with a CD-RW and packet-writing software, but I would recommend against it—the possibility of data loss is too high when your CPU is attempting to perform video-editing duties and read/write data to the CD-RW at the same time. Save your CDs for the project results (VideoCD [VCD], Super VideoCD [SVCD], or storing the final clips).

- **DVD burners**　As I mentioned in previous chapters, there's no single DVD burning standard at the moment, but certain companies like Sony are making DVD burners that do both DVD+R and DVD-R formats. That said, although DVDs are great storage mediums for your final projects and for archiving raw footage, you should never use them for active project storage space (for the same reasons mentioned above). Use DVDs to share the final production or to archive your final footage—you should have enough space to store roughly 20 minutes of high-quality uncompressed DV footage in case you want to edit it again later or save it in another format.

- **Cartridge storage**　This category encompasses Iomega Zip drives (100 MB, 250 MB, and 750 MB), Iomega Jazz drives (1 GB), Castlewood Orb drives (2.2 GB), and any other sort of storage system that uses removable cartridges (with the exception of cartridges containing hard drives like the Iomega Peerless products). The formats with larger capacities are adequate storage alternatives, but the problem with all cartridge-based systems is the sometimes unreliable data transfer speeds and cost/benefit ratio when compared to hard drives (on a per-MB basis, cartridges are quite expensive). Tape drives also fall into this category, but this format is ill suited for any video work.

- **Hard drives**　The last one on the list, hard drives are the only real choice for a digital video workspace. The newest drives are fast, spacious, and the chance of data loss is very minimal. With capacities currently hitting 200 GB in a single drive (the Western Digital "Drivezilla"), hard drives also represent the best cost per megabyte value.

Internal Hard Drives

Now that we know hard drives are the way to go, the question becomes what kind of hard drives are the best for digital video? The hard drive market, like all technology markets, has its own set of jargon and technology. Here are some of the things that you should know before you go hard drive shopping.

When buying a hard drive you'll run into three factors: capacity, rotation speed, and cache. The capacity is straightforward—the higher the number, the more storage space you have. Rotation speed is the number of times that a hard drive spins around per minute (much like a tire on a car): 5400 revolutions per minute (RPM) is standard, and 7200 RPM is what you'll see on high-performance drives. For video work, and indeed for a faster-performing computer in general, 7200 RPM is the best choice. The last element is the cache size—cache on a hard drive is much like RAM on your computer. The cache acts as a buffer for the data, and since the cache can respond much more quickly than the hard drive itself (nanoseconds instead of milliseconds), the more cache a drive has the better overall performance it will give. Most hard drives have 2 or 4 MB of cache— the Special Edition Western Digital 120 GB (Figure 5-4) drives have 8 MB of cache, which makes them top performers (and my recommended internal drive—find out more at *www.westerndigital.com*).

Figure 5-4 The fastest hard drive around is the Western Digital Special Edition 120 GB.

There's another class of hard drive called a "SCSI drive" (pronounced "skuzzy"). SCSI (Small Computer System Interface) hard drives offer some performance advantages over most standard hard drives, but SCSI hard drives are vastly more expensive and require special know-how to configure on a PC. SCSI drives are very popular in the server world and high-end workstations, but for you and me, they're too expensive and too complex. And the good news is, a high-speed SCSI drive benchmarks roughly the same as the Western Digital Special Edition drive, so there's no reason to take on the expense of a SCSI drive.

One of the new standards for hard drives is called Serial ATA (Advanced Technology Attachment). It's been in development for several years, but the first drives are just starting to ship with it. The 200 GB Western Digital "Drivezilla" is based on Serial ATA, and support for Serial ATA was just recently added to Windows XP with Service Pack 1. Serial ATA is definitely the standard of the future—the drives using Serial ATA will be able to handle up to 144 petabytes. How big is that? 1000 GB equals 1 terabyte, and 1024 terabytes equals 1 petabyte. 144 petabytes is a staggering amount of information, and I think that the concept of magnetic-based hard drives will be obsolete before we reach that barrier anyway!

Note   If you think 200 GB is big, just wait until early 2003. Maxtor has announced that they'll be shipping a 5400 RPM hard drive with an incredible 320 GB of storage in Q1 of 2003, and a faster 7200 RPM version with 250 GB of storage. Even with multiple video projects on the go, you'd have a hard time filling up that much space!

External Hard Drives

Easier to install than an internal hard drive and more than fast enough for video work, external hard drives are one of the best investments you can make in upgrading for your digital video. I didn't use one until I started working on this book, and I didn't realize what I was missing—the ability to move a hard drive full of data between computers is very convenient, and with capacities currently reaching to 160 GB, they're large enough for any task. They come in two flavors: USB 2.0 and FireWire. Various types of external hard drives are on the market, and I took a few of them for a spin.

The Iogear Ion drive (Figure 5-5) is a USB 2.0-based hard drive that uses a 2.5 inch hard drive—the same size you find in laptops. In fact, it's ideally suited for a laptop—the hard drive is powered by plugging directly into the mouse port on the back of a laptop (but it can also be used with a desktop computer). Laptop hard drives typically don't have the sheer performance of a full-sized 3.5 inch hard drive, but the Iogear Ion drive performed fairly well—sufficient for video capture. I would, however, recommend upgrading an internal laptop hard drive before getting an external drive like this.

Figure 5-5 This is the Iogear Ion USB 2.0 external hard drive.

By far the best-looking external hard drive I looked at, the Western Digital external FireWire hard drive (Figure 5-6) boasts 120 GB of capacity and blazing 7200 RPM speed to match. It has an extra FireWire port on the back of the drive, allowing you to connect the drive to your computer and then connect your DV camera to the back of the drive. I tested the drive by capturing video from a DV camera directly to the drive, and the process was perfect—this drive is a winner, and it's large enough to last you for quite a while.

Figure 5-6 The Western Digital 120 GB FireWire drive is sleek and sexy.

Maxtor has been in the hard drive business for a long time now, and they know what they're doing—the 3000XT shown in Figure 5-7 is a massive 160 GB of storage that uses a FireWire interface and includes a bonus port on the back.

Figure 5-7 The Matrox 160 GB FireWire hard drive has massive storage space.

The drive is fairly expensive, but what a drive it is! The 3000XT spins at 5400 RPM (the 3000DV offers a 7200 RPM speed), but I found it fast enough to capture, render, and play full-quality, DV-quality AVI files. The 3000LE (not shown) is the USB 2.0 version of this drive but tops out at 120 GB.

Hard Drive Partitions

Having a big and fast hard drive is only half of the equation—knowing how to use it intelligently as part of your workflow process is the other half. Why does it matter? Well, when you're working with video (capturing, editing, or rendering) your computer can work faster if it can load and unload segments of the video directly to and from the hard drive without having to work around other files. When you have a partition specifically for video work, with nothing else on it, you'll see performance gains over doing video editing on your C drive partition (which is full of files).

So how do you create these partitions? There are two ways: the free but slightly complex way or with software that you purchase. PartitionMagic is software created by PowerQuest Corporation (*www.powerquest.com*), and it allows you to move, delete, expand, shrink, or add partitions on the fly from within Windows. The software is very impressive, and it makes working with partitions a breeze. I also like that PartitionMagic creates boot disks, allowing me to format and partition hard drives on computers that don't have Windows on them yet. This software is extremely useful to have in your toolkit, but it's not absolutely necessary for getting a new hard drive set up—Windows XP has some tools that will allow you to do some basic partition functions.

At the beginning of this chapter I talked about the Computer Management Console and how it gives you a snapshot of your hard drive status. It also allows you to create and delete partitions on a new hard drive—here's how:

Caution   Unlike PartitionMagic, using the Windows XP drive partitioning tools is a destructive process. This means that when you delete a partition and re-create it, your data will be lost permanently. I advise using this procedure only on blank hard drives with nothing on them.

---

1   Start up the Computer Management Console as described earlier in this chapter. Let's assume you've just added a new external 160 GB Maxtor FireWire hard drive (what a superb product!) and you want to break up the hard drive into three partitions of roughly 50 GB each: one for capturing the video, one for editing the video, and one for rendering the video. Select the drive in the lower window—it will usually say "Unallocated" in the section describing how the space is used (Figure 5-8). The drive will also never be exactly the size you thought you were buying—a 160 GB drive actually has 152.66 GB on it. It's a long story that involves math, so I won't get into it, but suffice it to say that your hard drive isn't "broken" if you're not seeing the exact number you thought you should.

Figure 5-8 Here is our fresh drive with unallocated space, just waiting to be partitioned.

2   Right-click on the Unallocated section and select New Partition. This opens the New Partition Wizard.

3   Click Next to get past the introduction screen, and then select Extended Partition. Primary partitions are only for hard drives that you want to boot from. Since this is strictly for storage, an extended partition will be perfect for our needs.

4   On the following screen it asks you how much of the drive should be an extended partition—the default is all of the drive, measured in MB. Leave this number alone and click Next. You'll see a summary screen to confirm your choices. You should see Partition Type: Extended Partition, a disk you've selected (it will have a name like "Disk 2" or "Disk 3" depending on how many hard drives you have installed), and the partition size in MB (remember this should be 100 percent of the drive size). Click Finish to complete this step of the process.

5 It takes a few seconds to create the partition, after which you should see something similar to Figure 5-9. This is now "free space," but until we create logical drives in the next step, you can't access that space.

Figure 5-9 Shown above is the free space on a partition, waiting to be sliced up into logical drives.

6 Right click on the Free Space section and select New Logical Drive. A new wizard starts up, and after you click Next you'll see your only choice is to create a Logical Drive. Click Next.

7 Now you have to assign a size value to the drive (Figure 5-10). Remember—we wanted to have three partitions of roughly 50 GB each, so we'll use a value of 50,000 MB (1,000 MB = 1 GB). Click Next.

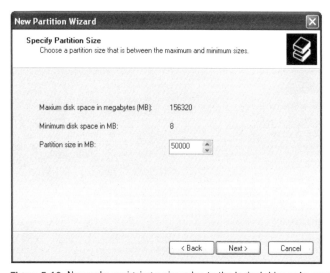

Figure 5-10 Now we're assigning a size value to the logical drive we're creating.

8 The next step asks you what drive letter you want to assign it to. You can accept the default or pick your own drive letter—it's a good idea to have your drives be sequential, so don't pick "Z" for this first drive. Once you've selected the drive letter, click Next.

9   Now that you've assigned the drive size and letter, it's time to prepare
it for accepting data by formatting it. This next step (Figure 5-11)
defines how you will format this drive. By default, NTFS will be
selected in the File System drop-down menu—if it's not, select it. NTFS
is the only format capable of capturing video files beyond 4 GB. The
Allocation Size should be left at Default, and the volume label can be
whatever you wish (the volume label is simply the name of the drive
when displayed in My Computer). In this case I'm going to call it
"Capture" to indicate that this is the drive I'll be using for capturing the
video. Select the "Perform Quick Format" box before clicking Next.

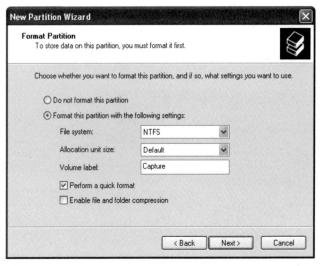

Figure 5-11 You should see this screen when setting the drive up to format.

10 This wizard's final screen reviews the changes you've requested—
make sure everything looks correct, and then click Finish.

The drive will take anywhere from 10 to 60 seconds to do the format, and
once it's completed you should see something similar to Figure 5-12. You can
see that the drive now has a letter assigned to it, is in NTFS format, is just under
50 GB in size, and the status is rated as "Healthy." Repeat steps 6 through 10 to
create other drives—when you're done you should have no free space left on
the partition.

Figure 5-12 Our drive is formatted and ready to go!

Note   When you're creating and naming your logical drives, it's a good idea to plan your strategy for working with video. For instance, I use my "Capture" drive for capturing the raw video files from the camcorder. I then use the "Render" drive when I'm outputting the final high-resolution, edited video file—and I'll usually have a "Scratch" drive meant for temporary storage for the video editing program.

Caution   Once you've created a partition and a drive, there's no way to resize it with the Windows XP tools—you'll have to delete it and start over. This can be a big hassle if you have 30 GB of data on it that can't be moved anywhere else. Take your time and ensure that you're 100 percent accurate. If you need to resize a partition or drive with data on it, you'll need PartitionMagic and its ability to perform nondestructive changes.

Caution   If the drive takes substantially longer to format, it means one of two things: you either forgot to select the "Quick Format" box or your hard drive may be failing. Run a Scandisk on it to check for faults.

The Processor (CPU)

The key to a high-performance video-editing system is balance between the components, and the CPU is a cornerstone in this equation. Ideally, the CPU should be waiting for everything else to catch up to it—it should be one of your fastest components (relatively speaking). In today's market of 2.8 GHz CPUs, here's a general rule of thumb: If the amount of RAM in MB is anywhere near your CPU speed in MHz, it's time to upgrade that CPU!

How Many MHz Are Enough?

Most video-editing packages require a minimum CPU speed of 500 MHz, and some I've seen recommend 1 GHz. One of my computers is a 1 GHz AMD Athlon, and it's a capable video-editing machine (if a bit aged)—with prices on CPUs being so low, there's no excuse not to have something in the 1.5 GHz or higher range if you want to have an enjoyable video-editing experience. Unless you're doing your video editing on a secondary computer that no one is using, you'll quickly grow tired of waiting for your CPU to finish encoding the video. Intel loaned me a 2.54 GHz CPU (Figure 5-13) for a test machine I built, and the CPU was simply amazing—the raw power and snappiness with which Windows operated was very impressive. Rendering times were more than cut in half from what I was used to, and previewing my video was nearly instantaneous. Intel packs a lot of power into their high-end P4 CPUs, and it had a huge impact on how enjoyable my video-editing experience was.

Figure 5-13 The 2.53 GHz Pentium 4 CPU from Intel is impressive.

How much of a difference does CPU speed make when rendering digital media? Here's one example: turning a 178 MB WAV file into an MP3 using a Pentium 4 1500 MHz CPU would take 243 seconds. That same file encoded using a Pentium 4 at 2200 MHz (2.2 GHz) would take 165 seconds—a speed savings of 47 percent! That might not mean much with a single audio file, but take that speed gain and apply it to a 60-minute project, and you have a time savings of hours. Unfortunately, there's no accurate way to predict how much a faster CPU will improve your video rendering speed—many factors influence this. But it's safe to say that a faster CPU will always help your project.

Intel CPUs vs. AMD CPUs

In the battle for CPU dominance, Intel and AMD trade leadership spots several times each year. Intel has released a 2.8 GHz processor and will have the crown for raw MHz. AMD, never one to be outdone for long, will likely have released their Athlon 2800+ which will perform on par with Intel's latest offering. In terms of performance, AMD processors perform better than Intel's P4 on a per-MHz basis, but AMD hasn't been able to match Intel's clock speed in terms of sheer MHz. Both processors have special acceleration features or multimedia playback and encoding—on the Intel Pentium 4 processors, they're called MMX and SSE2 instructions, and on the AMD side of things they're called 3DNow! Since it's not possible to get a CPU without these special accelerations, there's not much point in discussing them—they just work to accelerate multimedia functions.

So what does all this mean to you, the end user? Either processor will perform beautifully in all scenarios, and there are no longer any issues of compatibility, so your decision should be based on price and compatibility with your current hardware. If you have an Intel CPU in your current machine, you may be able to upgrade to a faster CPU with little hassle. The key factor is your motherboard—you'll need to find out what type of CPU speeds it supports. If you're currently using a Pentium 4 CPU, it likely means your motherboard will support any current Pentium 4 CPU. If you have an older motherboard, like one using a Pentium III CPU, you'll probably need to upgrade your motherboard. And when it's upgrade time, you can pick any motherboard and CPU combination you want.

Note   One of the biggest revolutions in the CPU world is coming late this year or early next year— the 64-bit CPU. Current CPUs are 32-bit—the move to 64-bit processors and 64-bit software will have a profound impact on the video-editing world. Both AMD and Intel will be releasing 64-bit processors in late 2002 or early 2003, and once the software catches up, we'll see tremendous speed increases across nearly all computing tasks. This isn't something that will happen quickly, though—it will likely take until late 2003 for all the pieces to be in place. Do a Google search for "AMD Clawhammer," "AMD Opteron," or "Intel McKinley," and you'll find a lot of great information on what's happening with 64-bit CPUs.

System RAM

Next to the CPU, RAM is one of the most speed-critical elements on your computer. In fact, in some cases even with a fast CPU, a system without enough RAM will be very sluggish. The more RAM a system has, the less it has to access the hard drive to swap out data and the longer that hard drive will last. Think of RAM like this: when your CPU requests a file, the hard drive delivers that file and puts it into RAM where it can be manipulated with greater speed. The next file you request will also need to be loaded into RAM—and if there's not enough RAM to store both files, you have to wait while the computer puts the first file back onto the hard drive before it loads the second file. This takes time and slows your computer down a great deal.

Wondering if you need to upgrade your system RAM? I'll make it easy for you: if you have less than 512 MB, add more—and that's without being specific to video editing. Windows XP needs 256 MB of RAM just to breathe on a system, and once you start loading up several applications it's hungry for more. 512 MB is a sweet spot that will allow you to have multiple applications open and everything will still be snappy. 512 MB is a good starting point for a video-editing system, and the sky's the limit when it comes to adding more—768 MB to 1 GB is a great amount to have when editing large projects, but you may want to see if 512 MB suits you first before upgrading.

Many types of RAM are on the market, but you only need to worry about getting the type compatible with your motherboard. The fastest RAM on the market currently is RDRAM 1066, a high-speed RAM type found in high-end Pentium 4 motherboards. Although it's certainly the best in terms of speed, it's expensive—Double Data Rate-Synchronous DRAM (DDR) is a more common type of RAM and is less expensive. DDR PC2700 is the current top of the heap, so if you want to strike a balance between performance and price, PC2700 is the way to go.

Caution   Most motherboards will support RDRAM or DDR—not both. When you're buying a motherboard, you should think ahead about the type of RAM you want to use, since you won't be able to switch RAM types later.

Is Generic RAM the Way to Go?

In a word, no. When you're out shopping for RAM, you'll come across two types of RAM: generic RAM, often called "unbrokered," and name-brand RAM from companies like Crucial Technology (Figure 5-14). The unbrokered RAM will always be less expensive, but that's for a reason: that RAM is usually made up of memory chips left over from the larger name-brand buyers like Crucial. The reality is, only a few factories in the world create RAM chips. They resell the chips to other companies, and not all the buying companies have the same standards for quality. I've had problems with RAM going bad on me in the past, and diagnosing bad RAM is one of the most frustrating processes there is. The bad RAM has always been the less expensive, generic type.

Since switching exclusively to Crucial-brand RAM (Figure 5-14) a few years ago, I've never had a problem. And interestingly enough, I found that ordering online from *www.crucial.com* gave me prices almost the same as what the local vendors were selling the generic RAM for and quite a bit less than they were selling the Crucial RAM for.

Figure 5-14 Pictured above is a stick of DDR PC2700 RAM (*www.crucial.com*).

You can cut out the middleman by ordering Crucial RAM directly from Crucial. I installed 1 GB of Crucial-brand DDR PC2700 RAM in the test system I used for this book, and I was thrilled with the results—the RAM is blisteringly fast and I've had zero problems. I strongly recommend Crucial RAM; it's not a very expensive upgrade to get 512 MB or even 1 GB of RAM. Your computer will thank you!

> **Tip** Always try to buy the largest single stick of RAM that you can. For instance, if your computer has two memory slots on it and you want to put 512 MB of RAM in it, you have the choice of buying two 256 MB sticks or one 512 MB stick. The 256 MB sticks may be a few dollars cheaper, but what happens if you want to add more RAM later? You're out of slots. If you have two memory slots, buy your RAM in 512 MB sizes. If the motherboard has three or four memory slots, you can get away with 256 MB sticks of RAM.

Your Monitor

It breaks my heart to see someone take a beautiful new computer and hook it up to an old 14" monitor from 1995. Considering that the monitor is the most-often used component on your PC, it's important to get a monitor that not only gives you a great picture, but also one that is easy on your eyes, both from a size perspective and the quality of the display. If you have anything under 17", it's time to upgrade—although it's certainly possible to do video editing on a 15" monitor, it's not very enjoyable. Here are some things to think about when it comes to your monitor:

LCD or CRT?

This is the year of the *LCD* monitors—prices have fallen and the display quality is up. LCD monitors take up less space, emit less radiation, are easier on your eyes, and have a brighter picture than *CRT* monitors. They're still more expensive than a CRT monitor, but LCD monitors are the future, no doubt about it. A high-quality CRT monitor will still get the job done, but if you can afford it, look into getting an LCD monitor.

> **Lingo** *CRT.* The term used to describe typical computer monitors (the big, heavy ones). Cathode ray tubes are the technology these monitors are based on.

> **Lingo** *LCD.* Liquid crystal display monitors are based on the same technology as laptop screens.

Monitor Size

In the world of computer monitors, bigger is better, but only up to a point. 15" monitors are too small, so you should have something between 17" and 19" for your monitor. 21" CRT monitors are utterly enormous, and in most cases you'd be better off with a second monitor. CRT monitors are always about one inch smaller than you'd think—a typical 19" CRT monitor actually has 18" of display space. LCD monitors, on the other hand, are the size they say they are—a 17" LCD offers 17 full inches of display space. If you can afford an LCD monitor, get a 17". If you're buying a CRT monitor, get a 19". I'm so impressed with LCD monitors that I'd even recommend a 15" LCD over a 17" CRT. The larger sizes of monitor will allow you to see more on the screen at one time, and when you're editing video, the more you can see, the better off you are.

Screen Resolution

Most video-editing programs require a minimum resolution of 800 x 600, as does Windows XP, but the interface will be extremely cramped unless you're running at 1024 x 768 or higher (the higher the resolution, the smaller everything is on the screen, and hence more will fit). It's important to run in a resolution that is easy for you to see, however, so don't get caught up in "higher is better." If you have a 19" CRT monitor, you should be at 1280 x 1024 resolution or 1152 x 864 if the former is too small. If you have excellent vision, you might even try 1600 x 1200. When it comes to LCD monitors, the decision is already made for you: LCDs function optimally only at their native resolution. A 15" LCD usually runs at 1024 x 768, and a 17" LCD runs at 1280 x 1024.

Tip   If you're sharing a video online, it's a good idea to preview your video at the resolution most people will be using: 800 x 600 and 1024 x 768. You'll get a better feel for the quality of the video and how it will look to them.

Dual Display Nirvana

Having two monitors will give you a new way of working—instead of having to use keyboard shortcuts all day to switch applications, you can leave applications open on each monitor. In a video-editing environment dual displays can be even more useful, but it depends on the application. Some applications are designed for dual displays and will give you a highly optimized workspace. Other applications won't stretch across the second screen. You can still use that second screen for locating your media files, checking your e-mail, etc. Dual displays aren't for the technologically faint of heart, though—they require a bit of knowledge to get working properly. Still, if you're up for it and have the desk space, adding a second monitor is often more useful than upgrading to a single larger monitor. I've been using twin 17" LCDs for several months now, and I found they drastically increased my productivity—I have a hard time working on a single display computer now.

Note   Some video cards have a TV-out port on them, and for video editing this can be very useful to check your work if you hook it up to a small TV set. Remember that your video will look very different on a TV than on your computer monitor—the aspect ratio may be different, the colors will be different, and the quality will also look better on the TV set (because TVs are low-resolution devices compared to a computer monitor).

Video Card

The video card is also an important part of your system, but it doesn't necessarily do much of the work when it comes to video-editing (there are exceptions though—keep reading). Video cards perform their duties in 2-D and 3-D—2-D imaging is everything you see within Windows. 3-D performance only comes into play when you're running a game based on a 3-D engine, so it has minimal impact on video editing. It does, however, have a huge impact on any rendering tasks that involve 3-D effects. Quite a few transitions involve 3D effects, so having a powerful 3-D card will speed things up quite a bit. In the manual for Hollywood FX, a transitions package that comes with Pinnacle Studio Deluxe, it states that a 3-D acceleration card will result in 200 percent to 500 percent performance gains when 3-D transitions are used.

A system with a cheap and underpowered video card will be very sluggish, however, in all Windows tasks, including video-editing applications. So although a 3-D video card won't truly "accelerate" your video-editing, a capable 3-D video card will make your entire computing experience much easier and will accelerate the rendering process if you're using 3D transitions. It will also help with DVD playback and reduce the CPU load when playing back video files.

Two main video card companies are battling it out for supremacy right now: nVidia and ATI. I was an ATI user for many years, but I was frustrated at the constant problems I was having with the ATI drivers—my system would crash regularly when I tried to play a video, and it was always the ATI drivers that did it. Out of sheer frustration, I replaced my high-end 64 MB ATI Radeon video card with an nVidia GeForce4 MX-based video card. The overall speed increase in my system was noticeable, and the crashes stopped—I'm an nVidia man now. For the purposes of this book, nVidia gave me a new card that incorporated their top-end graphics processor: the GeForce4 Ti 4600 (Figure 5-15) with 128 MB of RAM.

Figure 5-15 Pictured above is the nVidia GeForce4 Ti 4600 graphics processor (on a reference card).

This card is a powerhouse in the 3-D world, but it also made for a very snappy Windows experience. Screen redraws were quick, even while the CPU was under the heavy load of video editing, and rendering with some of the more complex 3-D transitions was also accelerated. You certainly don't need a high-end GeForce4 Ti 4600-based card to do video editing, but if you're using an old video card you would be well served to upgrade to at least a GeForce4 MX card—you'll like the difference it will make in your system performance, even if you're not a gamer.

The Importance of Audio

Try this little test: put your favorite movie into your DVD player, press Play, and jump to the most action-packed or emotional moment in the movie… then turn off the sound. Watch the scene—even if the dialogue were put back in, without the music or sound effects, the movie just isn't the same, is it? People forget how important audio is, and they also forget how good audio is supposed to sound. Most computer systems today ship with average-sounding speakers. They're good enough to hear the "bings" of Windows XP, and you might even listen to music on them, but are they going to do your digital video production justice? Probably not.

People forget how important audio is, but if there's one application that demands great speakers, it's digital video editing. You need to be able to hear everything in your video production—especially things that won't show up on cheap TV speakers but will be glaring on a home theater system. Having a solid set of speakers allows you to do this.

Many brands of speakers are on the market today, but ultimately only a few are worth owning—most are low-end speakers that sacrifice quality for good looks (most of the "flat" speakers fall into this category). Logitech has opted to focus on performance (although their speakers still look great!) and the results are some good-sounding speakers. The flagship of their speaker line, the Z560's shown in Figure 5-16, are a 4.1 (four speakers and one subwoofer) speaker set capable of cranking out 400 watts of power—I found the audio to be crisp and clean, although some music was a bit hollow-sounding for my tastes. The four speakers give you excellent spatial effects, and the Z560's are good for every-thing from digital video editing to game playing—and they're affordable to boot. 4.1 speakers require a fair bit of desk space, though, so if you're looking for something a bit smaller, consider a 2.1 speaker set.

Figure 5-16 The THX-certified Logitech Z560 speakers are powerful.

Try This!   If you're interested in getting a new set of speakers, go to a local computer store. Most computer stores have a "speaker wall" where you can hear how various speakers sound. If you want to compare speaker quality, spend a few minutes listening to how each set of speakers play the same song—you'll be surprised at the differences among them all!

Consisting of two speakers and a sub-woofer, 2.1 speaker sets still give you good sound while not using up much desk space. The Logitech Z340's offer 6.5 watts in each speaker and 20 watts from the sub, and I found the sound to be vastly superior to the cheap, thin sound most computer speakers can generate.

If you're not shy about spending money and like having the best, consider speakers by Klipsch. Their 2.1 ProMedia speakers (Figure 5-17) cost as much as the 4.1 Logitech speakers, but the sound quality is absolutely stunning. Rich, vibrant tones with powerful bass, they never sound muddy or distorted—truly worth the investment. I bought the ProMedia 2.1 set myself in early 2000 and they're still going strong, so they're also built to last. I haven't heard any computers speakers that sound this good—they're simply that good. Find out more online at *www.klipsch.com*.

Figure 5-17 The Klipsch ProMedia 2.1 computer speakers are stunning.

Caution Consider plugging in some headphones if you're doing any late-night video editing. I love immersing myself in audio when I'm working, but when I used to live in a condo I got into trouble from a neighbor on more than one occasion for having my speakers too loud. Even at very low volumes, bass from a subwoofer can move up a wall and be surprisingly loud.

USB and FireWire Ports

Having the right ports on your computer is a must—unfortunately, most PCs today don't come with FireWire ports, and only the newest PCs are starting to ship with USB 2.0 functionality. The addition of these two high-speed *protocols* is easily one of the most important developments in digital video editing over the past few years. FireWire and USB 2.0 allow you to manipulate and save data at high speeds, and until these protocols were developed, external storage options were very limited (and slow). If you don't already have a FireWire port on your computer or laptop, you're going to need one to work with a DV camera. You don't need a FireWire port to capture analog video from a VCR or old camcorder, however (just a special analog video capture card).

Lingo   A *protocol* is a method of communication, usually between two electronic devices. USB and FireWire would be considered protocols.

You May Already Have the Right Ports

Depending on how old your computer is, you may already have the right types of ports. The easiest way to check is to look at the computer—Figure 5-18 shows the front of a computer with both USB and FireWire ports. The two ports on the left are USB, and the one on the right is a FireWire port. They're similar in size, but the cables are not compatible with each other. If you can't visually identify the ports, check your invoice for the specifications.

Figure 5-18 The USB ports are on the left, and the FireWire port is on the right.

Caution   There's no way to visually determine whether a USB port is 1.1 or a 2.0 port. You'll need to check your computer manual to be sure, but if you plug in a USB 2.0 device and it gives you an error about being plugged into a "non-USB 2.0 hub," odds are it's a USB 1.1 port. USB 2.0 requires specific drivers to function within Windows, so make sure you install them first.

Adding USB 2.0 and FireWire Ports

If you don't have FireWire or USB 2.0 ports, don't worry—it's easy to add them to your computer. Because of the speed requirements of both FireWire and USB 2.0, these add-on ports always come in the form of PCI cards—a card that plugs directly into your motherboard. It's certainly not difficult to follow the included instructions and install the card yourself, but if you're not comfortable opening up your computer's case, it's best to take your computer and the card to a technician to get it installed. Several companies on the market offer add-on ports, but the most prolific is Adaptec—they make several USB 2.0 products, one of which I looked at below. The FireWire cards are discussed in Chapter 6 when we get into capturing video.

Note Although it's easy enough to add in a PCI card with FireWire ports, it's even easier if they're already there out of the box. If you're buying a new computer, make sure it has at least one FireWire port and two USB 2.0 ports, preferably more.

Adaptec USB 2.0 Upgrade Kit

If you're looking for a basic way to add USB 2.0 (Figure 5-19), this kit is a good solution. It sells from *www.getadaptec.com*, and includes a PCI card with two USB 2.0 ports and a four-port USB 2.0 hub. Hubs are useful to have when your USB cables don't quite reach to the back of your computer, because they act as a one-to-many bridge, and the Adaptec USB 2.0 hubs are stackable, allowing you to easily add multiple hubs.

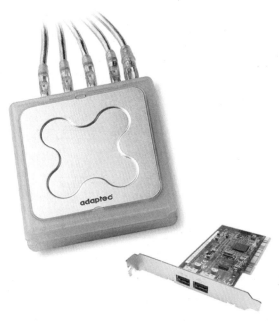

Figure 5-19 Shown above is the Adaptec USB 2.0 Upgrade Kit.

Tip   USB 1.1 devices can plug into USB 2.0 ports and hubs, but they still function at USB 1.1 speeds. USB 2.0 devices function when plugged into USB 1.1 ports, but at the speed limits of USB 1.1 (20 times slower than USB 2.0).

Use Hubs for Easy Access

If you have a lot of devices, USB or FireWire, it's time to invest in a hub when you no longer have any ports on the computer. Sometimes, especially if you have devices that need to be fairly far away from the computer, it's best to get a hub even before you run out of ports. Hubs are designed to act as a bridge, allowing multiple devices (up to seven with most hubs) to connect, and use only one port on the computer. Hubs can also be daisy-chained together—you could have two 7-port hubs connected, allowing you to have 13 devices connected (one port is needed to bridge the slave hub to the master hub) and still only use one port on the computer. You may need two types of hubs: USB or FireWire. I looked at two hubs on the market today: one from Adaptec (USB 2.0) and one from Iogear (FireWire).

Adaptec XHub 7+

The Adaptec XHub 7+ shown in Figure 5-20 is the USB 2.0 hub to end all hubs: seven connection ports, light-emitting diode (LED) lights to show connection and activity, beautiful design, a picture holder for a small photo, and a cable holder to keep things neat and tidy. It's a great hub, but quite expensive. I also wonder why they didn't have it accept a more standard 4x6 vertical photo to cover the cables at the back. Still, if you're looking for a classy hub, this is the best I've seen.

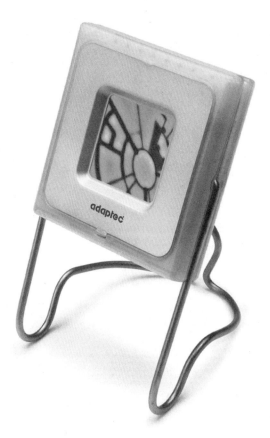

Figure 5-20 The Adaptec XHub 7+ is a great hub.

Iogear FireWire Hub GFH600

This tiny hub shown in Figure 5-21 offers six FireWire ports and supports speeds up to 400 MBps. It's not cheap, but in my tests I found it worked perfectly. Like all hubs, it requires no configuration—it simply plugs in and works. In most cases you shouldn't need a FireWire hub (since many devices include a spare port), but if you do, this is one of the only FireWire hubs on the market.

Figure 5-21 The Iogear FireWire Hub (GFH600) has six FireWire ports.

Final Video Output

Now that you've learned everything there is to know about video-editing hardware and your computer (well, the important information at least!), there's one final element you need to consider: how you're going to share the video physically. If you're planning on sharing the video on a CD, DVD, or even VHS tape, you'll need some special hardware. Let's look at the scenarios.

If You Want to Share Your Video in VCD or SVCD Format...

...you'll need a CD burner. Most computers today ship with a CD burner (often called a CD-RW), but if you need to add one they're quite affordable. Plextor-brand (*www.plextor.com*) CD burners are very popular—I have an old 12x and it has never failed me. With speeds currently at an amazing 48x (it will burn a full CD in under 3 minutes), CD burners are a great way to save not only your digital video but also to make audio CDs and back up your data. If you're looking for a less expensive solution, look for a LITE-ON (*www.liteonit.com.tw*) CD burner—they're rated just as highly as the Plextor drives but cost as much as 50 percent less.

Tip   If you want to minimize the number of CD drives you have in your system, consider getting a combination DVD-ROM reader and a CD-R burner. Several brands on the market today will give you the ability to play DVDs at 16x speed and burn CDs at 32x speed. These drives give you great value for your money.

If You Want to Put Your Video in DVD Video Format...

...you'll need a DVD burner (of course!). We discussed the various formats in Chapter 2, so you have two choices: DVD-R or DVD+R. DVD-R used to be the undisputed leader, but the companies behind the +R standard have made tremendous strides in the past six months and +R is now a serious competitor to -R. So what do you buy? That depends—the Pioneer A04 is one of the top-rated DVD burners on the market today (and they have a rumored A05 coming out soon that will burn twice as fast). I purchased one myself and I've been quite pleased with it so far—it burns DVD-R, DVD-RW, CD-R, and CD-RW. The ability to burn CDs sets it apart from a Panasonic DVD-R I had for a week—make sure to check that your DVD-R drive will also burn DVD-RW (the Panasonic would not). The +R side of the fence is a bigger mystery to me—despite repeated phone calls and e-mail messages, I couldn't get Hewlett-Packard (hp) to loan me an evaluation DVD+R drive. Their dvd200i drive burns DVD+R and DVD+RW, as well as CD-R and CD-RW, so it seems like a very capable drive.

One of the things still hindering the mass adoption of DVD burners (beyond the price of the media) is the two warring standards: DVD-R and DVD+R. Consumers are caught in the middle, and for the life of me I can't figure out why the two groups can't see this—their inability to arrive at an agreement is holding back the DVD-burning industry. However, there is some good news on this front: Sony has recently announced a DVD burner that will burn in DVD-R/RW and DVD+R/RW. You can have the best of both worlds! This is a surprising move coming from Sony, but it ends the confusion—the question is, how affordable will this drive be? At the time of this writing there is no pricing information, so I can only hope it's affordable.

Note   Getting a drive that supports rewriteable DVDs is very important. DVD media is still quite expensive, so the last thing you want to do is be burning a project over and over. Using rewriteable discs means you can burn your DVD, view it and look for flaws, and then go back and use the same disc again to correct them.

If You Want to Share Your Video in VHS Format...

...you'll need a video editing card that supports analog outputs. Most video cards will not, but certain products like the Pinnacle Studio Deluxe (discussed in detail in the next chapter) have analog output ports for both video and audio. There are some video cards on the market that have TV-out ports, but this will only carry the video signal. In order to get the audio you'll need to connect a cable from the audio-out port on your sound card to the audio input port on a VCR. It's not difficult to do, but it will require the right type of cables (usually a

3.5 mm headphone jack connector coming out of the computer into an RCA connector going into the VCR).

Name Brand Computers vs. Custom Built

So if you're beyond upgrading and looking for a new system, where should you look? Name brand computers like HP, Dell, and Gateway offer some great prices and bundled value with software, printers, etc. But these machines are often not the best performers, and you don't have the freedom to pick the parts you want. Quite often, the best choice for video-editing machines is a smaller vendor capable of building a custom machine based on your specifications. You tell the vendor what kind of CPU, RAM, hard drive, etc., you want, and they build it for you. This gives you the freedom of designing a computer perfectly matched to your needs, but it also has the benefit of getting you a computer assembled by professionals and a warranty (you probably won't get the 24x7 tech support that the bigger brands can offer, however).

DIY (Do-it-Yourself) Computers

Another option is to build a computer yourself—depending on your level of knowledge, this can be a great idea or a complete disaster. If you're going to build your own computer, you'll be responsible for putting all the pieces together yourself, and the only warranty you'll have is on the individual components. There's no one to call for tech support if your computer doesn't boot one day. If those things don't bother you, then you're just the kind of person that would enjoy building a custom machine. You get to pick exactly what you want to go into the machine, and you can assemble and tweak it to your heart's content. There are some easy ways to get started—the bare-bones systems from Shuttle (*www.shuttleonline.com*) are a great way to get started. The bare-bones systems are a motherboard already mounted in a case, so you only need to add the CPU, RAM, hard drive, and CD or DVD drive. The Shuttle motherboards include built-in audio and video, and are very compact as well. I have a Shuttle SS51G and have found it to be a very capable machine—it was used as the testbed computer for this book, and I had quite a bit of fun putting it together.

Computer Artistry

As with all things in life, there are people who build and people who *create*— true computer artisans are those who not only plug in the pieces of hardware but also finely tune the machine for performance. One of the finest computer artisans in North America is Voodoo Computers (*www.voodoopc.com*). They've won awards from almost every major magazine for having the best-performing machines on the planet. Their craftsmanship goes beyond technology—the computer's interior cabling (often a cause of airflow problems that can make a machine overheat) is designed based on principals of origami. That's right, the art of folding paper—Voodoo technicians fold and bend cables in a way that optimizes airflow and makes the interior extremely clean and easy to work with (not the snarl of cables most computer makers have). Voodoo PCs are not cheap, but if you want to have a machine with deadly performance, this is the company to talk to. Oh, and did I mention that their computers are so physically beautiful you may actually *want* to keep it up on your desk for people to see? Voodoo paints their aluminum-alloy F-Class series computer cases with the same high-gloss paint found on luxury sports cars, creating a deep, lustrous finish. Their computers are a work of art in every way.

Dedicated Video Workstation

Depending on how serious you are about digital video-editing and how much you do it, you may find that a dedicated workstation for video editing is a good solution. If you want to start large editing projects but still be able to work on other things, you'll probably need to devote a machine to just video editing. The biggest challenge is the temptation to use the powerful video-editing machine for everything else, since it will likely have the best hardware. You don't want to start doing your e-mail and playing games on this machine, however, because you won't be able to do these things while the video-editing workstation is churning away on a video project.

There are no hard and fast rules about building a dedicated video-editing workstation—it should be powerful enough to perform every video-editing procedure you need, but it should be used only for those tasks. Don't install unnecessary software or beta applications—system speed and stability should be your paramount goal. The hardware should be focused on video editing and nothing else.

You can save money by reusing your current monitor, keyboard, mouse, and speakers. How? By using a KVM—"Keyboard, video, and mouse" switch. Iogear (*www.iogear.com*) has an innovative KVM (Figure 5-22) that even includes audio support! It allows you to share your peripherals, and with a simple keyboard shortcut you can switch between computers (there's also a button on the KVM). The MiniView Plus KVM is a fairly expensive component, but I strongly suggest a quality KVM over the cheap "A/B switches" you'll find in most computer stores—a physical switch like that will get worn out in a few months (I went through three A/B switches before I gave up).

Figure 5-22 The Iogear MiniView Plus KVM switch includes audio support.

One serious limitation with every KVM I've found so far is the limitation of one monitor—if you have a dual-monitor setup, you won't be able to use a KVM to flip back and forth between monitors. I have yet to see a KVM switch that supports two monitors, but perhaps as that setup becomes more common over the next few years we'll see increased support for it.

Key Points

- Having the right hardware will speed up video editing.

- Hard drives are preferred over removable storage.

- Creating hard drive partitions just for video editing is a must.

- Both Intel and AMD CPUs will do the job.

- Crucial RAM is better than generic RAM for computer stability and speed.

- LCD monitors are great choices for video editing.

Chapter 6

Capturing Your Video

Capturing your video is an important step in the process of working with your video. It's a fairly straightforward process, but in order to capture your video at a good quality you'll need to have the right kind of hardware and understand your software's capture settings—I'll show you everything you need to know.

What Type of Video Do You Need to Capture?

The first question you'll need to answer is what type of video you're capturing—analog or digital. This is an easy question to answer: if you have a DV camera, it's digital, of course. If the source tape is VHS, an old camcorder, or almost anything else, it's considered analog video. Each type of video requires a certain approach and hardware to match. Let's start with analog.

Analog Video Capture

Analog video, unlike video from a DV camera, is likely going to be fairly low quality, depending on the source. If you have an old VHS tape full of home movies, the video will be highly dependent on the quality of the original video camera, the type of the VCR used to dub it to tape, and the age of the tape. As you can imagine, these factors vary widely, so there are no guarantees as to what kind of quality you can get from a tape.

Analog Cables

You'll likely encounter two types of cables: composite (usually called "RCA") and S-Video. RCA cables can be used to carry video or audio—you'll typically see a three-prong cable, with the yellow for video and red and white for audio. The tips are single-prong and quite thick. The cables are electrically the same, so you can use any color for the signal—you just need to ensure that you use the same color at both ends. VCRs use RCA cables, so if you're connecting your VCR to your computer you'll need to have the right kind of cabling. If you are connecting to a *break-out box*, you should be able to go RCA to RCA. I'll talk about connecting your VCR to your computer later in this chapter. The other type of cable you'll sometimes see with analog devices is S-Video. S-Video is a video-only cable that can sometimes be tricky to connect—there are four small pins that need to align properly in the connection, and it's easy to bend them. S-Video offers higher signal quality than RCA, so if you have the option, use S-Video for transferring your video.

Lingo   *Break-out box.* A generic term used to describe any sort of external box that has audio/video ports and connects to the back of the computer. The goal is convenience—rather than putting the ports on the back of your computer, they're on the box, which can be placed up on your desk for easy access.

Capturing Video from a VCR or Camcorder

Capturing from analog ports requires a little more care than straight digital video capture—you need to be aware of a few things. The first is the capture resolution—if you're going to be archiving this footage, you'll want to capture at 720 x 480, the standard National Television Standards Committee (NTSC) television resolution. Video capture software often gives you different options for the type of file it captures the signal to, but you'll always want to selectAVI. Since you'll be editing this video later, you don't want to pick a precompressed format like MPEG—if you do, you'll see a significant drop in video quality. This will mean, however, that you'll need a fairly large hard drive to capture the video—analog video at 720 x 480 resolution takes up just as much hard drive space as video from a DV camera (roughly 13 GB per hour of video). Here are a few other things to keep in mind:

■   When capturing, it's a good idea to start the recording process on the computer before pressing Play on the VCR—you can always edit out any "blank space" later.

■ If there are logical breaks in the footage, consider capturing it in batches. It's easier to work with five 2 GB files than with a single 10 GB file.

■ Capture all the video off the analog tape as-is—don't worry about editing out the "junk" by manipulating the source tape. Some people prefer to record for a bit on the computer, pause the recording, cue up the analog tape, and then record again, but I think this is a waste of effort. In addition to adding even more wear and tear to your potentially fragile analog tape, I find it's much easier to edit the video once it's digital. The only advantage to this "record, pause, record" method is that it uses less hard drive space. If you have a big hard drive, it's simply not worth the effort.

■ If there's a break in your tape, you can fast-forward the tape while the computer is still recording. You can edit out the break afterward, but remember not to go past the clip that you want to record!

Tip   Old VHS tapes will typically have slight distortions in the tape, usually manifested by white lines of static at the bottom or top of the image. You can usually fix this by adjusting the tracking on a VCR—look at your VCR manual for more information. If you have a VHS tape with multiple scenes on it, you may need to watch the video capture preview window and continually adjust the tracking. It may be impossible to completely eliminate the distortions, but if you can minimize it, your footage will look much better. Another option is to trim the edge of the video with the distortion, using the crop function found in most video-editing software.

Analog Video Capture Hardware

Unlike video coming from a DV camera, analog video must first be converted into a digital form before the computer can store it on a hard drive. This is why you need an analog video capture card—special chips on these cards convert the video. The quality of the conversion depends heavily on the capture card—some are better than others, and there's usually a direct correlation between the quality and the price of the card. You always get what you pay for, and that adage is particularly true in the computer hardware world.

■ **D-Link DSB-V100**   The DSB-V100, shown in Figure 6-1, is fairly representative of a whole class of video capture devices. It's low in price, simple to use, and based on USB 1.1. As you might imagine, at this price the video capture is passable but nothing to write home about. The resolution is limited to 352 by 258 so although you can capture a clip suitable for e-mailing to Grandma, this isn't the hardware you should pick for archiving your old videos. It has S-Video and RCA video inputs but no audio input—you'll need to connect a cable directly to your sound card input in order to get any audio. If you're on an extremely limited budget, this hardware will do the trick, but if you can afford anything better, look for something that offers better quality.

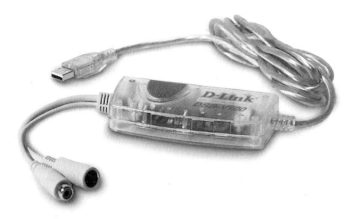

Figure 6-1 The D-Link DSB-V100 is low in price and simple to use.

■   **Pinnacle Studio Deluxe**   One of the best all-around packages I've seen for both analog and digital video capture, Pinnacle Studio Deluxe (Figure 6-2) is a good solution for someone who needs to do a little of everything. It consists of three components. There's a PCI card that goes inside your computer and has two FireWire ports, a large connection port for the break-out box, and an audio cross-over port (to connect the outgoing audio on the Pinnacle card to the input on your sound card). The break-out box is very impressive—full inputs and outputs are offered in both RCA and S-Video formats. This means you can also use this system to output your video to VHS tape if necessary. The bundle includes the superb Pinnacle Studio 8 video-editing application, along with a copy of Hollywood FX Plus. When I started down the road of archiving my old home movies, I tried several products, and this was the product I settled on—it's a versatile, powerful, and flexible package that I recommend highly if you have analog video you need to capture but you eventually want to get a DV camera.

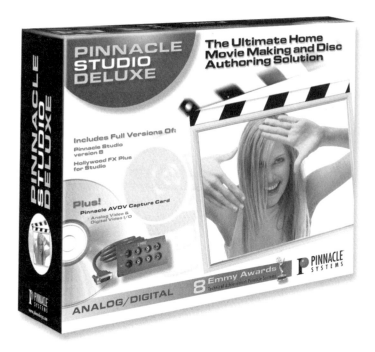

Figure 6-2 The Pinnacle Studio Deluxe is an excellent all-around package for analog and digital video capture.

■   **Video cards with capture features**   Several brands of video cards on the market today have video inputs capable of capturing analog video signals. The most popular are probably the ATI All in Wonder series of cards and the nVidia Personal Cinema—multimedia cards capable of a huge variety of functions. The video input on these cards is usually substandard in quality when compared to a dedicated capture solution like the Pinnacle Studio Deluxe. The resolution is also limited to 640 x 480, so the video captured is ill suited for a DVD. You could use the video for a VCD or SVCD, and it's suitable for online distribution, but I would consider capturing video in this manner to be a last resort. If you have old memories that you want to preserve, you want to save them in a high-quality format.

Try This!   Want to capture analog video without needing a special analog capture card? Give this a try: most DV cameras have RCA video inputs meant for VCRs. You can connect a VCR or an old camcorder to these RCA ports with a simple RCA to RCA cable. Once you have it all connected, press Record on your DV camera, and then press Play on the VCR or camcorder. The DV camera will record that analog signal in a digital format onto the MiniDV tape. Then you can connect your DV camera to your computer and pull the video down over FireWire and edit it just like any other digital video. This method ensures that you'll get maximum-quality video, it eliminates the need for a dedicated analog video capture card, and you don't need to fuss with the capture settings on your computer. With the 60-minute limit of a MiniDV tape in standard play mode, you may need to do this process in batches if the analog source video is long. Every DV camera has a different quality level for recording video inputs, so this tip may not work well with every camera.

Digital Video Capture

Digital video capture can be summed up in one word: easy. The existence of FireWire and large hard drives has made the process of capturing digital video extremely worry-free and surprisingly simple. FireWire allows for up to 400 MB of data to be transferred per second—in real-world numbers, that's 50 MBps, faster than any hard drive on the market. It's also enough data to accept a full-quality DV camera signal without any added compression. Before FireWire, video capture was fraught with compromises in compression and storage—you've picked an excellent time to dive into the world of video capture and editing.

FireWire Capture Cards

We'll cover the exact steps you need to follow when capturing digital video later in this chapter, but it's almost as simple as connecting the camera and clicking Record. Before you can connect your camera, however, you'll need to have a FireWire capture card. If you're not sure that you need one of these cards, look back to Chapter 5, "Examining Your Computer Setup," where I told you how to identify FireWire ports. Odds are you'll need a FireWire card, so here are some of the cards on the market today.

Adaptec DVPics Plus

Featuring three FireWire ports, the DVPics Plus (*www.getadaptec.com*), shown in Figure 6-3, is a good choice if you have multiple FireWire devices (like a DV camera and a FireWire hard drive) and you don't need USB 2.0. It also includes video-editing software (MGI VideoWave SE) and software to burn your DVDs (Sonic MyDVD 3).

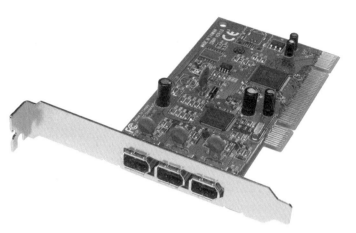

Figure 6-3 Adaptec DVPics Plus is a good choice when you have multiple FireWire devices.

Tip   Some FireWire peripherals, like hard drives, have "pass-through ports"—it's like a one-port FireWire hub. This means you can not only connect the hard drive to the FireWire card on your computer but also connect a FireWire device to the back of the hard drive. This allows you to daisy-chain together many FireWire devices (up to 63, the limitation of the FireWire specification), and it may save you from having to get a FireWire hub. And in case you're curious about limitations around reading and writing from the same FireWire interface, in my tests involving both a desktop PC with a FireWire card and a laptop with a PCMCIA card, I was able to accept FireWire input from a DV while simultaneously capturing that video on a FireWire hard drive.

Adaptec Fireconnect for Notebooks

If you have a notebook without FireWire ports, there's only one option: a PCMCIA card. The Adaptec Fireconnect for Notebooks card shown in Figure 6-4 (*www.getadaptec.com*) gives you three FireWire ports and takes up only a single Type II PCMCIA slot (most notebooks have at least one of these slots). It requires Cardbus support, which most laptops have, but this means it can't be used in a Pocket PC (which lacks Cardbus support). The Fireconnect for Notebooks is a good value, and I had no trouble when I was using it to power two external FireWire hard drives (simultaneously) and to capture video from a Canon GL2. It has 6-pin FireWire ports like a normal desktop FireWire PCI card.

Figure 6-4 The Adaptec Fireconnect for Notebooks card has three FireWire ports.

Adaptec DuoConnect

My personal favorite of all the Adaptec products I looked at, the DuoConnect (Figure 6-5) solves the problem of not having either USB 2.0 or FireWire: It gives you a PCI card with three USB 2.0 ports and two FireWire ports. This single card will upgrade any computer with a free PCI slot to be able to use either high-speed technology, so it's a great value. The bundle also includes a 6-foot FireWire cable.

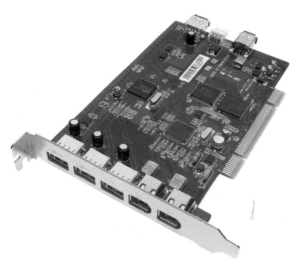

Figure 6-5 The Adaptec DuoConnect solves the problem of not having USB 2.0 or FireWire.

ADS PYRO Digital Video 1394DV

I wanted to mention the ADS PYRO Digital Video 1394DV (*www.adstech.com*) for one specific reason: the software bundle. Most FireWire cards are similar in design and construction, but one thing that often sets them apart is the software they include. In this case, the ADS bundle is all Ulead software: VideoStudio 6.0 SE, DVD MovieFactory, and DVD PictureShow. All three applications are excellent, and for beginners this bundle would be everything they'd need for basic video-editing and sharing through DVD and CD. The ADS card (Figure 6-6) has two standard 6-pin FireWire ports.

Figure 6-6 The ADS PYRO Digital Video 1394DV offers an excellent bundle for beginners.

Note Some video-editing packages include FireWire cards, so you may not need to buy a separate card. Pinnacle EditionDV is a high-end video-editing package that includes a two-port FireWire card and cable. Before buying a FireWire card, check to see if the video-editing package you want to buy includes one (I wish more software companies would do this).

Capturing Video from a Web Cam

If you have a Web cam, using it to capture video is a pretty straightforward process: the video is recorded directly to your hard drive. Every Web cam has its own application for recording video, but most Web cams are installed into Microsoft Windows XP as a camera device—which means Windows can access the camera directly. This is very useful because it means that other applications can also access the camera directly. In most video-editing applications that have an interface for capturing video, you'll be able to make live recordings and edit them instantly. Why would you need to edit video taken with a Web cam? Well, imagine you're selling an antique clock on eBay—using a Web cam, you could make a presentation directly to the viewer, talk about the clock, and hold it up while you're describing it. Since you're recording this video directly into your editing program, it will be a snap to add music and titles and edit out mistakes you've made. I haven't seen people doing this on eBay yet, but I'm sure it's only a matter of time.

Other Uses for a DV Camera

Here's something I didn't know would work until I tried it: when you connect a DV camera to Windows XP, it becomes a part of the system in the same way that a Web cam does. What does this mean in practical terms? It means that you don't need a Web cam for videoconferencing or even a digital camera for still photos—as long as your subject is within range of your FireWire cable connecting the camera to the computer. When you connect your DV camera to a Windows XP-based computer, the DV camera appears as a device in My Computer (Figure 6-7). You can right-click the icon and get the Properties for the camera—the details are minimal, though, as I think this interface was primarily designed for digital still cameras.

Scanners and Cameras

Canon DV Camcorder

Figure 6-7 Your DV camera will appear as a device in My Computer.

If you double-click the icon of your camera, you'll interface directly with the camera through Windows XP. This interface looks like Figure 6-8, and it allows you to do several things:

- The main window has a live video feed coming from your camera. You can use this preview to compose your shots or even try out effects and adjustments on the camera to get a real-time preview of how the image will change.

- On the left-hand Camera Tasks, you can click Take A New Picture to snap a digital picture with the camera. The resolution is fixed at 360 x 240 (1/2 DV resolution), but the image quality is much better than the digital still photos you'd take with the camera on its own. Why? Because Windows XP snaps a still frame from the high-quality video feed, and your camera takes photos by switching into a lower-quality mode specific to still pictures. You can store the photos taken through this interface in the My Pictures folder by right-clicking on each image and selecting Save In My Pictures.

■ As you take your photos, their thumbnail preview appears below the main video feed. On the window's left side, under Details, it indicates what type of camera is connected to the computer and how many photos have been taken.

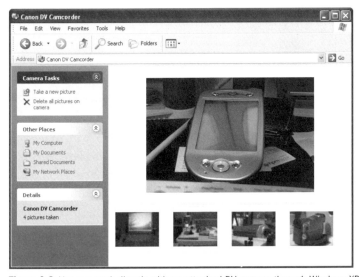

Figure 6-8 You can work directly with an attached DV camera through Windows XP.

In addition to taking still photos, you can use your DV camera as a Web cam in applications like Microsoft Windows Messenger. Here's a quick step-by-step on how to accomplish it (this tutorial assumes you already know the basics of using Windows Messenger):

1 Connect the camera (make sure the battery is charged) and let Windows XP identify and connect to the camera—this should take no more than 10 seconds.

2 Make sure the camera is pointed in your general direction. Tripods work well for this, but you can also put the camera on your computer desk and prop the lens up toward you by placing a book underneath it.

3 In your Windows Messenger list of contacts, find the person you want to videoconference with and double-click his or her name. This will open a new window like the one shown in Figure 6-9. If you don't see the sidebar with the option for Start Camera, you'll need to look on the View menu and select Show Sidebar.

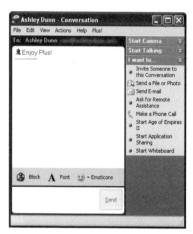

Figure 6-9 When you click on a person's name in your Windows Messenger list of contacts, you'll see a blank message window.

4   Click Start Camera on the sidebar. This will send the following message to the person you are inviting: "Jason Dunn would like to have a video and voice conversation with you. Do you want to accept or decline the invitation?" It will have your name in it, of course, not mine. If this is the first time you've done this, the Audio and Video Tuning Wizard will start and step you through setting up your camera.

5   Once the person accepts the invitation, your chat window will look similar to the one in Figure 6-10. The upper-right corner of the window will be the video window—if the other person has a video camera, you'll see his or her image there. In the bottom-right corner of that image, you'll see a preview of what your video camera is sending—a picture in picture.

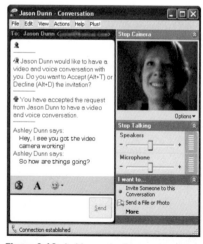

Figure 6-10 A video and voice conversation is initiated through your chat window.

Caution   As concerns about Internet security grow, an increasing number of people are installing firewalls (hardware or software designed to block intrusions into your computer). Firewalls are great for security, but they complicate video and audio conferencing. It's too complicated to cover here, but in order to share video and audio over the Internet, you'll need to modify your firewall to allow the communication to take place. With software firewalls, it can be as easy as clicking Yes to a warning dialogue box. Hardware firewalls are a little more complex and require you to open ports (virtual doorways).

Preparing to Capture Your Video

Before you connect your DV camera and transfer the video to your computer, you should check a few things. The biggest concern is another application taking up processing power (sometimes referred to as "CPU cycles")— if your CPU is working hard on another task, it won't be able to process the incoming video stream. This usually results in dropped frames—remember when I explained earlier that video is simply a series of still images (usually 30 images per second)? These images are also referred to as "frames," so a dropped frame is a missing frame in a video sequence. If one drops, you won't be able to perceive it—but if your video has hundreds of dropped frames in the space of a few minutes of captured video, it may not appear as smooth as it should. Dropped frames are the enemy of a smooth video-capture! Follow the tips below to combat this problem.

Turn Off Complex Screen Savers

Fancy 3-D screen savers are fun to watch, but the more complex they are, the more CPU cycles they take to run. And while you're capturing video (analog or digital), your CPU shouldn't be dominated by a screen saver—if it is, you'll see dropped frames. To disable your screen saver, right-click on the desktop, select Properties, switch to the Screen Saver tab, and select None from the list (or a simple screen saver like the Windows XP screen saver).

Close Other Programs

Other than your video-capturing program and applications running in the system tray (like Windows Messenger), no other applications should be open. This is both to preserve available RAM and to minimize the chance of an open application taking up CPU resources.

Deactivate Antivirus Software

Most antivirus software is configured, by default, to scan newly created files for viruses. This has the net effect of causing a lot of CPU cycles to be wasted while the antivirus software scans the video file as it's created on your hard drive. While capturing, temporarily deactivate the antivirus software (in most cases you can do this by right-clicking it in the system tray).

Check for CPU-Intensive Tasks

For the same reasons mentioned above, you'll want to ensure that you have no CPU-intensive tasks. To check for this, simultaneously press the Control, Alt, and Delete keys. The Windows Task Manager appears, and you should click the second tab in from the left (Processes). Your Task Manager will look similar to Figure 6-11—the CPU column shows what percentage of the CPU power the current tasks are taking up. If you click the word CPU, it will sort the list from lowest to highest—click it again and you'll get the list from highest to lowest. *System Idle Process* should be taking up nearly all the CPU power—this effectively means the CPU is doing "nothing." If you do see a task that's taking up significant CPU cycles (more than 5 percent), and you've already closed other applications, select the task and click End Process. If the task won't close, try rebooting. Be careful about closing tasks—you run the risk of closing a program that Windows requires. Rebooting is often a better alternative.

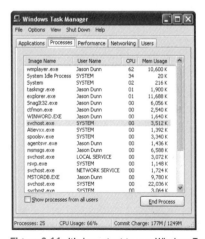

Figure 6-11 It's important to use Windows Task Manager to check for CPU-intensive tasks.

Capture to an Empty Partition

If at all possible, always capture to an empty partition. Move or delete files to clear it off and remember to empty the Recycling Bin (files aren't actually removed from the drive until the Recycling Bin is emptied). This ensures the smoothest possible video capture because the hard drive has a continuous block of space on which to capture the video. If you're really feeling determined, you can even format the partition to ensure that it's nice and fresh—formatting completely wipes out all the files, whereas deleting them only deletes the file "markers" (technically your files are still there). You can do this by opening up My Computer, right-clicking on the drive in question, and selecting Format. Remember to keep the drive in NTFS format!

Defragment Your Hard Drive

If you don't have the option to capture to an empty partition, make sure you defragment the drive prior to capturing. You can do this by opening up My Computer, right-clicking on the drive you want to use, and selecting Properties. Switch to the Tools tab, and then click the Defragment Now button. Running a defrag moves all the files together and gives you a continuous piece of blank space on which to capture the video.

Capturing Video from a DV Camera

Compared to the complexity that video capture required in the late 1990s, transferring video from a DV camera to your computer is a snap. This tutorial assumes that you have a FireWire card or FireWire port on your computer and that you have your DV camera ready to go with a fully charged battery. For the purposes of this example, I'm going to be using Pinnacle Studio 8 because it's simple to use, but nearly all video-editing applications function the same. They have a capture interface, are designed to interface with a DV camera over FireWire, and have controls very similar to a VCR—Stop, Record, Play, Rewind, and Fast Forward. Here's what the capturing process looks like in Pinnacle Studio 8.

1 Turn on the DV camera and put it into Camera mode (the mode for video playback).

2 Connect the FireWire cable to the camera (the 4-pin end), and then connect the 6-pin end to the FireWire port on your computer.

3 Windows XP identifies the new hardware (as Figure 6-12 shows) in multiple stages. You may see it install "AVC Device" and "AV/C Subunit"

and others. Allow this process to continue until you see the words every computer user longs to see: "Your New Hardware Is Installed And Ready To Use." On subsequent connections, this process will be almost instantaneous—you'll be able to connect and start recording from the camera in a few seconds.

Figure 6-12 Windows XP identifies new hardware in stages.

4   Now that the camera is connected, you should see a window that looks like Figure 6-13. The Windows XP "action list" contains functions that the user can choose from depending on the media. In the case of a digital video device, there's only one option: Record The Video To The Computer. Pinnacle didn't quite finish their programming work with this aspect of Studio 8—you'll notice it says "Pinnacle Studio Using <Need Provider>." Most applications will say something more helpful like "Record Video Using." This has no function other than to save you the time of starting the application on your own. You can tell Windows XP to always start up your video-editing application when you connect your DV camera by selecting the Always Perform The Selection Action check box. Click OK to start up the video-editing application if you haven't already.

Figure 6-13 This Windows XP action list shows a digital video device.

5   Once Pinnacle Studio 8 has started, make sure you're in the Capture tab—if you're not, click the word Capture at the top of the screen (see

Figure 6-14). The controls allow you to manipulate the tape in your camera—you can rewind the tape, fast-forward, and generally cue it up to the point where you want to record from. In most cases you'll simply want to click the Rewind button and start recording from the beginning of the tape. Before you start recording you'll want to make sure you're recording to the correct location.

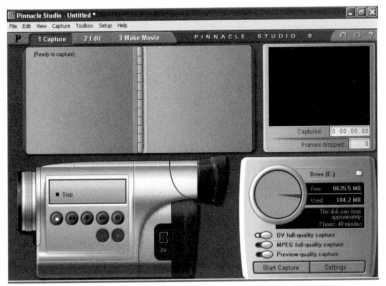

Figure 6-14 In Pinnacle Studio 8, the Capture tab allows you to manipulate the tape in your camera.

6 By default, the storage folder for capturing will be the C drive, so we'll want to change that to a drive with lots of space. There's a small white folder to the right of the drive letter—left-click it, and a new window appears. This is where you specify the file's name and where you want it stored. The name is saved only for this session, so the next time you load Pinnacle Studio 8 it resets to "Video 1." I'm going to specify my E drive, which has just under 9 GB of space. It's not a lot, but it's sufficient for my needs.

7 When you select a drive for the first time, the software runs a Data Rate Test on it—this tests the read and write speed of the hard drive to make sure it has the performance needed to work with digital video. This test is automatic, and when it's completed you'll see something like Figure 6-15. If you have a reasonably performing hard drive, it will pass the test and you can click OK. If for some reason the drive test fails, it's time to get a new hard drive—you won't have good results if the drive can't keep up to the video stream. See Chapter 5 for hard drive recommendations.

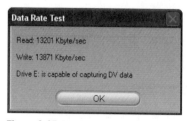

Figure 6-15 The Data Rate Test tests the read and write speed of a new drive.

8   Once the Data Rate Test is completed, click Settings. We'll need to make sure that the video capture settings are set to what we want—which is maximum quality. The first tab, Capture Source, is fairly straightforward: the capture device for both video and audio should be DV Camcorder (see Figure 6-16). The Capture Preview box should be selected, or you won't be able to see your video as it's being captured. TV Standard should be set to NTSC. *Scene Detection* During Video Capture is an important option—I normally have this set to Automatic Based On Video Content because I find it easiest to edit that way, but if you want to select the scenes yourself manually, select No Auto Scene Detection—Press Space Bar To Create Scene.

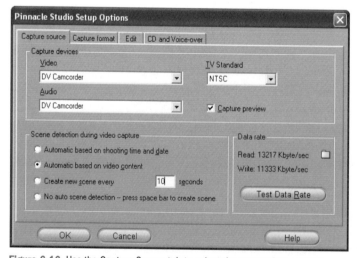

Figure 6-16 Use the Capture Source tab to select the appropriate settings.

Lingo   *Scene Detection.* This is a technology built into most video-editing applications. The software is able to tell when the camera is capturing a new scene, and it marks that segment as a "scene" for easier editing. Typically you'll see a series of thumbnail images, each representing a new scene, and you can edit your video by simply dragging and dropping the video segments that you like. This detection isn't perfect, though—if a strong camera flash goes off, the video camera perceives that as a "scene break" and starts off on a new scene the frame after that flash. You'll learn more about this in Chapter 7.

9   The next Settings tab is for Capture Format (see Figure 6-17). There are several presets (DV, MPEG, Preview) and a series of options to configure for each one. Unless you have an extremely small hard drive, always use DV—the other options sacrifice time or quality to save on storage space. DV gives you the full-quality video stream, and this means you won't have to capture it later. The Studio 8 DV capture takes up around 200 MB per minute, so make sure you have plenty of space before you begin. The other two tabs, Edit and CD And Voice-Over, don't relate to recording, but they're worth exploring once you start editing.

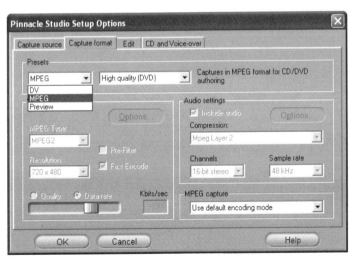

Figure 6-17 The Capture Format tab gives a series of options to configure for the presets.

10   Once you're finished with the Settings, click OK. You'll be returned to the Capture interface (Figure 6-14). Click Start Capture, and the Capture Video window appears (Figure 6-18). Give a name to your video clip, and if you know how long your video clip is, enter a number. If you don't know how long it is, leave the number at the default maximum (this will be different based on hard drive size).

Figure 6-18 Use the Capture Video window to give a name to your video clip.

11 Click OK and the video capture begins. Assuming you have the scene detection set to Automatic, as it captures you'll see thumbnails appear in the "book" above the camera, as shown in Figure 6-19. To the right of the book is the preview window, where you'll see your video as it's being captured. Below that window you'll see Frames Dropped—this number is what you want to watch. In ideal circumstances, it should stay at zero. If it's any more than 60 frames dropped per minute of video, you have a problem and should look for CPU-consuming tasks.

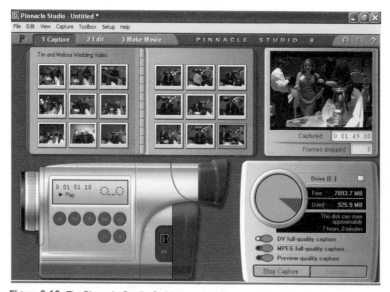

Figure 6-19 The Pinnacle Studio 8 video capture process is underway.

12 When you're finished capturing the video, click Stop Capture—you're done! The video file will be stored on your hard drive on whatever partition you specified earlier in step 6.

Capturing Analog Video (Archiving Home Movies)

The catalyst for a lot of people who are getting involved in digital video—archiving home videos to save them from the ravages of time—is something I encourage everyone to do. So many memories are truly "once in a lifetime" events, and it's a shame to have them be lost forever if your VHS tape breaks or the camcorder doesn't work any longer. Archiving them to a digital format preserves them for future generations, and it's easier than you might think. For the purpose of this exercise I'm using the Pinnacle Studio Deluxe described earlier in this chapter—most analog capture cards function on the same principles, however, so you can choose whatever product fits you best (although I highly recommend the Pinnacle Studio Deluxe solution). Let's get started!

1 Getting the proper cables is the first thing you'll need to do. If you're copying from a VCR, you need a three-prong RCA cable, as shown in Figure 6-20: one yellow prong for the video, a red prong for one audio channel, and a white prong for the other audio channel. The other end should also have three prongs. Remember that the signal always has to come in one end and go out the other—the easiest way to understand audio and video cabling is to pretend that *you are the signal*. The signal starts coming from the VCR, so where does it go from there?

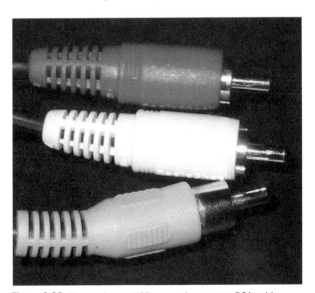

Figure 6-20 To copy from a VCR, use a three-prong RCA cable.

2 VCRs have audio and video output ports on the back—and sometimes the front—so that's where the signal will come out (see Figure 6-21).

Connect the RCA cables to those ports—yellow for the video and the red and white cables to the audio ports. Now the signal will be traveling down the cable.

Figure 6-21 You connect the RCA cable to the VCR outputs.

3 It needs to get digitized, so the signal has to go into the break-out box, which is already connected to the computer—connect the video (yellow) cable to the video port on the break-out box and the same for the audio cables (see Figure 6-22). With the audio cables, it's important to get the left and right channels connected properly—if you have the red cable plugged into the left audio channel output on the VCR, the red cable should be plugged into the left audio channel input on the break-out box. That's it! The signal now goes from point A to point B.

Figure 6-22 To digitize the signal, you connect the cables to the break-out box.

Now that the cabling is completed, we need to get the software capture configured. The software capture for analog video is very similar to the previous series of steps on digital video capture, so please excuse any repetition, but I want to give you the complete steps.

1   Once Pinnacle Studio 8 has started, make sure you're on the Capture tab— if not, click the word Capture at the top of the screen (see Figure 6-23). Unlike capturing through FireWire, there's no way to control your VCR with on-screen controls. Before you start recording you'll want to make sure you're recording to the correct location. By default, the storage folder for capturing is the C drive, so we'll want to change that to a drive with lots of space. There's a small white folder to the right of the drive letter—left-click it, and a new window appears. This is where you specify the name of the file and where you want it stored. The name is saved only for this session, so the next time you load Pinnacle Studio 8 it will reset to "Video 1."

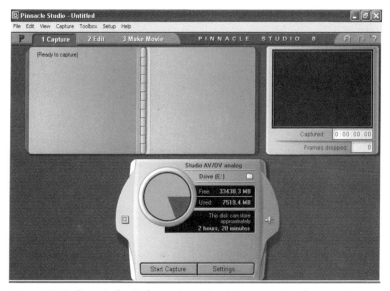

Figure 6-23 In Pinnacle Studio 8, use the analog video capture interface to make sure you're recording to the correct location.

2   When you select a drive for the first time, the software runs a Data Rate Test on it—this tests the read and write speed of the hard drive to make sure it has the performance needed to work with digital video. This test is automatic, and when it's completed you'll see something like Figure 6-24. If you have a reasonably performing hard drive, it will pass the test and you can click OK.

Figure 6-24 The software runs a Data Rate Test on a new drive.

3   Once the Data Rate Test is completed, click Settings. The first tab, Capture Source (Figure 6-25), is fairly straightforward: the capture device
for both video and audio should be Studio AV/DV Analog. The Capture
Preview box should be selected, or you won't be able to see your
video as it's being captured. TV Standard should be set to NTSC. The
Scene Detection is an important option—I normally have this set to
Automatic Based On Video Content because I find it easiest to edit that
way, but if you want to select the scenes yourself manually, select No
Automatic Scene Detection.

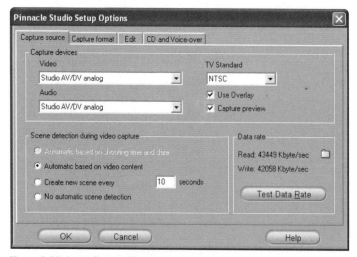

Figure 6-25 In the Capture Source tab, select the appropriate settings.

4   The next Settings tab is for Capture Format, as shown in Figure 6-26.
When it comes to analog capture, there's only one option: Full DV
Quality. The other two tabs, Edit and CD And Voice-Over, don't relate
to recording, but they're worth exploring once you start editing.

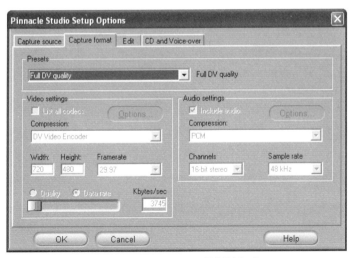

Figure 6-26 In the Capture Format tab, select Full DV Quality.

5   Once you're finished with the Settings, click OK. You'll be returned to the Capture interface.

6   Click Start Capture, and the Capture Video window appears. Give a name to your video clip, and if you know how long your video clip is, enter a number. If you don't know how long it is, leave the number at the default maximum (this will be different based on hard drive size).

7   Click OK, and the video capture begins. Assuming you have the scene detection set to Automatic, as it captures you'll see thumbnails appear in the "book" above the camera. To the right of the book is the preview window where you'll see your video as it's being captured. Below that window you'll see Frames Dropped—this number is what you want to watch. In ideal circumstances, it should stay at zero. If it's any more than 60 frames dropped per minute of video, you have a problem and should look for CPU-consuming tasks.

8   When you're finished capturing the video, click Stop Capture—you're done! The video file will be stored on your hard drive, on whatever partition you specified earlier in step 6.

Organizing Your Video Clips

After you've been working with digital video for a while, you'll likely build up quite a collection of video clips and movies. Keeping them organized, and having a backup in case of data loss, is very important. I should note here that the videos I'm talking about are in a format suitable for archiving on your computer—

you probably won't keep a 5 GB AVI file on your hard drive, but you may save it into a lower quality format and keep a 100 MB version (we'll talk about how to do this in Chapter 7). Everyone organizes and visualizes information differently, so pick a method that works best for you (or combine several). Here are some tips to help get you started:

- **Organize based on topic**   If you find yourself being the official videographer at family weddings, holidays, and birthdays, you're going to have a lot of events pile up on your hard drive pretty quickly. Organizing them based on topic may be a good solution for finding them easily in the future—in your My Video folder (found in My Documents) you can create folders like "Holidays," "Weddings," "Birthdays," etc.

- **Organize based on date**   If you're a linear thinker, this method may work best for you. Create folders for the year, and inside that folder don't put any subfolders—use descriptive names for your video files and sort by date when viewing them. This method works well when combined with topic sorting—you can create a "2002" folder and then inside that folder create the topic folders (Birthdays, Weddings, etc.).

- **Type of video**   If you find that you share your videos a great deal through e-mail, the Web, and VCDs, you may want to keep the versions separate. Create a folder for each type of sharing that you'd be doing and render your video in each format as you complete the project. When Aunt Martha says she'd just love to see a certain video in her e-mail, rather than having to rerender the video, you already have a folder with all your projects in an e-mail-friendly format. This method will use up a lot of hard drive space, and the rendering will take extra time, so this solution is only viable for powerful computers.

- **Use a third-party media organization tool**   Several media organization tools are on the market, but my favorite is ACDSee from ACD Systems (*www.acdsystems.com*). In version 5.0 as of October 2002, this application excels at managing photos, and, to a lesser extent, video clips. I searched for a video-specific tool, but I was unable to find one that was useful in any fashion. ACDSee offers some interesting features, however, for video clip management—you can attach keywords to your video clips and then use the search tool in ACDSee for finding any clips that contain those words. It's also possible to adjust the thumbnail size of the video previews, making it easier to browse for clips using ACDSee than using the normal Windows XP browsing.

ACDSee also offers some interesting features when it comes to capturing individual frames from a video clip—you can capture a single frame to a clipboard and then paste that frame into a document or image editing program. You can also export entire video clips as individual frames! This takes a huge amount of disk space, and it's difficult to envision a scenario where you'd need thousands of frames from your video, but it's nice to have the option.

■ **Backing up your video** An important part of staying organized is having an effective backup in case of data loss. There's nothing worse than having your hard drive fail and not having a recent backup. A friend of mine recently had his hard drive fail—just as he was in the process of backing up 5 GB of data for the first time in over a year! Data loss isn't something that just happens to "other people"—eventually it will happen to you as well. My personal choice for backing up all my data is Handy Backup (*www.handybackup.com*), a powerful but easy-to-use program. It's capable of backing up data to another hard drive, across a network, over the Internet to a File Transfer Protocol (FTP) site, or even burning it to a CD. Backing up your video files will likely take up a huge amount of space, so think out your backup strategy. If you want the security of knowing that all your video exists in two places, buy a large 160 GB Maxtor 3000 XT and simply back up your video files from one drive to another. My personal method of backup is to burn a CD or DVD with the final video files (the final AVI project file and the file in VCD/SVCD format).

Key Points

■ Capturing analog video from a VCR requires special hardware.

■ Capturing digital video requires a FireWire card.

■ Some FireWire cards ship with all the software you'll need to edit your videos.

■ DV cameras can be used as Web cameras and digital still photo cameras.

■ There are steps you should take to optimize your computer before capturing video.

■ Organizing your videos, and backing them up, is an important task.

Part III

Editing

The camera has been chosen, the video has been recorded, and now it's on your computer. What happens next? We edit! Video editing with the current crop of software on the market has never been so exciting—when combined with the sheer power of current hardware, editing digital video has never been so easy. I'm going to be looking at basic video-editing applications aimed at beginners, and then I'll delve into the world of advanced video editing, where almost anything is possible.

Chapter 7

Basic Video Editing

Once you've captured your video, the next big step is to edit it. There are different approaches to editing video, and we'll cover the basics in this chapter and get into advanced editing techniques in the next chapter. More than likely, video editing will be the lengthiest part of any project you do. Why? It involves the most creativity, and if you're a perfectionist like me, you'll find yourself correcting even the most minor mistakes. The upside to this is that digital video gives you that control—you can tweak and tune your video to be exactly what you want. Here are some key points to think about when you start editing your video.

It's More Than Just Fixing Errors

Too often, people think of video editing as being the "part where mistakes are fixed." In the 1980s, when camcorders were clunky and digital video editing didn't exist at the consumer level, editing consisted of simply trying to remove those shots where someone left the lens cap on or thought the camera was paused when they set it down on the table for 10 minutes. Editing out those mistakes gave you your "good" footage, but it certainly didn't do any-thing to improve the 5-minute shot of the family dog. Break out of this men-tality right now—editing is about more than just fixing errors.

Unedited Video Is Boring

Have you ever watched a "Vacation Video from Hell"? I think you know the type of video I'm talking about. You're over at a friend's house, you're told they took some great video footage of their recent trip to some exotic locale, and you say you want to see it. Uh-oh. Two appendage-numbing hours later, you swear to yourself that you're not going to ask to see another vacation video as long as you live. Here's the honest truth: No one will find your vaca-tion video as interesting as you do. They weren't there, so they won't have the memories you do. What people *are* interested in seeing, however, are the highlights. Editing an hour of video down to 10 minutes of highlights will give you something that you can show to others without apologizing afterward. And once you get the reputation for having great vacation videos, who knows, your friends and family may be *asking* to see it next time!

Shaping Your Story

Video editing is about shaping the story you want to tell. Every video has a story—a sequence of events—and it's up to you to make that story a good one. Part of editing is taking out the things that don't belong in the story, and rearranging the elements that are left to communicate to the viewer. It's better to have a 10-minute video that tells a story than a 60-minute video that doesn't tell any story at all.

Audio Adds Excitement

As I expressed earlier in the book, audio is a critical element in any good video production. Unless you're directly interviewing someone on camera or covering an event where the audio is an integral component (a speech or wedding), in most cases audio from your footage will be nothing more than background noise. Why not replace that with something more exciting? Most video-editing programs allow you to *rip* tracks from a CD. Having catchy, recognizable songs in your video will make it much more engaging and exciting to the viewer.

Lingo *Rip*. No, this doesn't stand for "Rest In Peace." To *rip* an audio track from a CD means to digitally extract the audio and convert it into a WAV file that you can use in your video. In most cases it's as simple as putting the CD in your CD-ROM drive, selecting the track you want, and clicking a button. We'll cover ripping audio in Chapter 8 when we discuss advanced editing techniques.

The First Editing Decision You Need to Make

This question wouldn't have come up even a year ago, but recent developments in the video-editing world have made this question an important first step in the video-editing process: Do you want to edit the video yourself, or do you want computer software to do it for you?

Enter Autoproducing

As incredible as the above question sounds, it's a reality today with some of the most impressive software I've ever seen. I'm approaching this as a category because there are several products on the market that approach autoproducing in different ways, although all of them are based on the same core technology. I'm convinced that in the next two years we'll see a whole new type of video-editing software appear, all of it based on the concepts I'm discussing here.

The basic idea behind autoproducing is simple: software analyzes the video and, with minimal input from the user, edits the video into a final form using predefined rules for professional-caliber video editing. To the best of my knowledge, there's only one company offering autoproducing technology: muvee Technologies.

An Interview with the Makers of muvee In discovering muvee, quite by acci-
dent earlier this year, I felt like I had stumbled onto something amazing—I was so impressed
with what the makers of muvee had accomplished that I thought a quick interview with them
would be the best way to share it with you.

How did the concept for muvee come about?

"Researchers at Kent Ridge Digital Labs have been pioneers in video and audio analysis
for the past 10 years. In the late 1990's a team from KRDL had a hunch that more people
would use video for informal and casual communication if only the production process could
be made easier. The key pieces were there—reasonably priced consumer DV camcorders,
FireWire and USB interfaces and big hard drives. The stumbling block was the enormous
amount of tedious work it takes to edit video using conventional editing tools.

Currently there are more than 50 million camcorders in the world (with another 10 million
a year being sold). However, only a few percent of people who shoot video actually ever get
round to editing it. This provided a huge opportunity—press a button to shoot video, press
'make muvee' to automatically turn it into a completely edited production. This was a compelling proposition, a bit like the way instant cameras opened up photography to most people in
the early twentieth century.

Several of these researchers were musicians, and they observed that in music videos,
unlike narrative videos or documentaries, the way the video is edited matters nearly as much
as the actual content—perhaps more. This meant it was possible for a program to create music
videos from home video automatically, without requiring any deep understanding of the
semantics or meaning of the original video material. The work has now progressed much further
than this with the use of other techniques such as more intricate analysis of the video—for
instance, this allows us to detect the presence of faces, which is used in some of the muvee
production styles that are included in the muvee autoProducer program."

What are some of the "rules" that muvee uses when autoproducing a video file,
and how does it know when to implement them?

"Professional editors rely on an 'editing grammar' to make captivating productions—dozens of rules that guide their editing decisions. Many of the rules are things that professionals
do unconsciously. Many are simple once you know them, but nonobvious to the vast majority of
amateurs, even if they've been watching professionally edited video all their lives on television.

One important rule is that the video should be edited to the rhythm of the music: the pac-
ing (number of different shots in a given time) should follow what we call the 'Emotional Index'
of the music. For example, a fast-paced video has a cut or transition every 1 to 4 seconds—if

it's less frequent than that, the production will feel slow, almost regardless of how much action there is in the video footage itself. And when there is a strong driving beat, the cuts and other transitions should mostly fall on the beat—but not rigidly so. The types and speeds of the transitions (e.g., how fast to dissolve from one shot to the next) are also important. Like the music itself, it only feels right if it hits the right balance between being too rigid and too loose.

There are many other rules governing which segments of the raw video are chosen and how they are sequenced. There are also special rules for which video segments can be juxtaposed. For example, where possible the software avoids 'jump cuts.' These are sudden and unpleasant cuts from one shot to another similar but nonidentical shot. Professional editors go to considerable lengths to avoid jump cuts.

In order to apply these and other rules, muvee autoProducer first analyzes the music and raw video. The video analyzer finds shot boundaries, color, texture, motion, the presence of human faces, etc. The music analyzer finds the tempo, rhythm, and Emotional Index. The Constructor uses this information, plus a muvee Style which the user selects from a choice (currently of 24), to create the best possible production—one that's stylish and artistically coherent.

Getting the techniques to work well with a wide variety of input video and music is an enormous challenge. It's not just knowing the rules, but knowing how to apply them and when to break them. Done right, it allows users to create near-professional quality productions from home video footage—even if they have no prior experience in video editing. That's the power of what muvee calls Artistic Intelligence.

So there are many parts to this. muvee has filed several major patent applications and is scoping out others."

What is the ultimate evolution of muvee? What features are coming next?

"Many users have asked for greater control over the production process so that they can influence or override the automatic editing decisions. However, what they clearly don't want is full manual control—that's readily available in various NLE (Non-Linear Editing) products, which are generally far too tedious and complex for amateurs (and even professionals sometimes!). We plan to offer the best of both by automating the vast majority of tasks, with the user providing only as much input as they want to.

The great thing about video editing is that it's changing all the time. If you look at video productions from 10 years ago and compare them with what's produced today, you'll see huge changes. Some of it's a matter of improved technology—some effects that are commonplace on TV today were simply impossible 10 years ago—but it's also a question of fashion. muvee's products will continue to evolve to keep pace with the best practices of professional editors."

Autoproducing Software Products

Three products on the market today allow you to autoproduce your video, and all three are based on the core muvee technology. I took a close look at two of them: muvee autoProducer Cobalt and ACD VideoMagic. The third, Roxio VideoWave Movie Creator Cinemagic, simply isn't ready for prime time—it had too many limitations to be useful (it shows promise, though—perhaps the next version will be better). Although all are based on the same core technology, each is quite different in implementation, so it's worth looking at each one when making a decision on which one to choose.

Caution One thing to be very aware of is that the process is almost entirely automated—you have no control over the transitions, the timing, or even the scene selection. Although I'm a big fan of this technology, I've found through much trial and error that a product based on muvee simply isn't a good choice for editing events with specific shots that you want to keep. Although muvee-based products do a remarkable job of getting the best footage from your clip, they still have a bad habit of cutting that one important shot. muvee also assumes that the video you feed it has a lot of content worth throwing away—if you've already done some preediting to remove the bad shots, there's no way to tell it to lay off the heavy editing. It can't hurt to run your video through muvee—you might just get lucky—but if you have a very specific idea in mind for how you want the video to look, it's probably better to edit it manually. muvee excels at editing video where nothing "special" happens—video of your children running around at the local park, a soccer game where you don't care too much about including a specific goal. The more generic your goals are with the video, the more satisfied you'll be with muvee.

---

muvee autoProducer Cobalt

The "granddaddy" of this category, muvee autoProducer Cobalt (Figure 7-1) is the flagship product of muvee Technologies. When I first visited their Web site (*www.muvee.com*) I thought it was too good to be true—software intelligent enough to do something creative like edit video? I downloaded the free demo, and the rest was history—I became one of muvee's biggest fans. To understand why, you have to realize that out of the millions of hours of video shot every year on DV cameras, a very small percentage of it gets edited. Even with all the great digital tools we have now, for the average person video editing is a daunting process. My hope is that this book will help dispel that fear, but for everyone else not using this book, editing can be a scary task. muvee Technologies has the goal of changing that by eliminating the need for consumers to make complex video-editing decisions.

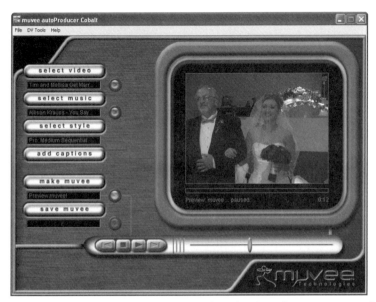

Figure 7-1 The muvee autoProducer Cobalt software interface allows you to autoproduce your video.

Using muvee is remarkably simple. Later in this chapter we'll do a short tutorial on using muvee, but it's quite honestly as simple as selecting your video clip, selecting some music, and selecting the style of the edit (you can chose from 24 different styles). You can combine multiple video clips and multiple audio files to give muvee more raw material to work with, and, once it's done the time-consuming initial analysis, you can preview your movie. If you don't like the style, pick a new one, and click Preview again—it will instantly show you a new version (no waiting). You can tell muvee how long you want the video to be, and blend the audio between the audio files and the real audio track from your video.

muvee autoProducer Cobalt also offers basic video capture over FireWire and a surprising number of export options. You can export your final project as a full-quality DV-format AVI file, MPEG, or WMV for streaming over the Web, or even in ASF (Active Streaming Format) specifically for a Pocket PC. It also offers the ability to record the video file back to the DV camera, which makes it easy to get onto a VHS tape (it's easier to connect a DV camera to a VCR than to connect a VCR to your computer).

muvee autoProducer Cobalt is a great deal and a tool I recommend that everyone purchase. If you're a beginner, this is a wonderful introduction to the world of video editing—it allows you to experiment with different styles and music clips without getting into the sometimes complex interface of a video-editing application. Even if you're an intermediate-to-expert-level user, you'll be surprised what fun you can have with muvee—it's so simple, but remarkably effective, that you'll probably laugh out loud like I did when you see the results of your first use.

I'm hoping that as they continue to develop the product they'll add the ability to tag certain scenes as being important, which would address one of the only limitations of the product: having important video scenes get cut by software that doesn't know any better. Some of the styles are sequential (meaning your video is presented in the same order as the original video file), and some aren't—it would be useful to be able to make any selected style sequential or nonsequential. And more styles would be great too!

ACD VideoMagic

ACD Systems (*www.acdsystems.com*), the maker of several excellent digital media products, licensed the core muvee technology and built its own application around it. Dubbed ACD VideoMagic, this product is very similar to muvee autoProducer Cobalt. It has the same 24 styles and produces the same results but offers a more advanced user interface, as Figure 7-2 shows.

ACD VideoMagic lets you combine photos and video clips—you can add an entire photo collection, put it to music, and have a nice photo slideshow. You can rearrange video clips and photos by clicking and dragging them; and adding new audio, photos, or video clips is as simple as browsing and dragging into the timeline. The interface is very easy to use, and even a beginner would have no problem creating a simple music video. It's a good entry-level autoproducing solution.

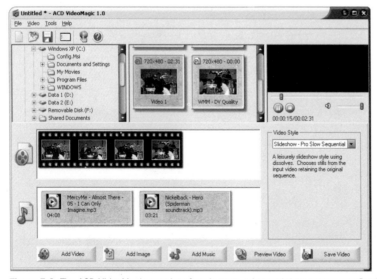

Figure 7-2 The ACD VideoMagic user interface is more advanced than muvee autoProducer Cobalt.

For all that it adds, however, ACD VideoMagic takes away a few things: You can't retain any of the original audio track, so every video is a "music video." In most cases that's fine, but I would have preferred to see the option to blend the two audio sources. It doesn't allow you to record video from a DV camera, nor does it allow export of the video back out to the DV camera. Lastly, it had a habit of crashing on me fairly frequently—this is a new product with a lot of potential, so I hope that ACD Systems keeps developing it because they're off to a great start.

Try This!   If you want to maximize the possibility of getting the "perfect" edit from a muvee-based software product, do a first pass at editing. By that I mean to open your footage in a simple video-editing application and delete all the junk. Delete the bad shots, the times when someone walked in front of the camera, etc. If you feed muvee nothing but good shots, the result will be much better, because muvee doesn't have the intelligence (yet) to determine a boring shot from an exciting one.

The Power of Manual Editing

As I explained above, autoproducing is wonderful for some types of video projects, but not for all of them. If you have a sequence of events that you really want to see in your video, in their entirety, manual editing is the way to go. Manual editing is a more time-consuming task, but with some of the newer software on the market today it's no longer quite as daunting. And, unlike the autoproducing software, when you've spent a few hours manually editing your video you can rightfully call it your own—your creativity will be stamped on the project. That's a good feeling!

Dozens of entry-level video-editing applications are on the market today, but to keep things simple I picked what I thought were the top programs. My goal in covering the products below was to give you an idea of what entry-level video-editing packages offer, what they cost, and what you can do with them.

Microsoft Windows Movie Maker 1.2

Did you know that Microsoft Windows XP came with a free digital movie-editing program? Probably not—it's one of the most overlooked programs in Windows XP. Windows Movie Maker is a very basic package, but for someone just getting started, it's perfect. The user interface is quite straightforward (Figure 7-3)—when you first use it, you can either import video clips from your hard drive or click the Record button to take footage off your DV camera. It offers basic scene detection that works quite well and has the ability to record a narration track or insert an audio file. You can mix the audio between the music or narration and the audio on your video track.

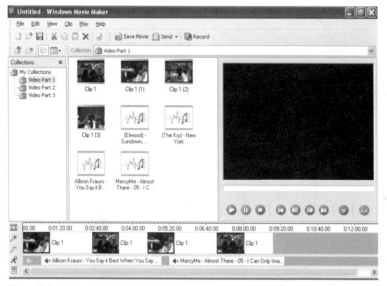

Figure 7-3 Windows Movie Maker 1.2 is a good choice for beginners.

Windows Movie Maker is a good choice for learning the basics of video editing without spending any money, and it's ideally suited for sharing video clips over e-mail or the Web.

Caution   There's currently a bug in version 1.2 of Windows Movie Maker that stops audio from being recorded when you have it set at maximum quality (DV AVI 25 Mbps)—your video will be recorded, but no audio. The workaround for this bug is to press Play to start the camera playback, and then to hit Record once the camera playback has started. I've heard this bug will be fixed in the 2.0 version of the software.

Ulead VideoStudio 6.0

Ulead has been a significant player in the multimedia realm for quite some time now, so it's no surprise that it has a large lineup of video products. VideoStudio 6.0 is the latest version of their popular entry-level video-editing package. It offers standard video capture, editing, and rendering. It also has 100 transitions, 30 special-effect filters that can be customized, and quite a few other features. As Figure 7-4 shows, the user interface is based on tabs that run along the top of the screen. This makes it easy to know what you're supposed to do next, but I found working within the tabs a little confusing—it wasn't immediately clear how to import video clips or do scene selection on them.

Figure 7-4 Ulead VideoStudio 6.0 offers a wide range of features.

VideoStudio 6.0 is an affordable package, but be on the lookout for possible bundles with your hardware. Ulead often has its software bundled with hardware like FireWire cards, so you may get this software for free. You can download a free trial of VideoStudio 6.0 from the Ulead Web site (*www.ulead.com/vs/trial.htm*), and I strongly recommend you take the trial version for a spin before buying the full version—you'll want to make sure it works with your hardware before buying it.

Pinnacle Studio 8.0

One of my favorite entry-level video-editing applications, Pinnacle Studio 8.0 (*www.pinnaclesys.com*) came out in August 2002, so it offers some very interesting features that the other applications have yet to catch up to. The application is divided into three main sections: Capture, Edit, and Make Movie. This application has one of the best user interfaces I've ever seen (Figure 7-5), and using it is remarkably simple. Editing can be done in one of three views: Storyboard, Timeline, and Text. Moving around elements is a drag-and-drop procedure, so it's easy to do. There are more than 100 transitions, with some great Hollywood FX 3-D transitions for those flashy productions.

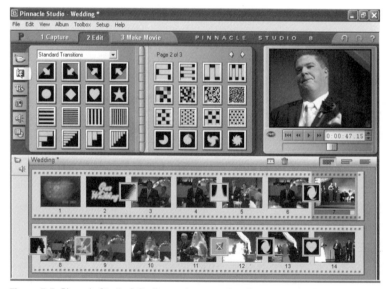

Figure 7-5 Pinnacle Studio 8.0 offers a clever user interface and many features.

It's also easy to add superb-looking text to your video (there are some wonderful presets), and the audio portion of Studio 8.0 is particularly flexible: You can import WAV or MP3 files, digitally copy tracks directly from an audio CD, or use the SmartSound feature to create background music that will line up with the length of your production perfectly. One of the new features added to version 8.0 is the ability to burn VCD, SVCD, and DVD-format discs. There are also 45 high-quality menu templates that you can use for professional-looking video discs. I was particularly impressed with how well Pinnacle was able to add these new features without adding complexity to the overall process.

There's one slight problem with Studio 8.0: It doesn't appear to be very stable yet. On two different computers, I've had several serious problems that ranged from being unable to capture analog video to complete system lockups when I tried to use the SmartSound feature. The latter error caused me to lose a portion of this chapter when my system crashed and took my document with it. *Note to self: save documents and shut down Microsoft Word before experimenting with new video-editing software.* Pinnacle is fairly regular about releasing software patches and upgrades, so I'm hoping that there will be a software update out soon that will address the stability problems. Despite these issues, this is the application I use most often to edit my video—it combines ease of use with great features and allows me to work the way I want to.

Caution   Pinnacle Video Studio works very well with the DV AVI files that it creates during the recording process, but it seems to have significant problems with DV AVI files generated by other programs. I was unable to import or work with DV AVI files created by muvee autoProducer Cobalt or VideoFactory 2.0. My hope is that they address this in a patch—it's frustrating to not be able to work with all the video files you have.

Sonic Foundry VideoFactory 2.0

I have to admit that before I started working on this book, I thought of Sonic Foundry as being strictly an audio software company. Was I ever wrong! Although they primarily make audio software, they have some great video software as well. VideoFactory 2.0 is a superb entry-level product that offers solid value. It's one of the least expensive packages I encountered but also one of the most capable from a pure editing point of view. With an impressive 170+ transitions, 115 special effects, and a bonus CD-ROM filled with stock video clips, this package offers a lot of options to beginners and intermediate users alike. The user interface is very clean and easy to work with (Figure 7-6)—everything is logically laid out, and although it doesn't offer the "tabbed interface" most entry-level programs do, I actually found it more efficient to keep everything on one screen at a time. It works well on less powerful computers as well—my moderately underpowered PIII-750 MHz laptop was able to keep up with the software quite well.

The software is very functional, offering users the ability to digitally copy songs from an audio CD, apply audio effects like reverb and delay, record video from video capture devices (including DV cameras), import photos, export to a variety of video formats (MPEG, AVI, DV AVI, Windows Media, Quicktime), and even burn a VCD directly.

One of the only things missing from VideoFactory was an easy-to-use scene detection feature. My contact at Sonic Foundry assured me it was there, but in searching through the help files I was unable to find a single mention of it, and the manual also had no mention. If it is there, they certainly made it hard to find,

and it's not automatic when importing video clips. I think this feature is important for beginners, because it saves them the hassle of having to manually cut up
all their video clips. If you don't mind a little extra manual labor after you capture your video, VideoFactory 2.0 is a fantastic tool. You can learn more and
order online from *www.sonicfoundry.com*.

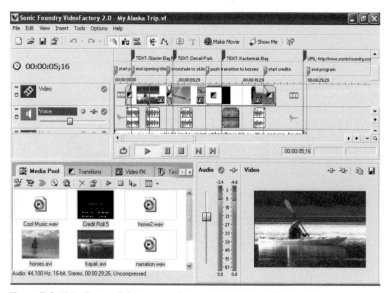

Figure 7-6 VideoFactory 2.0 is a powerful entry-level video-editing package.

Caution   Although the boxed version I received stated that the software was capable of MPEG1
and MPEG2 encoding, I discovered that once I did the upgrade to 2.0c (the latest version), I was
unable to do any MPEG encoding without taking further steps. The MainConcept MPEG1 encoder
is free to download and use if you register with VideoFactory, but if you want to use the Main-
Concept MPEG2 encoder, you'll need to purchase it. I hope Sonic Foundry updates their packaging to reflect the lack of MPEG2 encoding out of the box.

Roxio VideoWave 5.0

The VideoWave series of software has been around for years, and the latest 5.0
version adds some new features into the mix. The software bundle includes two
CDs full of titles, animations, background images, buttons, and audio clips—
everything you need to add a professional touch to your video. Roxio has made
it easy to do some of the more common effects like adding slow motion and fast
motion, creating picture-in-picture, and adding moving text. A basic set of filters
is included, and rendering time is enhanced through use of a technology called

SmartDV—it renders only the frames that have changed.Figure 7-7 shows the user interface of VideoWave 5.0, and as you can tell it's very different from any of the other products I've included here. I found the interface too obscure—there was no guidance from the software on where to go next, and trying to figure out the "next step" was a little frustrating. There are better options for your money.

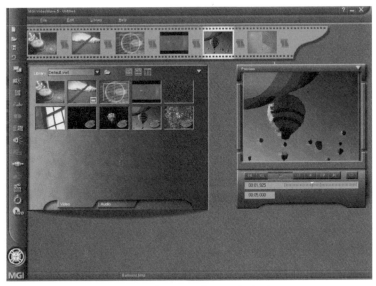

Figure 7-7 Roxio VideoWave 5.0 offers many features for beginners.

Using muvee autoProducer Cobalt

If you're interested in letting autoproducing software transform your video into a masterpiece, there's no better choice than muvee autoProducer Cobalt. In this step-by-step we're going to take a raw video file direct from a camcorder, transfer it to the computer using muvee, customize the show, pick a style, and let muvee go at it. If you want to follow along, download the free trial from *www.muvee.com* and get your DV camera ready—I guarantee this will be fun! You'll also need to have one MP3 or WAV file for the background music.

1 Connect your DV camera to the PC through FireWire, and once it's ready to go, start up muvee autoProducer Cobalt.

2 Once muvee has started, from the DV Tools menu, select DV Capture.

3 The Capture Video From DV Camcorder window appears (Figure 7-8), and the first thing you want to do is click the Browse button to make sure the target hard drive is the correct one. You want to pick your capture drive or any other drive with several free GB (depending on your video's length). The default file name of CapturedVideo.avi is just fine.

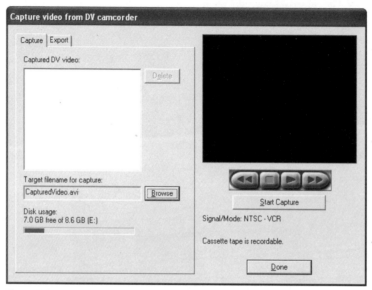

Figure 7-8 You use the Capture Video From DV Camcorder window to capture video from the DV camera using muvee.

4 When you're ready, and you've shut down other running applications, click the Start Capture Button. muvee puts the DV camera into Play mode and starts recording the signal to the hard drive. You can monitor the capture process by watching the video in the preview window (you should also hear audio).

5 Once you've captured the video segment, click Stop Capture. The DV camera continues to play the tape until you click the Stop button (just under the preview window). Why? Well, you can capture various video clips from this interface by starting and stopping the capture process as you watch the video. You can also use the controls to fast forward and rewind the tape in the camera.

6 Once you've finished capturing all your video, click Done, and you're returned to the main muvee interface.

7 Click Select Video, and when the window appears, click Add. Unless it's automatically selected, you'll need to browse to the drive where you captured the video clips in step 3. You can drag a selection box over multiple clips if needed, and once you have selected the correct video clips, click Add. You should see them appear in the Select Video window (Figure 7-9). If you want to change the order of the clips, you can click and drag them down or up in the list. Once everything is in order, click OK.

Figure 7-9 In the Select Video window, you choose the video clips to be included.

8 Now click Select Music, and a window similar to the Select Video window appears. Click Add and browse to a folder where you have a WAV or MP3 file saved. Select the music file you want to use and click Open. You'll be taken back to the Select Music window. The Audio Mix slider (Figure 7-10) should be all the way over to the left, which means we'll hear only the music, not the audio from the video. You can experiment with this setting later if you like, but for now we'll leave it at the default. Click OK to finish this step.

Figure 7-10 You select an audio file and the audio mix in the Select Music window.

9   Click Select Style and read through the 24 different styles by selecting
them from the drop-down menu (Figure 7-11). "Over-the-Top Music
Video" is a fun style, so select that one and click OK.

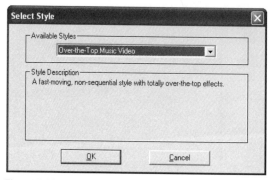

Figure 7-11 Look through the available styles and select one.

10 Next we're going to add some custom text—click Add Captions and
type your own text into the boxes (Figure 7-12). Opening titles can be
the event name, the date, or a greeting. The closing credits should be
your name or a closing statement. As you gain more experience with
muvee, you can try selecting your own fonts. For now, let muvee
choose the fonts and click OK.

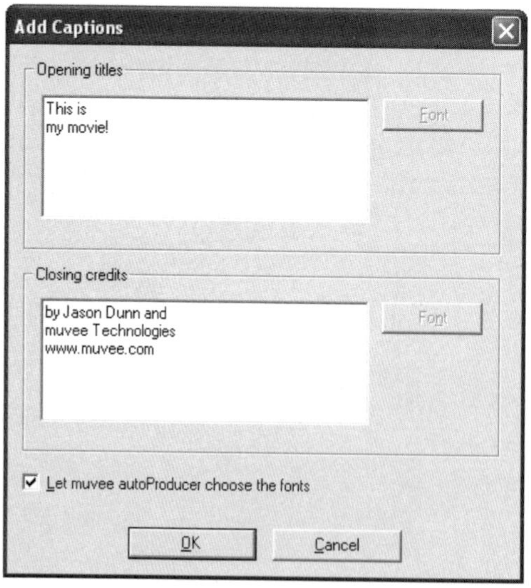

Figure 7-12 You can add custom captions to the video project.

Tip muvee uses different fonts based on the style you pick. When you're previewing your video in the final steps, you may find that the font is unreadable because it's too small (the "Over-the-Top Music Video" style is notorious for this)—in that case, you should override the automatic settings and make the fonts bigger or choose your own font. You'll have to select the Make Muvee function to see how the font will look in the video, but it's better to get this right now before the final rendering.

---

11 Click Make Muvee, and a new window appears. The basic setting simply tells you how long your production will be. If that looks fine, click OK. If you want to have more control over the production, change to the Advanced tab (Figure 7-13). In this tab you have control over how long the video will be and whether or not the video is repeated. By default, muvee will look at the length of the audio file and use the available video footage to make it match up with the music. If you tell muvee not to repeat any of the video segments, it automatically cuts the length almost in half. You can also select custom durations with muvee, so if you need to make a shorter version for e-mail, this is where you'd set it up. Once you've set up your options, click Continue.

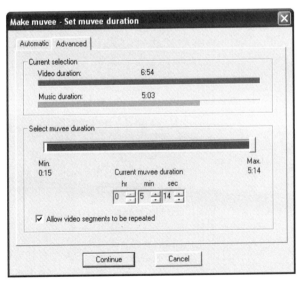

Figure 7-13 Use the Advanced tab to set up custom parameters for the video.

Tip   Even if you don't use muvee to create your video projects, it can be the perfect
tool to create fast-paced "trailers" of your work. Regardless of how long your video
project is, you can import it into muvee, select a fast-paced rock song, set the custom length to 30 seconds, and then see what muvee comes up with. You might be
surprised at how cool the trailer turns out to be!

---

12 muvee will now begin its analysis of your video and audio sources.
This can take anywhere from one minute up to an hour or more—it
depends on the length of your video clips and the speed of your CPU.

13 Once it has finished, you can click the Play button to preview the
project. This is a low-resolution version, so don't judge the quality.
Look at the shots, the transitions, and how the music you selected
blends with the images. At this point you can go back and change any
of the previous elements, and as long as you click Make Muvee again,
it will incorporate the changes. If you add new video or audio files, the
lengthy analysis will have to be done, but changing the captions or
selecting a new editing style won't add any time at all.

14 Once you're happy with the results, it's time to render the project to
the final format. Click Save Muvee, and when the window appears
(Figure 7-14), you can select the video format you want to render the
project in. The choices are self-explanatory: Computer Playback is for
archiving a reasonable-quality version of the video (29.97 FPS, 320 x
240, MPEG1), E-Mail is for sharing the video over e-mail (8 FPS, 208 x
160, ASF), Web Streaming is a good choice for putting up on your Web
site (30 FPS, 320 x 240, ASF), DV is a full-resolution AVI file appropriate
for burning to DVD or working further in other applications (29.97
FPS, 720 x 480, DV AVI), and VCD is what you'd use for burning a
video CD (29.97 FPS, 352 x 240, MPEG1). In most cases I select the DV
option to get a maximum quality AVI file—it's easier to work with
maximum quality and scale down than wishing you had rendered it in
a higher-quality format. Depending on what format you chose and
your CPU speed, the rendering process can take quite a while. Go grab
a cup of coffee and let muvee work its magic.

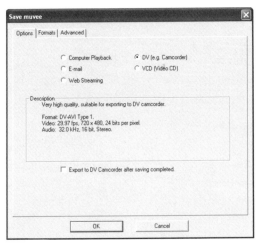

Figure 7-14 In the last step you render the video to a final format.

15 Once the process is complete you have your "muvee"!

Try This! If you want to take your muvee and put it onto a VHS tape, or even just watch it on a TV, render it as a DV AVI file. Once the rendering is complete, connect your DV camera through FireWire, and select DV Export from the DV Tools menu in muvee. Using this interface, you can push the video file back down onto the DV camera by selecting the DV AVI file and clicking Record. You can then easily connect the DV camera to your VCR or TV set.

Using Pinnacle Studio 8.0

In selecting the software to use for this step-by-step tutorial on doing basic video editing, I have to admit I was torn. Some excellent software bundles are out there, but ultimately I selected Pinnacle Studio 8.0 for two main reasons: It has a great user interface and the software is very full-featured—it's a one-stop application for beginners that takes them from video capture, through editing, to burning a DVD.

This project assumes that you've previously captured the video using the procedure outlined in Chapter 6 and that you have an audio CD handy with a song you want to use. I'm going to walk you through the basics of how to use Pinnacle Studio 8.0 to make basic video edits, add transitions and music, and output the project to a DVD. Pinnacle Studio 8.0 is capable of some advanced editing, but I don't want to get too complex in this chapter—Chapter 9 is where we cover advanced editing techniques. Regardless of what video-editing program you have, the general principles discussed in this walkthrough will be applicable to your software.

1 Start up Pinnacle Studio 8.0, and by default it should be in the Edit tab. The main workspace, which looks like a book, is called the Album. This is where you load clips and also where you'll access all the editing tools.

2 Unless you see thumbnail images of your video in the Album, you'll want to import the video so you can work with it. There's a small white folder immediately to the right of the drop-down video selection box (Figure 7-15). Clicking once on this folder gives you a browse window, and you should find your video file and click Open. The video is imported, and the scene detection tool is automatically applied. The net result is that you should have a series of thumbnails that represent your video clip. Studio 8 can fit 9 thumbnails per Album page and 18 on opposing pages, so if you have more scenes than that it will break them up into pages. There will be a small white arrow in the upper-right corner of the Album that will allow you to flip pages.

Figure 7-15 The main Edit window in Studio 8 is where you select the video clips.

3 Once you have your thumbnail scenes, it's time to create your video project! By default, we're in the Storyboard view, which is the simplest of the views. The storyboard is the series of gray blocks below the Album, and you add video to these blocks by clicking on a thumbnail from the Album and dragging the thumbnail into the Storyboard block. Figure 7-16 shows this in action—as you drag the scene down to the storyboard, the selected block has a green outline. Go ahead and drag several scenes onto the Storyboard. If you're not sure what exactly is in the scene, double-click the thumbnail and the video will play in the preview window (Figure 7-17).

Figure 7-16 You add video by dragging and dropping scenes from the Album.

Figure 7-17 Double-clicking a scene will create a preview of the video.

4   Once you're done adding scenes to the Storyboard, you should see
something similar to Figure 7-18: a series of thumbnails representing
the video you've assembled so far. If you'd like to watch it to make
sure you haven't left anything out, you can use the VCR-like controls
shown under the preview window in Figure 7-17. You're done with
phase one of this project: You've edited your video!

Figure 7-18 The Storyboard now has several scenes added to it.

Now that we've put together the pieces of video we wanted, it's time to
insert some basic transitions. A transition is a method of moving from one video

clip to the other, and Studio 8 has some very interesting transitions. To keep things simple, we're going to use a standard dissolve. Here's how:

1   To the left of the Album, there's a vertical row of small icons (see Figure 7-15 for reference). The second icon down, which looks like a lightning bolt, is the Show Transitions tab. Click it.

2   A new "page" in the Album loads, and you'll see 32 thumbnail images of the standard transitions that Studio 8 has (Figure 7-19)—and this is only page one of three. When you click a transition, the video preview window gives you a live preview of how the transition works. Select the second transition (Dissolve). You should see a preview that slowly fades from the "A" scene to the "B" scene. Think of it this way: transitions slide "between" the video clips. So the "A" scene will be whatever is to the left of the transition in the Storyboard, and the "B" will be the scene to the right.

Figure 7-19 In Studio 8 you'll see a collection of standard transitions.

3   To apply the transition, click and drag it onto the Storyboard, releasing the mouse button when you are positioned between two scenes— you'll also see a green box appear when the location is acceptable (Figure 7-20).

Figure 7-20 To apply the transition, click and drag into the Storyboard.

4 Drag and drop other dissolves onto the Storyboard until you end up with one transition between each scene as Figure 7-21 shows. You can apply only one transition at a time between scenes.

Figure 7-21 By dragging and dropping, you get one transition between each scene.

5 Use the playback controls under the video preview window to see the movie so far with the transitions. If it looks okay, it's time to add music.

Try This!   If you'd like to have your video fade to black at the end, insert a dissolve transition after the final scene. It will dissolve from "A" to "B," left to right, and since there's nothing to the right of the final scene, you'll get a nice fade to black effect.

Note   When faced with over a hundred transitions, there's the temptation to use as many as possible and the flashiest ones you can find. I can't stress this enough: resist the urge. Don't use more then two or three transitions per video project, and unless you want people to pay more attention to the transitions than to your video, don't overuse the flashy transitions (you'll recognize what I'm talking about when you preview the various transitions).

Adding music and adjusting the audio levels is slightly convoluted, but once you complete the steps the first time, you'll get the hang of it quickly. Music will greatly enhance the atmosphere of your video project.

1 Insert your audio CD into your CD drive. The Windows XP Autoplay window may start up asking you what you want to do with the audio CD. Select Take No Action.

2 From the Toolbox menu, click Add CD Music. A new window appears, saying that the CD isn't recognized and asking you the name of the album. Type it in, and then click OK.

3 A new tool panel slides into view, and it should look like Figure 7-22. Using the Track drop-down menu, select the audio track you want to add to the video. By default, the audio track will likely be longer than your video, so we'll want to trim it. It's easier to do that in another step, however, so leave the sliders where they are and click Add To Movie.

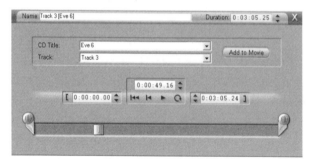

Figure 7-22 Use the Track drop-down menu to select the track you want to add to the video.

4   Before doing anything else, click Play in the video preview window.
The computer will now digitally copy the CD and insert the audio track
into the movie timeline. Depending on how fast your CD-ROM drive is
at audio extraction, this can take anywhere from a few seconds to several minutes (see Figure 7-23). Once the video has started to play, it
should include the new song we just copied over. You don't need to
listen to the entire song—click the Pause button to stop the preview.

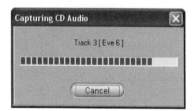

Figure 7-23 Digitally copying the audio CD track will take a few seconds to several minutes.

5   If you're in the Storyboard view, it looks like nothing has been added.
Switch over to the Timeline view by clicking the Timeline icon, found
just below the video preview window.

6   Now that you're in the Timeline view, on the very last line of the window you should see your song to the right of the treble clef (Figure 7-24).
The song will likely be longer than the video, so we'll need to shorten
it. Using the bottom scroll bar, scroll over to the right until you see the
end of the song. Move the cursor over the end of the song, and it turns
into a blue arrow. Click and drag to the left—this will shorten the song.
Continue to drag left until you see the end of the video. As you get to
the end of the video, the cursor will "snap" into alignment with the

ending, making the video and audio end at the same time. We're done adding and trimming our song, but there's one step left.

Figure 7-24 The audio track has been added to the timeline.

7   The final step in the audio process is to decide how to mix the volume levels of the two audio tracks we now have: audio from the video clip and audio from the CD we just ripped. From the Toolbox menu, click Change Volume. A new window slides into view (Figure 7-25). From left to right, the audio tracks are the original video audio, the sound effects, and the music. Clicking on the icons of the first two will mute them (you can see the line through them in Figure 7-25). If you have subtle music, you can mix the two audio levels, but since I picked a rock song, I'm muting the audio from my video.

Figure 7-25 If you have music, you should mute the audio track on your video.

Try This!   If you'd like the audio to fade out at the end of the video, there's a way to do it with Pinnacle Studio 8.0, but it requires some finesse. You should be in the Timeline view. Click once on the audio track to select it. Now click again on the audio track, near the end where you want the fadeout to begin. A blue dot should appear. This is a "pivot point" where everything after it will be altered but nothing before it. Now click again at the very end of the audio track—another blue dot should appear. Click on this blue dot and drag downward to the very bottom of the audio track. You should see a blue line sloped downward between the pivot point and this final point. It should look something like this:

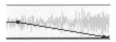

The final steps in this process involve taking our video, now in its fully edited form with transitions and music, and burning it to a CD. I'll be covering several stand-alone CD and DVD burning packages in Chapter 10, but since Pinnacle Studio 8.0 has built-in burning tools, we might as well get to know them!

1   Click the Make Movie tab, then on the last option in the vertical row: Disc.

2   Click Settings.

3   The Pinnacle Studio Setup Options window loads, and the Make Disc tab should be selected. Since we want to make an SVCD, we should select that as the Output Format. The Video Quality/Disc Usage should be set to Best Video Quality, and the Filter Video box should be selected (this enhances the overall quality of the video). Moving down to the Media and Device Options, we'll leave it at one copy, but change the write speed to 32X, the maximum speed of our CD burner. The final options should look like Figure 7-26.

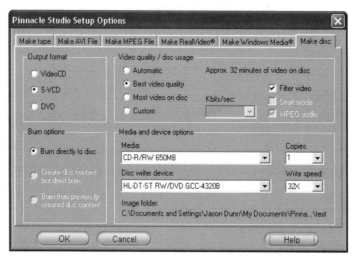

Figure 7-26 To burn an SVCD, you configure the options in the Pinnacle Studio Setup Options window.

4   Once the settings are complete, click OK. Now click the green Create Disc button (see Figure 7-27).

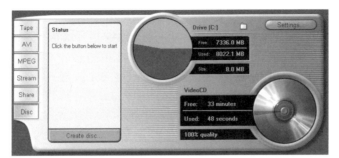

Figure 7-27 We're getting ready to burn our video to a CD.

5 The rendering process will now take place, and depending on the speed of your computer you may be waiting minutes or hours. When the rendering is finished, the computer will burn the results to disc (which shouldn't take more than a few minutes). Once that process is completed, the disc will be ejected from the drive, and you have your movie! Take it to a DVD player and test it out.

Although this process may seem very long and involved for a "basic video edit," I assure you that once you've gone through this process, subsequent attempts will be much easier. Pinnacle Studio 8.0 is a highly intuitive application, and we only scratched the surface of what it's capable of doing.

Caution   Be sure to preview your video before assuming that the burn was successful. The first SVCD I burned with Pinnacle Studio 8.0 was full of audio and visual errors, yet the software gave me no indication that there were any problems with the burn process or the video rendering to MPEG. See the end of this chapter for software products that will let you preview DVD, VCD, and SVCD discs on your computer.

Saving Your Video

Once you've completed your video editing, regardless of which application you're using, you have several options for saving the video. We'll discuss the proper formats for sharing video over e-mail and the Web in Chapter 9, but for now it's important to understand the differences between the two main types of video formats: "transient" and "final product." Those are my own terms, but "lossless" and "lossy" would apply equally well here. Basically, the terms are defined like this:

Transient

A work in progress. This is the format you would use to save your video and keep the quality high because you were planning on using it in another application or you wanted to archive it for future use. Transient video formats are those formats that don't force data loss when they are saved over and over: DV AVI is the best example of this. Transient data formats are largely uncompressed, so they take up a lot of storage space. Keep your video in this format until you're ready to complete the project and share the video in a "final product" format. If you have the space to keep a copy of the transient format, do so—you never know when you might need it.

Final Product

You should save the completed project, ready to share, in a highly compressed lossy format. Many formats fall into this category: MPEG, Windows Media Video, DivX, RealVideo, Quicktime, and almost any other format that is significantly smaller than the original DV AVI. VCD, SVCD, and even DVD formats all fall into this category. Formats like this are a one-way trip—you can't decompress them and regain the quality you lost, so before you delete your high-quality source file make sure the final product file you created is perfect.

Previewing DVD, VCD, and SVCD Videos

When you create a DVD, VCD, or SVCD, it's always a good idea to preview the disc on your PC before taking it to an external DVD player—you never know whether it's going to work. Video disc burning is still something of a game of chance—I've had several bad experiences with software packages that claimed the burn was complete, but when I watched the disc, the video was riddled with visual glitches and audio pops. Previewing them right away on your computer eliminates the guesswork and saves you the nasty surprise of putting your masterpiece into a friend's DVD player and having nothing happen.

Windows Media Player, even the new 9 Series version, can't play DVD, VCD or SVCD formats. I think this is a huge oversight by the Windows Media team, but thankfully there are third-party solutions close at hand to solve this problem. Two types of applications solve these problems. The first are applications that plug into Windows Media Player and give it the ability to play DVD files (not VCD or SVCD formats).The best package I've seen that allows this is the CineMaster DVD Decoder Pack from Sonic (*www.cineplayer.com/decoder*). It seamlessly installs itself into Windows Media Player (Figure 7-28) and allows you to view DVDs. It doesn't offer all the advanced features of the stand-alone software DVD players, but if previewing DVDs is your primary goal, this is the best choice. You can also add an MP3 encoder pack for ripping your MP3 files at a higher quality than Windows Media Player supports natively.

Figure 7-28 You can watch a DVD with the Sonic CineMaster DVD Decoder Pack.

The second category of software is external players. They typically offer more features for playback, support DVD/VCD (sometimes SVCD), and have a higher price tag. I recommend two products in this field.

WinDVD 4 from Intervideo

It's a bit pricey, but if you're looking for a full-featured DVD player that also sup-ports VCD and SVCD format, WinDVD4 is a great choice (Figure 7-29). In addi-tion to being a great player, it has some highly sophisticated features like Time Stretching (which will let you watch a 2-hour DVD in 1.5 hours), and Video Desktop (which displays a DVD where your desktop wallpaper is). You can download a free demo from *www.interview.com.*

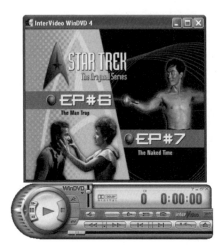

Figure 7-29 WinDVD4 from Intervideo also allows you to watch a DVD.

Sonic Cineplayer 1.5

An excellent DVD player from Sonic that also supports VCDs (but not SVCDs, strangely enough), this player supports taking screen shots of what you see on the screen, autoresume of playback, and Dolby Digital audio, and it doesn't take up many resources while running. It's available from *www.sonic.com*—unfortunately, there's no demo to download and try out.

Key Points

■   Autoproducing software edits your video for you, but it doesn't allow fine control over what scenes are included.

■   Manual video editing is time-consuming, but it allows you complete control over the elements of your video.

■   Pinnacle Studio 8 is a good software package for beginners and intermediate users.

■   Don't use transitions that are too flashy—they take away from your video.

■   Transient video formats like DV AVI are good for archiving, and final product formats like Windows Media Video are good for sharing.

■   Always preview your final projects before showing them to others.

Chapter 8

Advanced Video Editing

In the world of digital video, the sky's the limit when it comes to what's possible—a look at any of the top movies is evidence of that. A movie like *Lord of the Rings* combines live-action actors and computer-generated images (CGIs) in such a way that it's getting difficult to tell what's real and what's not. Of course, these effects are out of reach for you and me—today at least. Every year, video-editing software becomes more sophisticated, so it's quite believable that before this decade is through we'll be able to draw upon Hollywood-quality effects for our own video projects (it's the inevitable "trickle-down" effect of technology).

The Possibilities with Advanced Video Editing

My goal in the first part of this chapter is a bit daunting: to give you an overview of what's possible with today's high-end consumer and Prosumer-level digital video-editing applications—without turning it into a step-by-step tutorial (I'd need six chapters to do tutorials on all these concepts). The exact steps required to implement some of the things I'll be discussing vary from application to application, but if you know the terminology for what you want to do, looking in the application's Help file will get you going in the right direction. More than anything, I want this chapter to light up your imagination with what's possible.

Note   As you get deeper into advanced video-editing techniques and terminology, you'll encounter a concept that I wanted to save for this chapter: interlaced and non-interlaced video. Video you see on a television is interlaced—this means that for every frame of video you see, there are actually two fields of information. Each interlaced video field contains alternating horizontal lines, so when the two are shown at the same time you see a complete image—this effect allows television signals to display an effective 60 frames per second and reduce flicker. The reasons for this go back to the dawn of early television, but what's important for you to understand is that the video you see on your computer after rendering will look quite different when it's converted into a format meant for viewing on a TV set (like an SVCD or DVD format). When you save a video file as a DV AVI, it will be non-interlaced, and when you convert that same file for burning to a DVD, the video will be interlaced. Before judging the quality of your video, play it back on a TV set to get a feel for how it will really look to your viewers. If you're looking for more information, do a Google search for "interlaced video" and you'll find some excellent resources. One in particular that I found useful is here: *www.lukesvideo.com/interlacing.html*.

Tip   If you're like me and you enjoy testing new software all the time, you should get to know the System Restore feature in Microsoft Windows XP a little better—it will save you a lot of headaches because it allows you to restore your system to a previous state, before you installed that new piece of software. System Restore is found in the Program Files menu, then Accessories, and then the System Tools folder. By default, Windows XP makes a System Restore point once a day and before new applications or drivers are installed. If you test an application and you find it's not something you want to keep, use the System Restore to roll your system back to the point before you installed that application. Your personal files are completely unaffected, and the procedure is reversible, so it's a safe tool to use. It's also useful when installing hardware because it can undo changes made by hardware drivers. Don't wait too long to restore your system though—the restore points only last a few weeks.

Going from A to B: Transitions in Action

I explained transitions in the last chapter, but it bears repeating here: A transition is something that sits in the middle of two videos scenes and brings in the next scene while removing the previous scene. It's a very basic concept, but it's one on which all transitions are based. The great thing for us in our editing projects is the extremely creative methods that have been created to move from A to B. Most video-editing packages include basic transitions, but unless there's a lot of them, you'll quickly tire of the included transitions and long for something more exciting. That's where third-party transition filters come in. Many companies are making some very exciting transitions, and I chose to take a closer look at three different packages: Hollywood F/X, Boris RED, and VFXMask.

Note   Most transitions function as "plug-ins," meaning they aren't stand-alone applications (there are exceptions, though). They connect directly to your video-editing application and are available as an option from a menu in that application. Before buying a transition bundle, make sure it's compatible with your video-editing application.

Hollywood F/X

Offered by Pinnacle Systems (*www.pinnaclesys.com*), Hollywood F/X is an excellent bundle available in both a Plus version and a Pro version. If you own Pinnacle Studio 8, you may already have a version of Hollywood F/X—Pinnacle Studio Deluxe comes with the Plus version. The Hollywood F/X transitions were integrated smoothly into Pinnacle Studio 8, making them easy to access and preview. The Plus version of this bundle offers 288 presets, organized by category. Indeed, that's one of the best things about the bundle: looking at the "Weddings" category gives you 12 distinct transitions perfect for a wedding video, such as rings, hearts, and wedding albums. It also gives you the ability to control lighting, shadows, motion blur, and motion trails using the Control console (Figure 8-1). I used the Plus version with Studio 8 for a few projects, and I was really impressed with the quality of the transitions and the breadth of choice I was given. The Pro version is overkill for most users, but if you want to import 3-D objects created in outside applications like Lightwave 3-D, it's the bundle to get. Pinnacle had no information about compatibility, so my assumption is that these transitions only work with Pinnacle video-editing products.

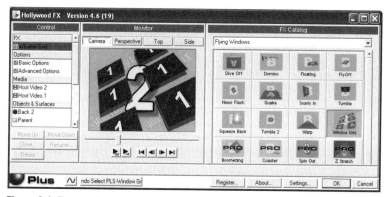

Figure 8-1 The interface for changing Hollywood F/X parameters lets you control several features.

Boris RED 2.5

Created by the team at Boris FX (*www.borisfx.com*), the RED 2.5 bundle is the mother of all transition and plug-in packs (see Figure 8-2). I'm not exaggerating: It boasts over 1,000 preset effects that are completely customizable and has an 878-page manual. This is not something the amateur would buy, but if you're serious about going deep into video editing and want a powerful tool to add to your belt, Boris RED is a must-have package. It functions as a stand-alone package but also plugs into popular editing packages on the market, including Ulead MediaStudio Pro, Adobe Premiere, Pinnacle EditionDV, and many others. It supports stand-alone rendering and is capable of producing Quicktime, AVI, or even Flash animations. If you're interested in learning more, go to their Web site and look at their video overview. If you're looking for a "taste" of the Boris quality, but are intimidated by RED, check out Boris Factory. It offers 100 high-quality transitions, plugs in to several popular applications, and is quite affordable.

Figure 8-2 Boris RED 2.5 is a massive collection of powerful transitions and plug-ins.

Tip   If you're interested in buying Boris Factory, go to *www.ulead.com* and look in their Partner Products section.

VFXMask Plug-in

If you use Ulead VideoStudio or MediaStudio, you'll enjoy this software (it works only with Ulead products). VFXMask transitions are based on masks (Figure 8-3)—a mask is a grayscale image that acts almost like a cookie cutter in that it discards everything outside its edge. VFXMask works on the same principle and offers over 300 masks, and you can easily import and organize your own masks. Masks can be created in image-editing applications like Ulead PhotoImpact or Adobe Photoshop, so you can customize your transitions by creating your own masks. Corporate logos, names, shapes—there are a lot of possibilities here for creativity. You can download a free trial version or purchase the software for a reasonable price. You may also want to check out VFXFlash Factory, a new collection of 170 preset transitions—based on the video clips I saw in their gallery, these transitions are beautiful, with soft wipes and interesting color effects.

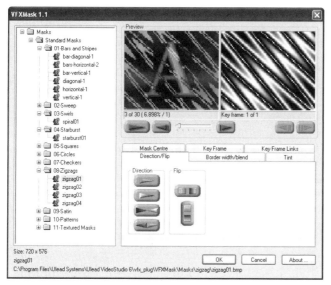

Figure 8-3 VFXMask Plug-in for Ulead offers over 300 masks.

Tip   When applying transitions, be aware of the need for "slack video." If you're applying a long transition, perhaps one that involves 3-D elements, you won't want people to miss something important from the video if it's playing while the transition has their attention. Instead, you'll want a few seconds of noncritical video playing during the transition to be leading up to the shot you want—that video is the slack.

Moving Paths

A moving path is a term used to describe the movement of an external element through a video frame. You see moving paths all the time in video—when the name and location of a news reporter slides into view during a news report, that's a moving path. Another use for a moving path would be bringing in another video clip for a picture-in-picture effect. Figure 8-4 shows a tool panel from Ulead MediaStudio 6.5's CG Infinity, the module used for text rendering and titling (I'll explain what titling is later in this chapter). After you've typed in your text, you can select one of these moving paths to be applied, and you end up with text that moves along based on the preset.

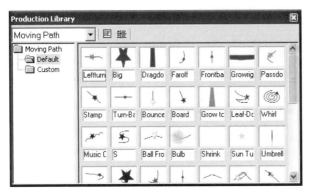

Figure 8-4 Ulead MediaStudio 6.5 CG Infinity has a wide selection of moving paths.

Batch Capturing

If you're trying to save space on your hard drive, batch capturing is a feature that you'll probably like quite a bit. In an application that supports batch capturing, like Ulead MediaStudio Pro 6.5, you're able to view your tape and mark capture points. Think of this as a first pass at editing—you're not shaping the story so much as cutting out the junk you don't want. When you've added all your capture points, the software goes back and captures the scenes. The advantage of this process is that you're not wasting space on video that you don't need. The disadvantage is the time it takes to set up the capture points, and the time it takes to recapture. I personally don't use this feature in any of the software I have, but for some people it's quite important.

Adding Narration

Have you ever watched a documentary and found yourself leaning forward in anticipation of what was going to happen next? Documentaries can be surprisingly engaging, and part of that is a strong voice from the narrator. The narrator weaves the story together, and regardless of what types of media are used (video, audio, photos), the narrator is a critical component of the story. In the same way, narrating your own videos can add that special touch and bind the story together. Every video-editing application I've seen supports narration in one form or another. At the most basic level, you can use the Windows Sound Recorder to record yourself talking as you watch a preview of the video. In some applications (like Pinnacle Studio 8—see Figure 8-5), an actual narrating function allows you to mute the audio on the video track, record your own voice as you watch it, and then place the audio file on the timeline. If you want to combine narration and music, the application you're using would need to support more than one audio track (most do).

Figure 8-5 Pinnacle Studio 8 gives you an interface for recording a narration.

Tip   If you want to learn how to combine multimedia elements to form a coherent and compelling story, look at documentaries. *The Civil War*, a PBS documentary that can be ordered from *www.pbs.org*, is considered one of the greatest documentaries ever made on the subject. Ken Burns, the documentary filmmaker who spearheaded the project, has an amazing knack for combining different media to tell a story. You stand to learn a lot by watching well-done documentaries.

Importing Photos

Using the documentary example I mentioned above, think about how much impact a still photo can have in a video production. Seeing a still photo in the midst of video clips has a powerful effect—the eye focuses from tracking movement to tracking a single still object, and the effect can be dramatic when accompanied by music or a voice-over meant to represent the subject of a photo. Photos should be in JPEG format, but most applications will also accept BMP, GIF, and TIFF formats. Check the Help file for your application if you're not sure or use a simple photo-editing tool like FotoCanvas (*www.acdsystems.com*) to save it in a compatible format.

If you're working on archiving old home movies, consider scanning in some old pictures from the same time period. Most video-editing programs have the ability to capture still frames from your video, so if you have no photos to scan, this method would also work. If you're doing a period piece, you could investigate using public domain images from historical records and documents. Authenticity is key.

Try This!   Want to get creative with your photos? When you insert photos into your video time-line, insert the sound of a camera flash or camera shutter (often included with the video software, or you can search the Web for the sounds) and use a very fast transition that fades from A to B, possibly going to white in between. The goal is to give the photos the effect of being taken by a camera inside the video. You can also try making a video presentation with nothing but photos—you'll need a strong narration voice or compelling music, however, to keep it interesting.

Importing Videos

Beyond the basic task of importing your own video clips when making a compilation, there are other sources of video clips than can greatly enhance your project. Whether they're from the Web, commercial video clips, or something you create in another application, external video sources can enhance your projects. Video formats supported usually include AVI and MPEG but rarely final output formats like RealVideo.

Videos Filmed by Others

If you're looking for a video clip of something specific, a great tool to use is the All the Web search engine (*www.alltheweb.com*). It has a search tool specifically for videos—you type in your keyword, and it attempts to find videos based on your requested topic. It's surprisingly accurate and definitely worth trying. Keep in mind that the quality of the video will likely be extremely low, and you should always ask for permission before using someone else's video. Just because someone put their videos up on the Web doesn't mean he or she wants others using it.

Royalty-Free Media

A good alternative if you want high-quality video and don't mind paying to get it, royalty-free video has been around for several years, but with the proliferation of high-speed connections like DSL and cable modems, it's finally practical to get it through the Web. Ulead has created a special Web site to sell royalty-free video: *rfm.ulead.com*. The concept is compelling and affordable: The videos are "broadcast quality" (Type 1 DV AVI) and come in packages of 16 or 17 clips. The clips are organized by category, such as sunrises and sunsets, city lights, and transportation. If you're putting together a presentation and quality is important, it's likely easier to buy a few clips online than to try to capture all the concepts yourself.

Videos Created in External Applications

A lot of programs on the market today are capable of exporting files as video. As an example, consider Cool 3D from Ulead (*www.ulead.com*), a 3-D rendering program. Cool 3D is able to render text and objects and move them along a path, and it comes with an assortment of special effects like explosions, lightning, and fire. From within Cool 3D, you can export high-quality AVI files and insert them into your current video clip. The Cool 3D gallery on the Ulead Web site has some great examples of how you can combine 3-D movies with digital video projects.

Adding Text Titles (a.k.a. "Titling")

Adding text to your video is a fairly basic function, but there are so many types of text and ways in which it can be used that it deserves some discussion. Most video-editing applications have a text tool—Figure 8-6 shows the tool from Pinnacle Studio 8—but not all text tools are created equal (Studio 8 has great quality text). Text quality will be primarily about one thing: the smoothness of the text. With low-quality text rendering, the text will have jagged edges. With high-quality text rendering, the text will have smooth edges. The smoothness is usually called "antialiasing"—and it means to soften the pixels so that the edge isn't as obvious.

Figure 8-6 You can create text elements using Pinnacle Studio 8.

So when should you use text in your video? There are any number of instances, but here are a few to get you thinking:

■ **Introduction**   Most videos benefit from some sort of introduction. Displaying the year and day helps give users a frame of reference—is what they're seeing a recent event or one that is decades old? Introduction text can also convey elements of the story ("A long time ago, in a galaxy far, far away. . .") or give the users a perspective on what they're about to see. And if your video covers subject matter not suitable for all ages, the introductory text can contain a warning or rating.

■ **Subtitles**   If you've ever seen a foreign film, you'll know why subtitles are important. Without understanding what's being said, viewers would quickly lose interest. Language barriers can create problems for viewers, even if the subject being filmed is using the same language as the viewer—I've seen documentaries where the people being interviewed are speaking English, but have such heavy accents that the filmmaker added subtitles.

■ **Scene identifiers**   Moving from scene to scene can be a good place to use text. If you're putting together a biography on someone, text identifiers for the major events in that person's life can help draw the viewer into your story.

■ **Closing credits**   Most of us like to take credit for our hard work, and the closing credits are where budding videographers can claim credit for the hours they put into making the video. If the production is a simple one, a simple "Filmed & Edited by John Smith" will suffice. If the project is more complex (perhaps involving a script, makeup, and lighting), you should break out each of the elements. Try to avoid the "ego effect" of listing the job and then your name, over and over. If you did several tasks on the production, list them all together, then your name.

Alpha Channel Effects

Sometimes called "green screen" or "blue screen" effects, alpha channel effects have given rise to a whole new method of filmmaking. The basic theory is simple: take an actor and put him or her in front of a screen. Make sure that screen is a color not matching anything that actor is wearing, and then, using computer software, digitally remove that color from the scene and replace it with an image of something else. The key to an effective alpha channel effect is to remove a color that isn't present anywhere else in the image. That's why blues and greens are chosen—they aren't present in the hue of human skin tones. The details behind alpha channels get very complex, but I think it's more important to understand how they're used rather than how they work.

Removing a background color is usually fairly simple in most video-editing applications—entry-level applications like Pinnacle Studio 8 don't support this function, but a tool like Ulead MediaStudio Pro 6.5 does. The process usually involves choosing a scene, selecting the color you want to remove, and applying that effect throughout the entire scene (which can take a while).One of the most innovative uses of green screen effects that I've seen is from a company called Serious Magic (*www.seriousmagic.com*). It makes a product called Visual Communicator (Figure 8-7) that allows the user to sit down in front of a Web cam or video camera, and, using an on-screen teleprompter and some superb visual effects, create a video communications piece. The key to this is the included green backdrop—Visual Communicator removes this color, in real time, and can insert any number of included template images or videos (or you can customize your own). There are some innovative uses for this type of technology, including corporate video releases, video "letters" to friends and family, training videos, and product demonstrations. The quality of the video rendering and on-screen effects is impressive—I could hardly believe they were being generated in real time when I saw them. This package is worth checking out if you want to add to your toolkit.

Figure 8-7 Serious Magic's Visual Communicator allows you to add alpha channel effects.

Try This! It's not always necessary to have a green or blue screen behind your subject to eliminate the background. If you want to see an interesting effect, apply the alpha channel effect to a background or surface in your video—it removes some, but not all, of that surface. The net result is eerie looking, which you can use to great effect in certain videos.

Time Stretching and Time Compression

Time stretching and time compression are just fancy terms for "slow motion" (slowing down the video) and "fast motion" (speeding up the video). Fast motion isn't used all that often, and if it is, it's usually for comical effect (think Charlie Chaplin). Slow motion, on the other hand, is very effectively used to convey emotion and "hold the moment." In fact, I've seen quite a few videos presented entirely in varying degrees of slow motion.

The key to using slow motion effectively is to know what types of shots it works well on—don't select your entire project and slow it down by 200 percent, expecting it to look good. Slow motion is most useful when capturing a moment—the bride walking down the aisle, the smile of wonder when a child looks up with glee after opening a birthday present she's always wanted. Differing levels of slow motion can also have an impact on the tone of your video—a subtle slow motion effect (say, 15 percent slower) can give your video a more personal touch without making it drag. But if there's a key moment you want to capture, crank it down to 80 percent or more—almost like a freeze frame, but not quite. Each application approaches applying these effects in different ways—Vegas Video 3.0 from Sonic Foundry offers a "Velocity Envelope" when you right-click the video track, and with a simple drag downward you can slow down the video (Figure 8-8 shows this in action). Unlike speed-altering effects I've seen in other applications, the Velocity Envelope doesn't eliminate or alter the audio—it keeps the audio at full speed, which creates an interesting effect that wouldn't be effective in all scenarios. Vegas Video 3.0 has a robust suite of audio-editing tools, however, so it's easy to bring these two elements into sync.

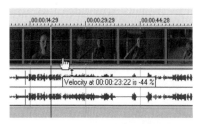

Figure 8-8 Vegas Video 3.0 offers a Velocity Envelope for altering playback speed.

Pinnacle Studio 8 approaches this a little differently—and offers a strobe tool to boot. A strobe tool effectively freezes the image and slowly fades it while the next image is displayed. This effect is difficult to capture with a still image, but in Figure 8-9 you can see that the head and torso of the piano player are in two places at once, with one being more faded than the other. This is the strobe effect in action. Do you remember that old TV show from the 1970s, *The Bionic Man?* By combining slow motion with a strobe effect, they were able to visually convey that the actor was actually moving faster than normal. Have fun with it!

Figure 8-9 Applying a strobe effect can create interesting results.

Try This!   Slow motion effects can often have limits within the software. Pinnacle Studio 8 can slow the video down to 10 percent of the original speed, but what if you want to go even slower? Apply the effect, export the video segment as a DV AVI file, import it again, and reapply the effect—you'll effectively get up to 1,000 percent slower than the original file, and there's no limit to how many times you can do this effect. Realistically, though, going slower than 10 percent of the original speed is not advised unless you have something specific in mind.

Caution   When using slow motion, eliminating the audio is usually a good idea. If both the video and audio are slowed down the same amount, nightmarish sound qualities will be the result. Of course, that can be an interesting effect in and of itself—scary Halloween video, anyone?

Try This!   If you have a shot where you were unable to keep the camera steady, and the video is quite jumpy, try adding a slow motion effect to that segment—the slow motion won't erase the instability of your shot, but the movement will be slower and therefore less visually jarring to the viewer.

Picture in Picture

I mentioned this briefly above when discussing motion paths, but it's interesting enough to warrant some further discussion. Picture in picture is a simple concept that you can use in some very interesting ways. Watch the local news: That graphics box that goes in the upper right corner, above the newscaster, is a classic picture in picture effect. That box is essentially another video window that can be loaded with any sort of content.

Another common use of picture in picture effects is digitally superimposing a video onto a display surface like a monitor, TV set, or PDA screen. In fact, in most Hollywood movies where a PDA is used, they overlay a fabricated video segment because the interface of the PDA is very hard to shoot and usually visually boring. I've also seen some shots where the main video segment is played inside a container like a computer screen—the rest is a still photo. There's no end to the type of shots you can produce using this method, so get creative!

Note   There's a category of hardware that I opted to leave out of this book due to its advanced nature: real-time hardware. Essentially, real-time hardware is a piece of dedicated hardware, usually in the form of a PCI card, that you add to your system to accelerate video effects. Unlike software rendering, which is based heavily on the speed of your computer's CPU, hardware-based rendering isn't as CPU dependent. The Pinnacle Pro-ONE is a real time hardware card that accelerates up to ten filters and transitions in real time—slow motion, motion paths, titles, and more. The Pinnacle Pro-ONE is typical of most real time hardware: fairly expensive, aimed at professionals, and geared toward saving video-rendering time. If you find yourself constantly frustrated with how long it takes your videos to render, even when you have a powerful computer, real time hardware may be the solution you're looking for.

Advanced Video-Editing Software Packages

If you're looking to step beyond the limits of entry-level video-editing packages, you have a lot of choices. Companies like Pinnacle sell video-editing systems to professional news organizations for tens of thousands of dollars, but that's not the kind of system that you'd be buying if you're reading this book. Instead the focus will be on applications that cost less than $1,000 US, geared toward high-end consumer and Prosumer users.

Ulead MediaStudio Pro 6.5

Ulead has nearly a decade of experience with digital media, so it's not surprising that their flagship video-editing product, MediaStudio Pro 6.5 (Figure 8-10), is a powerhouse application broken up into five core components:

■ **Video Capture**   Capable of capturing video from any source (with the appropriate hardware), this module features MPEG2 support, batch capture, and color calibration.

■ **Video Editor**   The heart of MediaStudio Pro, this module is where you'll spend most of your time. It's fairly light on resources and functions well even on less powerful hardware. From this interface you cut and splice your clips together, add transitions, import external audio and video elements, and render the project to its final form.

■ **Video Paint**   A powerful *rotoscoping* tool, the Video Paint component allows you to apply frame by frame special effects for some impressive video sequences.

■ **CG Infinity**   Want to create titles and motion graphics? CG Infinity is a vector-based graphics generation program. Vector graphics can be scaled up in size without any loss of quality, so the elements you create in CG Infinity will be useful at any size.

■ **Audio Editor**   No project is complete without audio, so this component allows you to edit and enhance your audio, remove background noise, and add a musical track. Because it's a multitrack editor, you can layer multiple audio tracks over one another—like a narrator's voice talking over an audio track.

MediaStudio Pro 6.5 is a powerful application, but like most applications of this type, it can take some time to learn. The user interface feels a little dated and counter-intuitive in some ways, so spending some time with the manual is a good idea. The quality of output from MediaStudio Pro is beyond reproach, though, so if you can master the tools, you'll be happy with the results. This product is a good choice for those who have a limited budget but want a high-end tool.

Lingo   *Rotoscoping*. Painting on effects to part of an image, frame by frame. Rotoscoping allows you to create some impressive effects by creating special effects but applying them in a manual and controlled fashion. A good example of rotoscoping is the light sabers from *Star Wars*. In reality, they're just thin poles, but by "painting on" the glowing light effect, you end up with a highly compelling video effect.

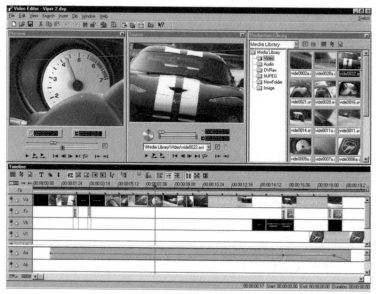

Figure 8-10 MediaStudio Pro 6.5 is a powerful, multifaceted package.

Adobe Premiere 6.5

The granddaddy of all digital video-editing applications, Adobe Premiere (*www.adobe.com*) is in version 6.5 as of August 2002. Because Adobe Premiere has been around for several years, the user interface has evolved into something that's highly user-friendly (Figure 8-11). This history also offers users an interface that's great for both laptop and desktop PC video editing. Premiere 6.5 supports MPEG-2 encoding, which can crunch 60 minutes of DV AVI from 13 GB down to 1 or 2 GB (depending on quality settings).

If you're the type of person who likes to take a simple home video and turn it into something a little more special, Adobe Premiere 6.5 has several great tools to help you do that, like creating broadcast-quality title sequences in your video. The storyboard layout allows for intuitive arrangement of your clips and speeds up the workflow process. Perhaps one of the best features of Adobe Premiere 6.5 is the ability to edit video in real time (with adequate hardware, that is). That means you can preview titles, effects, or even transitions in real time. No more waiting for things to render! I should note, however, that the final export of your video will likely require rendering and will take time.

A very useful component of Premiere 6.5 is its compatibility with Adobe Photoshop, Illustrator, and After Effects software packages. If you have graphics you've created in one of these other programs, Premiere allows you to easily import them into your video footage, so you can make your home video even more personal. When it comes time to show off your video to family and friends, Premiere 6.5 can output video to DVD and VCD, in addition to file formats like MPEG2 and Web-friendly formats.

Premiere offers a lot of value for the money and is the closest thing to an industry-standard video-editing application there is. This can be important to some because it means there are more resources (books, videos, Web sites) out there to support the learning process.

Figure 8-11 Adobe Premiere is one of most popular video-editing applications on the market today.

Sonic Foundry Vegas Video 3.0

Sonic Foundry must have some of the most talented user-interface designers in the industry, because every program they make is highly intuitive and doesn't take long to figure out. Vegas Video 3.0 is no exception, boasting a user-interface that is logical and well laid out (Figure 8-12).

Vegas Video 3.0 features video batch capture with scene detection and the ability to print to a tape from the timeline (good for VHS exports). Vegas Video 3.0 is great for video editing, but also for video compositing, audio recording, advanced encoding, and CD burning. You can record audio along with your video for, say, a wedding video or a Christmas video. With Sonic Foundry's pedigree in audio applications, it's no surprise that the audio tools are top-notch. Eighteen free audio plug-ins are part of the package, including EQ balancing, chorus and modulation effects, and even pitch bend (if that vocal performance you recorded has a few bad notes, this is how you'd fix it).

Not only can you record audio, but you can also input credit rolls and text animation to make your video project look unique and special. As with many of the video-editing packages, MPEG2 is supported in Vegas Video 3.0. A different feature from most packages, however, is dual processor-DV rendering support. If you have two CPUs in your computer, this package can use both of them for enhanced rendering speed. (In fact, video rendering is one of the best reasons to get a dual-CPU computer). Vegas Video 3.0 also supports all aspects of video, up to and including 16:9 (the same aspect ratio used in movies you see on the big screen).

You can purchase Vegas Video 3.0 from *www.sonicfoundry.com,* and it's in the ballpark of other editing suites. If you don't care about the pretty box, you can save a few bucks and get the electronic version that you download from their Web site. And speaking of downloads, I suggest you take their 30-day demo for a spin to see if you like the features. I really enjoyed using Vegas Video 3.0 and think it's one of the stronger packages in this lineup.

Figure 8-12 Vegas Video combines a brilliant user-interface with solid features.

Pinnacle EditionDV

Another professional video editor's package, Pinnacle EditionDV is great for creating ultra-high-quality video, with features like a proprietary subpixel rendering process that ensures that all motion effects are executed without image degradation or flaws (see Figure 8-13). This package (available from *www.pinnaclesys.com*) is a good solution for someone wanting to move up from another Pinnacle Product (like Studio 8) for professional-quality results. EditionDV recently won an Editors Choice award from *PC Magazine*, and with innovations like display presets for those of us with dual monitors, it's easy to see why.

Many video editing projects, both personal and professional, deal with raw footage that's in bad shape. Pinnacle EditionDV was created with this in mind—the editing and output process won't add any further damage to your footage, and, in some cases, EditionDV can help salvage footage through adjustments to brightness, contrast, and other visual elements. This product has powerful capture and logging tools as well as the ability to adjust audio input levels during capture, so you'll get the best input possible from footage that's less than stellar. An included FireWire card with two ports lets you start capturing your video right away, and the massive manual will make for some gripping reading as you learn the program (if you like that sort of thing).

The EditionDV interface is a little strange—it takes some getting used to. The program runs in a full-screen mode, actually overlapping the taskbar and Start menu in Windows XP. There was an irritating flicker while the two elements fought each other, but once I set the task bar to "Auto-Hide" mode, the problem was solved. All in all, Pinnacle EditionDV is a worthy tool capable of highly professional results.

Figure 8-13 Pinnacle EditionDV has a unique user interface and powerful editing features.

Adobe After Effects 5.5

Adobe After Effects 5.5 (Figure 8-14) is a great package for those out there who are semiprofessional or professional video editors looking for professional quality results with their video. It's primarily used to create motion graphics and visual effects, like text or shapes that move in a predefined path. I'm oversimplifying things, but suffice it to say that if you can imagine it, odds are Adobe After Effects can make it happen. You can switch any layer from a 2-D to 3-D space by simply clicking the mouse. Then you can manipulate the 3-D layer properties controlling the camera angles and lighting. With more than 90 plugins to blur, sharpen, or distort images, to correct color, and to create other cool stylistic effects, After Effects 5.5 is diverse and full of great features.

If you're at all familiar with Adobe products, you'll know about the standard palettes, menus, tools, and keyboard shortcuts that are generally included in all their software. After Effects 5.5 is no exception. Your work will be that much easier if you're familiar with all these standard Adobe features. And if you're not, well, they're easy to learn, and then you'll be equipped to use any Adobe products.

It might seem strange for an add-on package like After Effects to cost more than Premiere, but this is truly a package with almost limitless features. I highly recommend getting a third-party book or learning tool for this application, because it will take some serious learning before you're able to truly take advantage of all it has to offer.

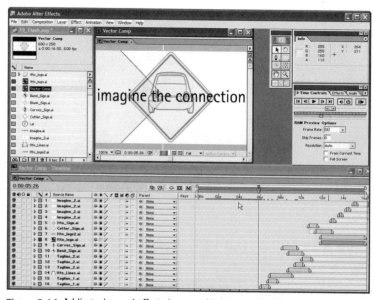

Figure 8-14 Adding advanced effects is easy with Adobe After Effects.

Advanced Video Manipulation Tools

If you spend any time hanging around people who are experienced and "hard-core" about digital video, you'll pick up on one fact: when it comes to encoding quality not all programs are created equal. Many experts use one program for capturing, another program for editing and rendering, and yet another for converting the video to MPEG (for VCD and DVD purposes). Why, you may ask? According to some, the dedicated programs do their respective jobs better than those all-in-one applications. How true is that? It's tough to say—it's quite a challenge to compare the encoding of dozens of software packages (it's not something I've done yet), and often the differences between them are subtle. There's no disputing, however, that if you want the ultimate in control over your encoding and have the knowledge to understand it all, these types of applications are very useful to have.

TMPGEnc Plus

Originally dubbed the Tsunami MPEGEncoder, TMPGEnc Plus (*www.pegasys-inc.com*) is the commercial version of the wildly popular TMPGEnc freeware application (*www.tmpgenc.net*). This application provides incredibly fine control over the MPEG encoding process, allowing you to adjust the bit rate, quantize matrix, GOP structure, and a slew of other things that I don't fully understand (this is complex stuff!). It has a nice wizard-driven interface, so even if you don't know exactly what you're doing, the defaults should work well for you (see Figure 8-15).

The major difference between the freeware version and the commercial package? The freeware version is an MPEG1 (VCD) conversion tool, with a 30-day trial for MPEG2 (SVCD and DVD) conversion, and the commercial "Plus" version provides unlimited MPEG2 encoding. The quality of the output is very impressive, and the application is specifically optimized for Pentium 4 CPUs, so you'll see the best speed results if you're using a P4 (though it will work with any Windows-compatible processor). If you want the best quality encoding available in this price range, TMPGEnc is the way to go.

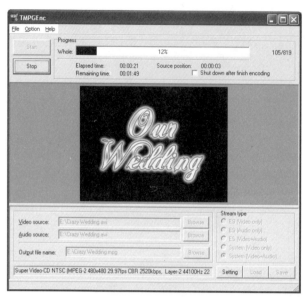

Figure 8-15 TMPGEnc Plus is a powerful MPEG toolkit for advanced users.

Tip   If you're looking for an alternative to TMPGEnc, I highly recommend the Main Concept MPEG Encoder (*www.mainconcept.com*). I discovered this encoder late into the book writing process, but it's an excellent application—full support for MPEG1 and MPEG2 allows you to create video suitable for VCDs, SVCDs, and DVDs. It's highly optimized for the Pentium 4 processor, and in some cases the video can be encoded in faster than real time—meaning a 60 minute video can be converted to MPEG in under 60 minutes, which is quite a feat. It also supports batch encoding, perfect for converting folders of AVI files to MPEG. This is a fairly expensive package, but the quality is excellent and well worth the price of admission. Main Concept also has a suite of other video products, including a full-fledged video-editing application (MainActor), an introductory video-editing package (MainConcept EVE), and a high-end compositing program (MainVision).

FlasK MPEG

FlasK MPEG, a freeware application developed by Alberto Vigatá, is a video conversion software utility with some highly useful features if you have a raw video file that you need to work with. It has no editing features, so the focus is on conversion—but while you're converting, there are some ways you can manipulate your video. Figure 8-16 shows the types of options you can choose from when converting, and, in addition to specifying the video resolution and frame rate, in other tabs you can crop the video and tweak the audio. It supports transcoding (going from one format to another) using any of the codecs you have installed on your system. Want to go from a DV AVI to a small DivX file? As long as you have the DivX codec on your system, no problem.

FlasK MPEG is a worthy addition to any power-user's video toolbox, and at a price of "free," it's tough to beat.

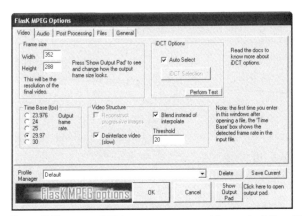

Figure 8-16 FlasK MPEG is an easy-to-use tool for manipulating video files.

Note If you're looking for a power-user tool for capturing video, check out ScenalyzerLive (*www.scenalyzer.com*). One of the most powerful capturing tools I've encountered, ScenalyzerLive allows you to capture video with real-time scene detection, and if you want to perform batch capturing, it will scan an entire MiniDV tape in under five minutes, showing you a thumbnail of every scene. Once you have the thumbnails, you can select which scenes you want. There is a free trial version, and the full commercial version is very affordable. If you're looking for the ultimate in control over your video capturing, ScenalyzerLive is a great tool. A freeware alternative to Scenalyzer would be VirtualDub (*www.virtualdub.com*). It offers far less features than Scenalyzer, but hey, it's free!

Music Creation and Audio-Editing Software

A critical component to any video production, audio is also one of the most difficult to pull off. It's easy enough to rip a song from a CD and use it for background music, but what if you want something unique? If you're planning on commercially distributing your video, you'll need to either license the music you used or replace it with something you wrote. Since most of us can't write songs like John Lennon could, it's time to look at some software that will help you create the music you need. And if you just need to clean up your audio track or mix in some sound effects, I've found some interesting tools for you to look at as well.

Sonic Desktop SmartSound Movie Maestro

Getting Hollywood quality music is only a dream for most of us when it comes to adding background music for our videos. It can be a real struggle to find the perfect song that's the perfect length. With SmartSound Movie Maestro from Sonic Desktop (*www.sonicdesktop.com*), you can easily achieve just that (Figure 8-17). Just three steps are all it takes to get your video, your soundtrack, and your final product ready for production!

Import the video by simply choosing it from the Choose Movie directory, and the three-step wizard guides you through picking the music you want. Then you can save the soundtrack you want directly to the movie clip, and you're done. If your child is playing in the soccer or basketball finals, what better way to enhance the memories than adding a thrilling music track? Movie Maestro is an inexpensive package that does only one thing but does it very well. Even the most novice users will have no trouble adding music to their videos.

Figure 8-17 Need some quick music for a video? Movie Maestro is a good solution.

Tip   Check to see if your video-editing package already has the SmartSound technology in it—you may not need to buy the package. For instance, Pinnacle Studio 8 has a version of this software integrated into it.

Sonic Foundry Sound Forge Studio 6.0

Audiophiles will love this software! If you need to do some quick tweaks to your audio to improve the quality or even record audio tracks from an external source, Sound Forge Studio 6.0 is a great choice. The user interface is intuitive and fairly easy to understand (Figure 8-18) so it won't take you long to get up to speed. If you have a keyboard and you want to hear what you sound like in a professional quality recording, hook it up to your computer, play your tunes and voila! If you're a musician, like myself, this feature is very cool. Anything that you can connect to your computer can be recorded—analog or digital in nature. You can create your own MP3 files and edit them, encode audio for the Web, or even produce audio for presentations at school, work, or home.

Video editors will love this feature: You can synchronize audio and video frame by frame using this software. Depending on the video-capture product used, the audio can sometimes get out of sync with the video. And you can work on one project while another is processing in the background! If you're a fan of ACID Music 4.0 software (described in the following section of this chapter), you're in luck: You can easily create loops and samples for ACID. You can also edit those loops and samples in 10 popular formats, including MP3 WAV and WMA.

Sound Forge Studio 6.0 is a good value, and if you find yourself wishing you could improve the audio quality of your audio, this is a good choice.

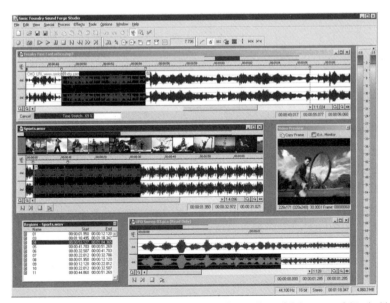

Figure 8-18 If you need to edit your audio tracks, Sound Forge 6.0 is a powerful tool with a surprisingly easy learning curve.

Sonic Foundry ACID PRO 4.0

Rated the number-one selling music creation software in 1999 and 2000, this software package not only allows you to make your own music but also to remix your favorite songs and publish them online! ACID is a loop-based audio program, which means it allows you to combine short audio samples (loops) and make a song (Figure 8-19). If it sounds simple, it is, but it still requires a lot of creativity—there are no "make me a song" buttons in ACID 4.0.

There are over 600 loops in nearly every music genre I can think of: dance, rap, pop, rock—the list goes on. And if you want to add more loops to your arsenal, Sonic Foundry has add-on collections that you can purchase. ACID lets you import audio files in over 10 formats, including WAV, MP3, and MIDI, so if you've already done some of your own music in another program, you can still work with it in ACID.

I could go on for a long time about this software, but the last feature I'll mention is the ability to adjust your music's tempo and pitch in real time, so you don't have to wait until the very end to hear what you've created. The music is too slow? Speed it up and hear the results right away. Not quite the right pitch? Click a button and you can instantly change it. ACID PRO 4.0 is a bit costly, but if you're interested in making your own electronic music, this is the package to get—I haven't seen anything quite like it on the market. And if you're looking for more of an introduction to this software, ACID Music 3.0 is a package that has fewer features than the PRO version but which still enables you to lay down some creative tracks.

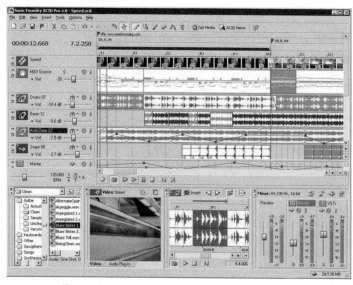

Figure 8-19 If you're in a creative groove, ACID is a fun and useful tool for creating music.

Sonic Desktop SmartSound Sonicfire Pro

With this easy-to-use software, you can effortlessly create custom soundtracks for any visual project. The greatest benefit that Sonic Desktop SmartSound Sonicfire Pro (Figure 8-20) has over other products is that it has evolved for some time into a conglomeration of many previous versions and has a wealth of knowledge all bound up into one package. Part of the growth of this product has been creating an easy user interface, and with this latest version, a stream-lined professional user interface is one of the features. This interface allows you to score videos automatically inside the software, as well as score multiple scenes and events. This last feature is critical—most videos have multiple scenes, but if they're different in tone you don't necessarily want the music to stay the same throughout the entire video. Sonicfire Pro includes markers that allow you to control where each scene begins and ends.

For someone who doesn't have a lot of experience when it comes to audio editing and compilation, this package is great because you don't have to build any loops and there's an automated soundtrack-creation feature that helps you create professional-quality audio with minimal experience. The bundle puts it out of the price range for most amateur video editors, but if you have even one paying project where you need a unique audio track, this software will pay for itself quickly. The bundle includes two CDs full of audio content, and it's easy to order more from a variety of genres such as "Far East" and "Contemporary Insights."

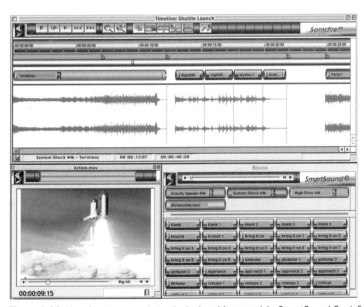

Figure 8-20 If crafting your music tracks by hand is your wish, SmartSound Sonicfire Pro is a good solution.

Sonic Foundry Sound Forge 6.0

One of Sonic Foundry's flagship products, Sound Forge 6.0 brings an almost unmatched variety of tools to the table. With over 35 real-time audio effects and 200 presets, track-at-once CD burning/ripping, and support for files larger than 4 GB, when it comes to audio this software does it all.

If you're doing a lot of audio editing at once, this tool is great, as it offers the ability to multitask. While one project is rendering in the background, you can be working on your next adventure in the foreground. You can import Windows Media and QuickTime files to use in your video projects, and with an unlimited number of undo/redo functions, you don't need to worry about making a mistake. Like every other Sonic Foundry product, the user interface is great—Figure 8-21 gives you an idea what it looks like.

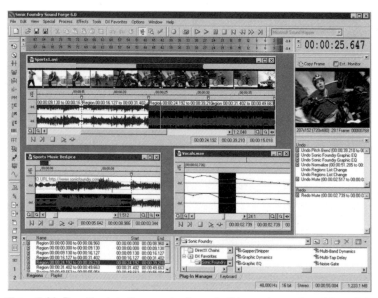

Figure 8-21 The ultimate in Prosumer-level sound editing packages, Sound Forge 6.0 is a virtual arsenal of audio weaponry.

This product offers so many features, I can't possibly list them all. A few of them are easy drag-and-drop operations, optimized video support, customizable toolbars, and three bonus applications (Acoustic Mirror, Batch Converter, Vegas Video LE 3.0). Even those few features are enough to get an amateur excited, but even more, they're enough to make a professional drool! It's not cheap, but with the included Vegas Video LE 3.0 (the "LE" means it won't be quite as full-featured as the normal version) this is a good all-in-one package, especially if you think the majority of your work will be in working with audio.

Getting Audio from a CD

Some video editing applications allow you to rip audio directly from a CD (like Pinnacle Studio 8), but I encountered several that don't yet have that ability. If you're looking to combine audio tracks in an audio-editing program, it's helpful to have them as WAV files instead of swapping CDs.

The 9 Series Windows Media Player has the ability to rip CDs to three different formats (WMA, WMA *VBR*, and WMA Lossless), but unfortunately it doesn't have an option for saving the audio in WAV format. WMA is a great format for storing your music, especially with the new 9 Series options. The problem lies in the fact that none of the video editing tools I tested had the ability to import WMA files—most were able to import WAV and MP3, but not WMA. Because of this, it's necessary to look to another application to extract WAV files from your CDs.

Lingo   Short form for "Variable Bit Rate," *VBR* files combine maximum-quality audio with file-size savings. Instead of creating an audio file at a fixed bit rate, VBR files have a "floating" bit rate. The reason? In most songs, the complexity of the sound isn't consistent. For instance, if there's an introduction with only a single voice singing, there's less audio data than during the chorus with a full band playing. VBR takes this into account by recording that introduction at a lower bit rate (perhaps 64 Kbps), then dramatically raising the bit rate in the chorus to 192 Kbps or higher. Depending on your application, it's possible to specify how high the bit rate will go. This results in having more bits where they're needed, and less where they're not, which means a smaller file size but better quality compared to a CBR (Constant Bit Rate) audio file.

My personal favorite for ripping CDs is Audiograbber (*www.audiograbber.net*). There's a freeware version that has the limitation of only allowing half the tracks to be ripped at any one time, but if you're only looking to rip one audio track, it should do nicely. Audiograbber has the capability to link to third-party audio encoders, enabling you to create MP3, Ogg Vorbis, and other formats. It has built in support for WMA audio up to 192 Kbps, but if ripping to WMA is your goal, the 9 Series Windows Media Encoder is a better choice. Because WAV files are our goal, Audiograbber is our tool.

Note   If you have the choice between using WAV or MP3, always go with WAV. MP3 files are compressed in a lossy fashion, meaning there is data lost. This loss of data can manifest itself as a hissing sound or distorted audio. If the MP3 is in a high bit rate (128 Kbps or higher) you likely won't hear it, but lower quality MP3s at 64 Kbps will have these problems. WAV files, on the other hand, are not compressed and have pristine audio quality. Whenever possible, use WAV files over MP3s.

Using Audiograbber to Rip CDs

Audiograbber is a simple tool to use, and it will allow you to get the song you want off the CD very quickly—pure audio extraction is much faster than extracting the file and then encoding it to WMA or MP3. This step by step assumes that you've downloaded the freeware version from *www.audiograbber.net* or you've purchased the full version, and that you have a CD with the song you want to use.

1   Insert the audio CD into your CD-ROM drive and start up Audiograbber. Assuming you're connected to the Internet when Audiograbber loads, it will connect to the FreeDB and automatically download the album information. FreeDB is a massive database of CD information that saves people from having to type in album information when they're ripping a CD. Figure 8-22 shows the Audiograbber interface when it first loads. By default, all the tracks are selected.

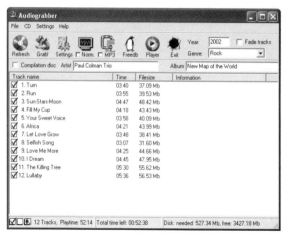

Figure 8-22 Audiograbber has downloaded the track names for my CD.

2   Since we only want to rip one song, not the whole album, click the empty white square in the bottom left hand corner. This de-selects all the tracks, allowing you to manually select the tracks you want to rip by clicking the white box next to the track number. Since I want the first track off the CD, I'll click the white box next to it and Figure 8-23 is the result.

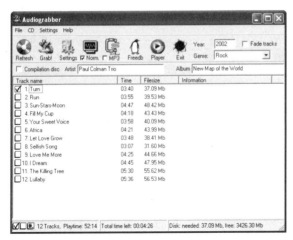

Figure 8-23 Selecting only one track to rip with Audiograbber is shown above.

3 Now click the Settings icon—Figure 8-24 is the result. By default, the ripped WAV files are stored on your C: drive in the Audiograbber folder. This path can be changed by clicking the browse button and selecting the location of the files. I'm satisfied with the default, so I'm going to click OK to close the settings Window.

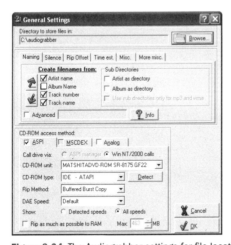

Figure 8-24 The Audiograbber settings for file location are shown above.

4 Now that everything is configured, click the Grab icon and Audiograbber will digitally extract the audio file from your CD. Figure 8-25 shows the progress indicator, and in most cases ripping one track from CD should take no more than 60 seconds (on a fast computer it should take less than 10 seconds).

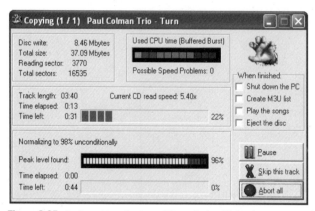

Figure 8-25 Audiograbber ripping a CD track shouldn't take more than 60 seconds.

5   Once the audio track has been ripped, the progress window will automatically close, and you can exit from Audiograbber. In your video-
editing application, import the file from the C:\Audiograbber location,
and you'll have the audio track you wanted.

Key Points

- Advanced video-editing tools support features like motion paths,
picture in picture, and alpha channel (blue screen) effects.

- High-end video editing packages like Adobe Premiere and Ulead
MediaStudio Pro offer a wealth of features and possibilities.

- If you want finer control over video capturing and encoding, there are
powerful stand-alone tools on the market like TMPGEnc, Scenalyzer-
Live, and the Main Concept MPEG Encoder.

- Adding unique musical tracks to your videos is simple when using
tools by Sonic Desktop like Movie Maestro, or Sound Forge's ACID.

- If you need to edit your audio or enhance it, Sonic Foundry's audio
tools (Sound Forge Studio) allow you to do just that.

- If your video-editing application doesn't support ripping audio from a
CD, Audiograbber is a useful tool to accomplish this.

Part IV

Sharing

So far you've beefed up your digital video knowledge, learned how to pick out a great DV camera, and become wiser about getting those great shots. You've also delved deep into the guts of your computer to understand what's required for powerful video-editing performance, and you've created your masterpiece with editing software. What's left? Why, sharing that masterpiece with others, of course! Creating video for yourself is satisfying, but having people tell you they loved your video is thrilling. And when you're creating that video *for* someone else (like a wedding video for a friend) the emotional rewards are even greater.

Chapter 9

Sharing Your Video with Others—the Digital Way

Whether you want to e-mail a video of your child taking her first steps to grandma or share your artistic vision in a short movie with the world at large, distributing your video digitally is the best way to do it. Technically, video on a DVD or CD is still digital, but the differentiating factor is that the digital file is tied to a physical medium instead of being purely digital. In an ideal world, digital video would always stay digital—we'd have no need to tie data made of bits to something physical made of atoms. Unfortunately, limitations around storage and bandwidth (transmission) still persist in this day and age, and until both are obliterated, we'll still be using physical objects to transfer digital information.

Tip   If you're interested in reading more about the nature of things digital, I highly recommend getting the book *Being Digital* by Nicholas Negroponte. The book was written in the early 1990s, but the author was incredibly accurate when talking about the digital future and the challenges we have in being purely digital.

The Advantages of Sharing Video Digitally

There are quite a few advantages to sharing video digitally, but they're not always immediately apparent. Below, I've listed a few of the most compelling reasons to share your video digitally compared to using a physical medium like burning it to DVD or CD.

Nearly Instant

As soon as your video is finished rendering to its digital format, it's mere minutes away from being shared with the world. There's a powerful allure here: the hassles of dubbing tapes, or even duplicating CDs and DVDs, aren't present. Once you have your file, you can e-mail it to groups of people with a few clicks. You can upload it to a Web site and share the URL through e-mail or instant messaging, and in seconds your video will be streaming onto their screens. It's also easy to distribute video "on demand"—if someone sends you a message asking about the event you taped, you can send them the video or URL to the video right away.

No Reproduction Costs or Loss of Quality over Generations

One of the beautiful things about anything existing in a digital medium is that, generally, it can be copied an infinite number of times with no loss of quality (the exception to this rule is digital content that's encrypted and can't be copied at all). In the analog world of tapes, duplication results in progressively inferior quality—you typically had to create several "master" copies and rotate among them. Contrast that with the digital world where the copy is an exact duplication of the original, with no loss of quality, and you'll see why digital duplication outstrips analog duplication in every way. Creating copies of video in the analog world always involves cost—you're paying for the tape, the two VCRs for the duplication, and most importantly your time, since most consumer-level analog duplication solutions duplicate in "real time." This means that if you want to make a copy of an hour-long video, it will take an hour. Now imagine needing to make 10 copies of that video for all your relatives, and you'll see why professional duplication services exist!

Immune to the Ravages of Time

Strictly speaking, digital video files are made up of 0's and 1's (binary), and numbers are immune to degradation over time. What can happen, however, is the failure of the storage medium where the video is kept. No one is exactly sure how long a video burned onto a DVD will last—it should easily last 50 years or more. Hard drives have a much shorter lifespan, but they'll easily last a few years. As long as you transfer your digital video files to a new hard drive before the older one fails, your files will always remain perfect. VHS tapes, however, start to degrade after a few years and, in some cases, are completely unplayable after 10 years. Keeping your video in digital format will help protect it over time—just remember to back it up and have multiple copies in case the storage medium fails.

Distance Isn't a Factor

Sending a file through e-mail to your next-door neighbor is just as easy as sending it to someone on the other side of the world—digital distribution tears down the barrier of distance. I was at a courier depot recently, and a gentleman there was trying to send a VHS tape to someone, presumably in a faraway location. He had to fill out a great deal of paperwork that included the length of the videotape, the length of the video on that tape, and what the contents were. What a hassle! Sending a video file digitally would have saved him a lot of time and effort.

Privacy and Security

Although nothing on the Internet is truly 100 percent secure, it's simple to upload your video to a Web site and password protect it, allowing only authorized individuals to watch it. If you really want to get serious about it, there are ways to apply DRM (digital rights management) to your video, only allowing it to be viewed once, for instance. To do this requires some complex technology, so I wouldn't suggest it for the average person reading this book, but the point is it can be done (check out the Microsoft Windows Media site at *www.microsoft.com/windowsmedia* for more information).

When you e-mail your video to a friend, the odds of that e-mail being intercepted are far less than your tape getting lost in the mail, opened by the wrong person, or damaged in transit. Digital video can also be secured on multiple levels—if you want to send it out through e-mail but secure the file from prying eyes, you can zip the file (*www.winzip.com*) and apply a password to it.

The Disadvantages of Sharing Video Digitally

Despite the reasons I've listed above, sharing video digitally has some disadvantages—many of them are more applicable to longer projects, so you'll have to look at your own project and decide if they have an impact on your goals.

No "Finished Product" You Can Hold

There's something very appealing about holding a finished video production in your hand with its nicely printed label, jewel case, and cover. The digital medium lacks that—you can store the video on your hard drive, but unless you decide to burn that video to a CD or DVD yourself and make the label, you won't be adding it to your video collection. In some cases, this isn't a significant limitation, but if the video is of something important (like a wedding), people enjoy having a physical keepsake. It's also safer to have the video in a physical format—hard drive failures are still a little too common for my tastes.

Limitations with Length of Video

If your video is quite long, it may be impossible to distribute it digitally due to the large file size. We'll talk more about how file size relates to distribution later in this chapter, but the reality is that once your file starts getting over 5 MB, you're going to run into trouble finding a place to store that video, and a 5 MB e-mail is only suitable for people who have broadband Internet access (and even then, their e-mail account might not accept a file that large). And even if you have enough space to fit a large file, your Web hosting provider may have limitations around bandwidth (how many times the file can be downloaded)—some Web sites will simply shut down a site for the day once its bandwidth allotment has been exceeded, while others will present you with a hefty bill at the end of the month. We'll talk more about this later in this chapter.

Playback is Computer-Centric

Unless you have exceptionally tech-savvy friends and family who have connected a computer to their TV set, most people will be viewing your digital video on their computer in an office or den, on a monitor 19" or smaller. This is fine for short, simple videos, but who wants to gather around a computer monitor to share in a special moment captured on video? Computers are usually designed for one person at a time, not a whole family. Video on a DVD or CD, however, will usually get put into a DVD player attached to a TV 30" or bigger—and I'm willing to bet there's a couch in the same room. Digital playback isn't very "user friendly" for large groups of people.

Usually Lower Quality than a Physical Medium

In the battle for balance between file size and quality, file size usually wins out. If you only have 10 MB of storage on your Web account, you have to make your video fit, regardless of how poor the quality will look. In a physical distribution medium like a DVD or VCD, you'll usually have more space than video, which means you can maximize the quality—most video productions won't reach the two-hour limit of a DVD.

As I explained earlier, in Chapter 2, DVD and VCD formats have templates for the data rates that they use, and most helper applications you'll be using to create them will take your video and put it into that format. Pure digital files, however, can be created in a huge variety of formats—and, unfortunately, that can sometimes result in poor decisions made by the creator. The result is a low-quality video that has you squinting at the screen trying to figure out what it is you're watching.

Compatibility and Tech Support

If you've just finished several hours of work on a video project and had the satisfaction of e-mailing it off to everyone you want to see it, the last thing you'll feel like doing is providing tech support to people who can't watch the video on their computers. There are dozens of reasons why they might not be able to see it: no video player, a corrupt installation of the video player, a missing codec, a badly behaved video or audio driver, or any number of other reasons. In an ideal world, none of that would happen, but if Aunt Edna e-mails you back wondering why she can't download your video over her 14.4 KBps modem on her computer running Windows 3.1, where do you even begin? We'll discuss some ways to create video that's as widely compatible as possible, but you should always be prepared for at least one person to e-mail you back saying that something isn't quite working right. But that's the burden of being a digital video guru, right?

Using the 9 Series Windows Media Encoder

Odds are, when you rendered your final video, you chose a high-quality format for storing on your computer or burning to a DVD or CD. If you want to share that video with others, a 600 MB file isn't very conducive to doing so. What's a video artiste to do? Use a tool like the Microsoft Windows Media Encoder to *transcode* the video into a format suitable for e-mailing to another person, putting up on a Web site, or displaying on a Pocket PC. The new 9 Series Windows Media Encoder is really simple to use, and gives excellent results—I think you'll enjoy using it as much as I do. Before I begin this walkthrough you'll want to make sure you have the 9 Series Encoder and player installed. Go to *www.microsoft.com/windowsmedia* and there will be a download link some-where on the page. If you want to work along with me in this step by step, make sure you have a video file handy.

Lingo   Taking one video format and reencoding it into another format is called *transcoding*. For example, if you were to take your DVD-quality video in AVI format at 720 × 480 and encode it to a highly compressed DivX video at 360 × 240, that process would be called transcoding. Transcoding to a lossy format results in a loss of quality, so don't transcode your file too often.

---

1   When you start up the Windows Media Encoder, the first thing you'll see is the New Session Wizard (Figure 9-1). We want to convert a file—I have a video I took on vacation, and at the moment it's a 621 MB AVI file. I'd like to share it over the Web, so let's see how small we can get it while still maintaining decent quality. After selecting the Convert A File icon, click Next.

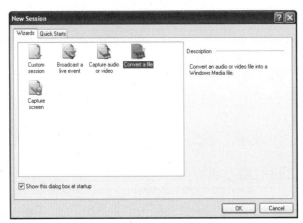

Figure 9-1 Shown above is the Windows Media Encoder New Session Wizard.

2   The next step (Figure 9-2) is where we pick our source file. It should be a file on a hard drive attached to your computer (internal or exter-nal). Encoding a video over a network isn't recommended. Once the source file is chosen, the output path is set to match it (the file we're creating will go to the same folder). If you want to change this for some reason, click the Browse button on the Output File line and select a new directory. Once this is set up, click Next.

Tip   The encoder can accept files in the following formats: ASF, AVI, BMP, JPG, MPG, WMV, MP3, WAV, WMA. That's right, you can transcode audio files too!

New Session Wizard
File Selection
Specify the source file and provide a name and location for the Windows Media file that will be created through this session.
Source file:
O:\RAW - Underwater Bob.avi
Browse...
Output file:
O:\RAW - Underwater Bob-1.wmv
Browse...
Tip
For best results, use the highest quality source file. Re-encoding previously encoded files can produce suboptimal results.
< Back
Next >
Finish
Cancel

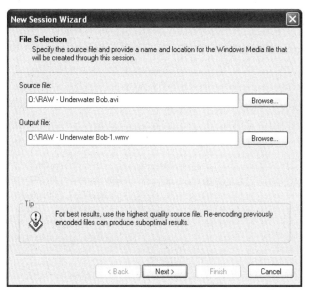

Figure 9-2 Now we pick the source file to be encoded.

3 The Content Distribution screen (Figure 9-3) is where we pick how we are going to share our file. There are seven choices which cover a huge spectrum of devices. For this exercise, we're going to pick Web Server, since I want to share the file over the Web. Click Next.

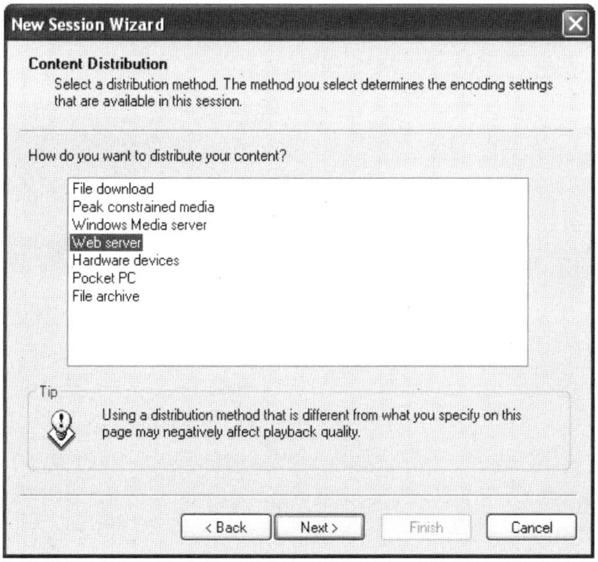
New Session Wizard
Content Distribution
Select a distribution method. The method you select determines the encoding settings that are available in this session.
How do you want to distribute your content?
File download
Peak constrained media
Windows Media server
Web server
Hardware devices
Pocket PC
File archive
Tip
Using a distribution method that is different from what you specify on this page may negatively affect playback quality.
< Back
Next >
Finish
Cancel

Figure 9-3 Choosing the way we're going to distribute our files is important.

4   Now we get to the real meat: the encoding options (Figure 9-4). This is
perhaps the most critical step in the process—you want to pick settings
that will match the method of distribution, but also match the quality of
the input source. In my case, I have a VHS tape with poor quality
audio. I'm also targeting people with broadband connections. To maximize the video quality, I'm going to select DVD Quality (CBR). The
"CBR" stands for "Constant Bitrate," and it simply means that the data
in each frame is constant. Because I know I have poor audio, I'm going
to select FM Quality (CBR) for the audio. In the Bit Rate box below, it
gives me several options—I'm going to pick the one in the middle
because I think it represents the best compromise between overall file
size and quality. 468.05 Kbps can be streamed over a broadband connection (and it's going on my fast server), and 320 x 240 resolution at
29.97 frames per second makes for good quality video that isn't too
small to see. Once you've selected the encoding options you want,
click Next.

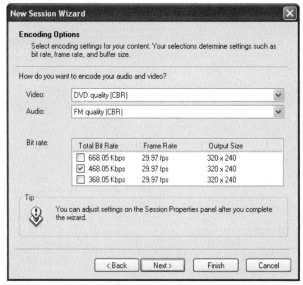

Figure 9-4   Selecting the encoding options is an important step in the process.

5   The Display Information screen (Figure 9-5) is where you enter the
information you want to be attached to that file. People will be able to
view this information in the Windows Media Player, so you'll want to
identify what the video is called (Title), who made it (Author), any relevant copyright information, a rating if it's not appropriate for all age
groups, and finally a description. As you can see in Figure 9-5, I went
into a fair amount of detail describing the video—I wanted people to

know what they're seeing, but if you want you can leave all these fields blank. Once you're finished with this step, click Next.

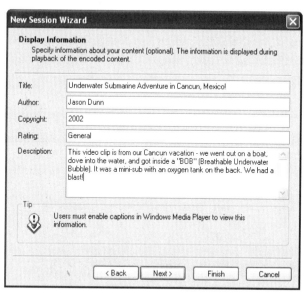

Figure 9-5 Entering in the appropriate display information for viewers to see is optional.

6 The final step in this wizard is the Settings Review screen (Figure 9-6). This screen simply summarizes the decisions you've made so far in the wizard. If something doesn't look correct, click the Back button to step backward through the process. If you're ready to start encoding click Finish.

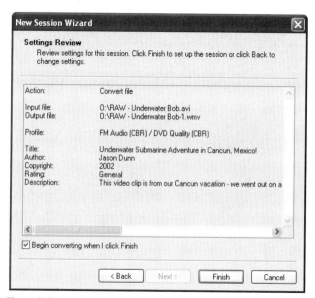

Figure 9-6 Review your settings to make sure they are correct before moving on.

7 Now it's time for you to sit back and watch. Figure 9-7 shows the encoding process underway. Depending on the speed of your computer and the length of the video file, this process can be quick or take a very, very long time. On my testbed computer with a 2.53 Ghz Intel Pentium 4 CPU, 1 GB of Crucial RAM, and a fast Western Digital 120 GB hard drive, the 2 minute, 48 second video took just under 7 minutes to encode. Imagine doing a 30 minute video on a slower computer—you may want to perform this process overnight in some cases. There's nothing to do at this stage but wait, although if you click on the Statistics tab (Figure 9-8) you can watch the encoding information on the total frames converted, determine whether any frames have been dropped, and what the exact bit rates are for the audio and video.

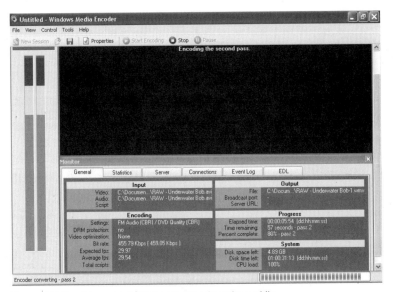

Figure 9-7 The video-encoding process can take quite a while.

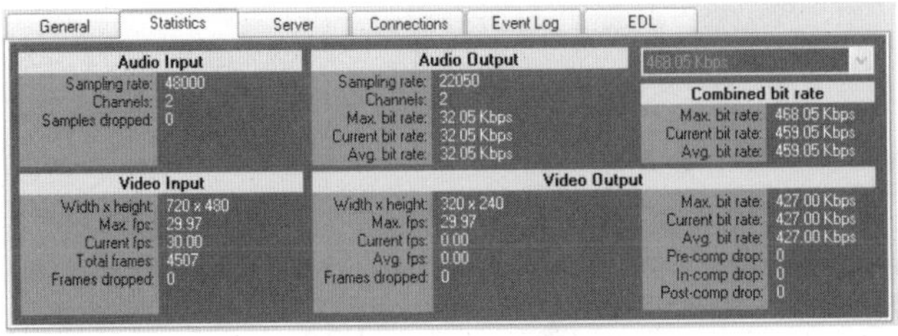

Figure 9-8 You can view encoding information in the Statistics tab while you wait.

8 Once the encoding process is complete, the Encoding Results window will appear (Figure 9-9). This window contains a lot of detail, but the important lines to look at are Bytes Encoded (which will tell you the file size of your new video), and the Frames Dropped (if you have more then a few hundred in a video that is less than 2 minutes long, you may want to re-encode). As you can see, my huge 607 MB video has been encoded into an incredible 9.58 MB—almost 64 times smaller! And if you can believe it, although the video resolution is lower than the original video, the quality looks better—there were some strange distortions present in the original video capture that were smoothed out when it was encoded.

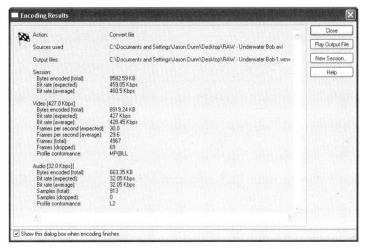

Figure 9-9 The Encoding Results screen displays all the detailed information you need.

And that's it—you've transcoded your video file to a new format using the 9 Series Window Media Encoder. The software has some other interesting features, so take your time and explore what it can do.

Putting Your Video up on the Web

Sharing your video by putting it up on a Web site is a great way to distribute it. Your Web site will (hopefully) be running 24/7, so people can access it whenever they want. With computers and Internet access being commonplace in North America and Europe, you're only a few clicks away from showing people your video-editing work anywhere you are. Sending someone an *URL* to a Web page is less prone to problems than sending them the video file itself. If your video is something you want to share with the wider community of Internet users, putting your video up on a Web site is the best way to do that. Search engines will eventually *index* your site if you submit it, or the URL will be passed around manually, and people from all over the world will come and see your videos.

Lingo   *URL* (Universal Resource Locator). Sometimes pronounced like the name "Earl," an URL is what you type into your Web browser in order to visit a Web site. URLs can also be sent through e-mail or even embedded in video files themselves.

Lingo   The process of *indexing* occurs when an automated program run by a search engine (called a "spider") visits your Web site. This spider will crawl through your Web site, following all the links it finds. It will look at the words on the pages and create an index of your site based on the content it sees. It then assigns a rank to your site based on the content, and when someone types in a search term (like "digital video"), your site may be one of the sites listed. Popular search engines that index content include Google, Lycos and AltaVista. Search tools like Yahoo! don't index content—links you find there are created manually by humans.

That's an important decision to make up front with your Web site: Do you want the things you put up to be available to the public? Or do you want to keep it private and share only with your friends? There are various ways to password protect your Web site, some of them more effective than others, but as a general rule of thumb you shouldn't put up videos on a Web site under the assumption that you have complete control over who accesses them. A determined individual can always bypass security. If you're going to put your video files up on the Web, you might as well start a community out of it—most community sites have tools to help you control who sees your videos.

Starting a Community

Now that you've encoded your video into a Web-friendly format, it's time to get it up onto a Web site for sharing. Assuming that you don't already have your own Web site (if you do, skip to the next section), you'll be looking for someplace to host your files for free and perhaps give you some basic Web tools that will help you create a virtual home for your videos. I scoured the Web and found two solutions, each offering a different approach to storing video online.

MSN Groups

MSN Groups (*www.msnusers.com*) is a Web site that gives you the basic tools to start up your own online community and store short (very short!) video clips online. The service is free, and with only 3 MB of storage (and a per-file limit of 1 MB), there's not much room for growth (Figure 9-10).

Figure 9-10 The MSN Groups home page is where you start things off.

However, if you're willing to pay a small fee per year for MSN Extra Storage Space, you'll get 15 MB of storage space for your files, and your Hotmail storage space also increases. If you want to use this service to share anything but the shortest video files, I recommend signing up for the extra storage. If you have a Microsoft Passport (*www.passport.com*), you can sign in and immediately get started creating your online community. Your Microsoft Passport information is usually the same as your Hotmail user information.

For a free service, despite the space limitations, MSN Groups have some surprisingly rich tools for community building (Figure 9-11). You can create custom Web pages, a message board for discussion, a documents folder for sharing files (this is where you'd put your videos), a photo album, a calendar for scheduling events, an e-mail list for keeping in touch, and a Web-based list for keeping things organized.

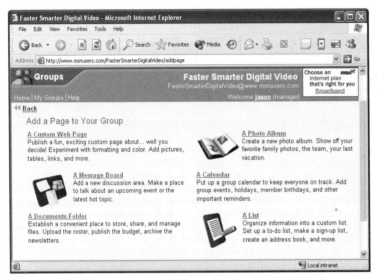

Figure 9-11 The MSN Groups community building tools help you create your site.

Creating an account is as simple as signing in with your Passport account and picking a community name, so I won't go into details on how to do that. You'll end up with a Web site address of *www.msnusers.com/YourNameHere*. I created a community called Faster Smarter Digital Video, and thus the URL I'd give out to people is *www.msnusers.com/fastersmarterdigitalvideo*. Once you have your community created, it's time to upload a video file to it. Let's get started!

1   Once you've logged into your account, on the left side you'll see a section with a blue background titled My Groups, and the group that you just created. Click on your group (Figure 9-12).

2   You're now in the community management area. Click Documents (left side). If you want to create a folder specifically for video files, you can click Create Folder and follow the steps to create a folder. I've already created a folder called Videos. You select the folder you want to upload files to by clicking on it.

3   Click Add File and you'll be taken to an upload screen (Figure 9-13). You'll need to browse to the location on your computer that has the video file you want to upload. Remember the 1 MB limit—if you select a video file that is either over 1 MB in size, or one that puts you over your 3 MB total size limit, a pop-up window appears reminding you of this. Once you've selected your file, click Upload Now.

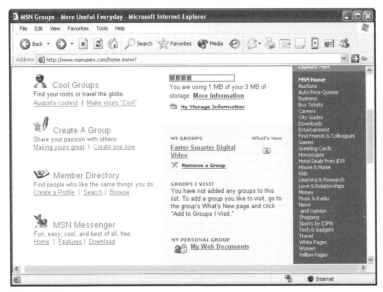

Figure 9-12 First you need to select your community.

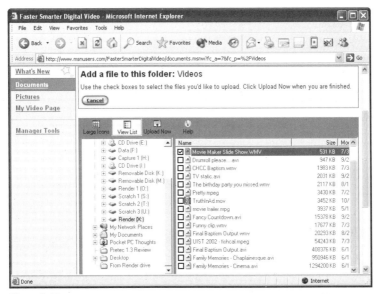

Figure 9-13 You need to select a file to upload—remember that 1 MB limit!

4 Depending on your Internet connection, uploading your video file may take 10 seconds, or it may take 10 minutes. Once the file is uploaded, you'll see it listed as Figure 9-14 shows.

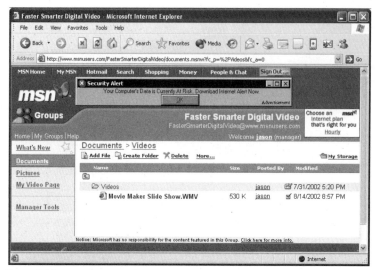

Figure 9-14   Your file should be listed once it's uploaded.

5   We need to get the URL that points to our video file, so right-click on the file name of the video you just uploaded, and then click Properties. You'll see a window like Figure 9-15—these are the file's properties. Select the Address (URL) by left-clicking in the area that starts with http:// and then press Control+A—this will select the entire URL.

Figure 9-15   Getting the file properties and copying them to the clipboard is the next step.

6   Press Control+C to copy that URL to the clipboard. You can keep it on the clipboard, but since we need it later, it's not a bad idea to open up Notepad (go to the Start menu, then All Programs, then Accessories, and then Notepad) and paste it in for safekeeping.

Now that we have a video file uploaded, we'll need to create a Web page that links to that video and tells people something about it.

1 When you're logged into your site, on the right-hand side you'll see a sidebar titled Manager Tools (Figure 9-16). These are the tools you'll use to control various elements of your community. Since we want to create a new Web page for our video, click Add A Page.

Figure 9-16 The MSN Groups Manager Tools help you control community elements.

2 You'll be taken to a Web page like the one shown in Figure 9-17. Since they don't have a specific template for video, we'll click on the Custom Page option. We'll need that URL you copied to your clipboard or Notepad, so have it handy.

Figure 9-17 This page allows you to create your custom page content.

3   This is the interface you'll use to create your custom video page. The
        tools are very similar to using a word processor, so don't be intimi-
        dated by anything. If you're an experienced Hypertext Markup Lan-
        guage (HTML) coder, you can click on the "Edit HTML" link at the
        bottom of the page, but I recommend staying in the default interface.
        There are two fields to fill out before getting to the page content: Page
        Name and Page Description. Each of these helps people navigate your
        site, so give them useful descriptions. In the large box (Figure 9-17)
        you'll be able to enter text and even include a photo by clicking on the
        Image icon.

4   Once you've entered your text describing the video, select a few words
        of text that you'd like to turn into a hyperlink to your video file. It can
        be obvious, like "Click here for the video," or integrated into the story
        you're telling about the video. Once you've selected the text, click on
        the Hyperlink icon.

5   A small window appears (Figure 9-18). This is the window you will use
        to link to your video file. Remember the URL we copied after upload-
        ing our video file? Paste it into the longest box in the bottom right.
        Because we're linking to our video file directly, ignore the top box that
        asks about linking a specific page. Leave the default of http:// in the
        other box. You may need to delete the http:// in the URL that you
        pasted into the window—you don't want to have two instances of
        http:// or your link won't work. Once you've finished, you should have
        an URL something like this: *http://www.msnusers.com/yoursitename/
        Documents/Videos/filename.wmv.*

Figure 9-18 Shown above is how to add a hyperlink to your video file.

6 Click the OK box. This returns you to the editing screen. The text that you had previously highlighted in step 4 should now be blue and underlined—this indicates that it's a hyperlink.

7 Click Save Page at the bottom of the screen.

8 You're taken to your page in its finished form (Figure 9-19). You should see your hyperlinked text. Click on it, and you should be presented with a box that looks something like Figure 9-20. This indicates that your hyperlink is correct. If you get a "Page Not Found" error, it means that you made an error in the hyperlinking process. Go back to step 4 and double-check your URL.

Figure 9-19 Pictured above is your custom page in a completed state.

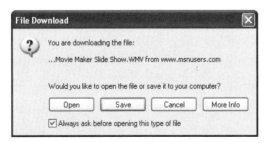

Figure 9-20 The download/open box indicates a successful hyperlink.

9 You're done! Your visitors will have the option of saving your video as a download to play later, or, by selecting Open, they will see the video stream and playback after a few seconds.

The MSN Users site has some great tools for budding community builders, so I'd encourage you to explore them. Suggest to your friends and family that they sign up for the newsletter feature, so when you upload a new video for sharing you can notify everyone with a single e-mail.

SingleReel

If you're interested in sharing your video with a wider community of amateur video editors and filmmakers, consider SingleReel (*www.singlereel.com*, shown in Figure 9-21). They offer video hosting, and I was unable to find any information about file size limits, so I'm inclined to think they'll host any number of reasonably sized clips (if you upload your 2 GB, six-hour remake of *The Godfather*, parts one through three, they may take exception to it). One snag is that, currently, they require the video to be in QuickTime (MOV) format. They're considering supporting Windows Media Video (WMV) in the future, but until then your video-editing package will have to support QuickTime exports (or you'll have to purchase QuickTime Pro from *www.apple.com*).

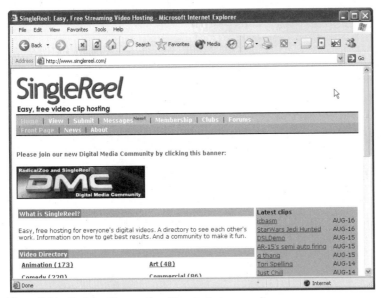

Figure 9-21 SingleReel is an online video sharing community.

SingleReel offers some great features, like a discussion forum, ratings on each video clip, a Video Messaging system where clips are made private and only those with a special URL can see them, and a privacy option for any or all of your clips. If you simply want to host your video files on SingleReel and not have anyone but authorized people see them, this is a good choice.

Caution   Always keep digital copies of any video you upload to a Web site. Never assume that the people running the site are keeping backups—hard drives fail, and Internet companies can go out of business overnight. If you're running short on hard disk space, burn them to a CD or DVD, but don't assume that the people running video hosting sites (especially free ones) care about your video clips as much as you do. There have been instances of photo hosting companies going out of business and people losing irreplaceable photos because they assumed they'd always have access to the site—don't make the same mistake they did! Keep a backup.

If You Already Have Your Own Web Site or Want One

Personal Web sites are becoming more common for the average user to own and operate—with one-year domain registrations costing a small amount (*www.dnscentral.com*), Web hosting being free or extremely cheap (*www.pair.com*), and content management systems like Blogger (*www.blogger.com*) making it easy to publish your thoughts online, now is a great time to have a Web site. I don't have any connections with the above companies, but I'd encourage you to go to *www.google.com* and type in "Web hosting" and see what you come up with. There are some great deals to be had! If you have your own Web site and you're interested in putting up your video, here are some issues to think about.

Note   Don't feel limited to finding a Web host in your local city or town. There's a natural inclination for people to find local businesses to host their sites. Although there's certainly nothing wrong with supporting local businesses, distance isn't a relevant factor when selecting a Web hosting provider. I can guarantee that whether you're uploading your files to a computer a few miles away or one on the other side of the planet, you'll be uploading your files exactly the same way. Pick a Web hosting provider based on service, price, and features—not location.

Tip   Speed is one of the most important factors to check when choosing a host, so spend some time clicking through its Web site. If their home page is slow to load, odds are yours will be too. Stay away!

How Much Space Do You Have?

More so than almost any other type of data, video files can take up huge amounts of space. So before you upload your video, make sure you have enough space in your Web hosting account—some Web hosts let you upload beyond your storage limit but charge you for it at the end of the month. Most Web hosts have a method for you to check your current storage space levels, so take advantage of that before uploading your video. In most cases, a typical Web hosting account will offer around 100 MB of storage space for an entry-level package, which is more than enough for several average-length videos at reasonable quality. If you need more space for storing multiple videos, Web hosts usually have account upgrades that offer more storage space at increased costs. Because large hard drives are so inexpensive, and most Web sites never use up their maximum allotment, I've seen some companies offering 500+ MB of storage space for under $20 US a month. Look around and see what you can find.

Beware the Bandwidth Monster

If you're running a popular Web site, you may have run into this already, but if you haven't, here's a simple warning: beware the *bandwidth* monster! It might sound melodramatic, but having been the victim of it myself, I can't stress this enough: keep an eye on your bandwidth. Bandwidth allotments are usually measured in gigabytes per month, although some Web hosts measure it on a daily basis in MB. Every Web hosting account will have a bandwidth limit, even if your Web host claims it offers "unlimited" bandwidth. I've been on several Web hosts offering "unlimited, unmetered bandwidth," only to be asked to leave when my site became popular and the bandwidth transfers increased dramatically. Worse, some hosts will slap you with a surprise bill for several hundred (or thousand) dollars at the end of the month. It sounds surreal, but it's true—I've seen it happen many times.

> **Lingo**   The term *bandwidth* is used to describe the transfer of data from a server to external computers. For instance, if I had a 1 MB file on my Web server, and it was downloaded 200 times in a 24-hour period, I would have used up 200 MB of bandwidth (file size multiplied by downloads).

Here's a true story on the subject: I put a funny video clip up on my Web site (*www.pocketpcthoughts.com*) because I thought people might like to see it. The clip was 17 MB in size, and within 30 days it had been downloaded nearly 17,000 times, resulting in a staggering 286 GB of traffic—just on that one file! At that time, I was checking my traffic stats only once a month, so I didn't see the results until later. It seems that once my visitors saw that clip, they passed the URL to their friends, and so on. It quickly became *viral*, and if it weren't for my generous sponsor who was hosting the site for free, I could have easily had a bandwidth bill over $2,000 US! Scary but true.

> **Lingo**   *Viral content* is something on the Web, whether it's a story, picture, video, or game, that gets e-mailed from person to person with amazing speed. One person likes it, and they want to share it with everyone they know, who in turn want to do the same. Within hours, you can have thousands of people viewing your video.

There are a few ways of monitoring your bandwidth. Some Web hosts have a tool that you can check to see how much bandwidth you're using on a daily basis, and most also generate raw *log files* for you. If you download these log files and use software like FastStats (*www.mach5.com*) to analyze them, you can discover some very interesting information about your Web traffic. The most important thing, however, is to keep a handle on how much bandwidth your site is using. If you put up a video file and notice that it's generating a huge spike in bandwidth, consider taking the file down or asking for a *mirror* for the file.

Lingo   *Log files* are text files that contain information about the Web traffic that your site generates. When someone comes to your site, information about their browser type, country, the time they visited, how long they stayed there, how much bandwidth they used up downloading things from your site—it's all recorded and stored in the log files.

Lingo   A *mirror* is another Web site that offers to host a file for you, giving visitors to your site a choice of locations to download from. The goal of file mirroring is typically to offset the bandwidth drain on a single site and to give visitors a choice of download location if your server isn't able to serve up the file.

Tip   If you think you're going to be using up a fair bit of bandwidth (say, more than 10 GB a month), before choosing a Web host that offers "unlimited bandwidth," e-mail them and ask them what would happen if you had a site that uses far more bandwidth than you're currently using (multiply your bandwidth requirements by 5 or 10). If that doesn't cause them to say no to having you as a customer, they'll likely have the capacity to host your site even if it gets popular. There are no guarantees, but it's better to ask up front than to find out later.

It's critical to keep a handle on your bandwidth usage, so make sure you have a monitoring system in place before putting up a large video file that could become popular very quickly.

HTML Code for Embedding the Windows Media Player

If you want to offer a video file on your Web site, there are basically two ways to do it:

1   Hyperlink to the video file.

2   Embed the Windows Media Player into the Web page.

The first option is quite straightforward for anyone with even basic HTML coding skills (`<A HREF=Óhttp://www.domain.com/file.wmvÓ>file name</A>`), but the second option of embedding the Windows Media Player control is a bit more challenging. By using the right code on your Web page, you can create an inline video control for the video player—instead of having the external video launch, the player loads as part of the HTML page and the video plays from within your Web page. It's less intrusive than an external player and has a certain "wow" factor that will make you seem like you know a lot about HTML. And best of all? It's simply a matter of using the following few lines of code between the `<BODY>` and `</BODY>` tags:

```
<OBJECT ID="Player" width="320" height="240"
CLASSID="CLSID:6BF52A52-394A-11d3-B153-00C04F79FAA6">
 <PARAM name="autoStart" value="True">
 <PARAM name="URL" value="http://www.domain.com/filename.wmv">
</OBJECT>
```

You'll need to change two things in this code sample in order for your own video clips to work:

- The WIDTH and HEIGHT numbers should be changed to match your video size. In the code above I have it set at 320 pixels wide by 240 pixels high. You can check the dimensions of your video file by right-clicking on it, selecting Properties, and then looking on the Summary tab. If you'd like a black border around your video, add 10 pixels to that number. If you want the video to display in a smaller box, you can use smaller numbers and the video will scale to fit.

- The URL value needs to be the complete path to your video file name, including the file extension (WMV in this case). You should confirm your file name path by typing it into a Web browser and seeing if the video file loads. If you get an error like "Web Page Not Found—Error Code 404," it means you have the path wrong.

This method works for any of the file formats the Windows Media Player will play: AVI, MPEG, WMV, or ASF. In case of files that can stream (like WMV), the embedded player streams for a few seconds and then starts playing the file. Figure 9-22 shows a simple Web page I made with nothing but the player on it. As you can see, the controls for the player are there, allowing the visitor to start and stop the clip and to control the volume. If you have video in another format, like QuickTime or RealVideo, try a search on Google and you'll find code examples to help you along.

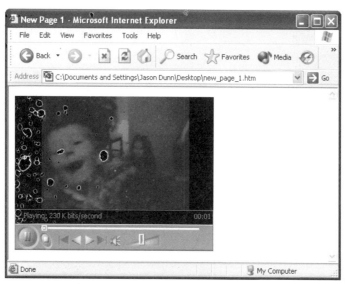

Figure 9-22 Shown above is the Windows Media Player embedded in a Web page.

Tip   If you're a Microsoft FrontPage user (Microsoft's Web design tool), there's a software add-in that will make embedding the Windows Media Player video really easy. It's found at *http:// www.microsoft.com/frontpage/downloads/addin/searchdetail.asp?aid=50*. The tool allows you to control how the Windows Media Player is loaded, whether or not the controls are shown, and how many times the video file loops. It's a great add-in!

Note   Another format that has been gaining popularity lately for streaming video is the Macromedia Flash format. Upward of 90 percent of all Web users have the Flash client installed, it streams easily, and file sizes are quite small even for video. There's an application called Boomer (*www.gfx2swf.com*) that converts video files to Flash files, and by the time you read this a new version that supports importing of AVI, MPEG, QuickTime, and WMV should be released. I'd really encourage you to look into it—it's a very simple tool but it makes converting video, audio, and images into Flash very simple.

Using an Online Storage Site

An online storage site is basically a "hard drive in the sky"—it's a dedicated data storage account that you can access through the Internet and store anything you want in it. In early 2000, at the height of the Internet boom, there were dozens of solutions for file hosting. You could get 100 MB of free storage and use it for whatever you wanted. The days of the great "Everything for free on the Internet" are long past. The bubble burst in 2000, and companies suddenly discovered that they needed a business plan and a strategy for profit in order to stay alive. Today things are quite a bit different. Most of those free services are gone, and those that remain have switched to a pay model. There are still a few free options, but to get any flexibility you'll need to get out the credit card.

Yahoo! Briefcase

One of the better options that I found, Yahoo! Briefcase (*briefcase.yahoo.com*) allows you to store up to 30 MB of video in a virtual "briefcase" that's accessible through your Web browser. Although 30 MB is a generous allotment for a free service, the file size is limited to only 5 MB, making it suitable for short videos only. You can e-mail a link to a specific file to others (see Figure 9-23), and control how long that link remains valid (two weeks, one month, or forever). The transfer speed when downloading my video file from Yahoo! Briefcase was decent at 35 to 50 KBps—not exactly "high speed" but, compared to some other services, quite good. They also have software currently in beta that will allow you to access your Yahoo! Briefcase directly as a hard drive letter—no Web interface needed.

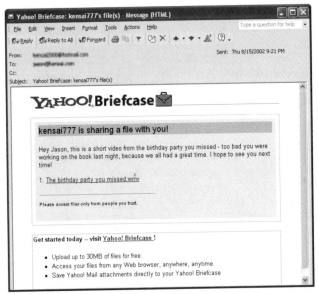

Figure 9-23 Pictured above is a Yahoo! Briefcase e-mail invitation for file sharing.

If you want to get more storage space, you can upgrade your account to 50 or even 100 MB. If you really need space, the account can be upgraded to a maximum of 300 MB. Your per-file cap goes up from 5 to 10 MB, making it better for longer or more high-quality videos. All in all, for sharing small video clips, this is a great free service worth checking out. And if you already have a Yahoo! e-mail address, you simply sign in at the Briefcase home page, and it's activated immediately.

Whalemail (A Swapdrive Company)

If you're looking for sheer simplicity, it's tough to beat Whalemail (*www.whalemail.com*). They offer a single service: You sign up for an account with 100 MB of storage, log in and upload your files (there appear to be no individual file size limits), and create a list of recipients to receive the special URL from which they can download your file. They support up to 400 MB of space, or even more if you contact them directly. Unfortunately, Whalemail offers no trial period or even screen shots of their interface—and uploaded files last only 14 days. It's also strictly a Web-based interface, which adds an extra step when it comes to uploading your files. If you need to share large video files and don't mind the 14-day limit, this is a service you should look into.

Xdrive

One of the original companies that survived the fierce competition among early online file storage services, Xdrive (*www.xdrive.com*) has managed to come out on top with one of the best-paid services I've seen. They offer a free 14-day trial, and if you like their service, you'll pay a small fee per month for 75 MB of space. Need more? For a higher fee per month you can get a massive 1000 MB of space, which is enough space for several high-quality and lengthy projects. Xdrive has a great Web-based interface with multiple folders and a very intuitive way of sharing folders. You can select people from your address book and give them varying levels of access to the folder, including read, create, edit, modify, delete, and share. If you're working on a collaborative video project, you could use Xdrive to download video clips, edit them, and upload them for others to work on further. The speed at downloading my files was impressive—between 300 and 400 KBps. Download speed of the service is an important consideration if you have large video files that you want to share—there's nothing worse than downloading a large file and seeing single-digit download speeds.

I found it very useful that Xdrive would let me select multiple files before clicking Download, which allows me to get all the files I want at once. There's also a piece of software that, once installed, will allow you to access your Xdrive as if it were a local hard drive (see Figure 9-24). Xdrive offers several other features (including a search function), and in terms of sheer value for the money,

I'd say this is your best bet for a paid service if you require more than the 30 MB that Yahoo! Briefcase can offer you.

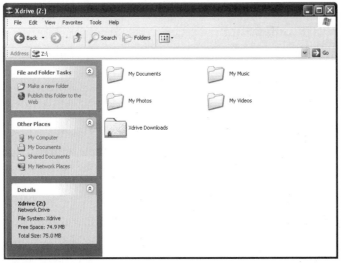

Figure 9-24 Xdrive adds a local storage icon for easy drag and drop transfers.

Sending Your Video Using Instant Messaging

Instant Messaging (IM) is a popular way of communicating with others online. Once thought to be a curious fixation only for teenagers, Internet users of all ages have quickly realized how useful it is to be in touch, real-time, with others. Part of that real-time communication is the ability to send files back and forth, and, you guessed it, videos! There's no faster way to send someone a video than a point-to-point communication between two computers, so take advantage of this when you see someone online whom you want to send your video.

Note   There's no perfect size or level of quality for your video file for IM transfer. The higher the quality, the longer it will take to transfer, so it's a decision you'll have to make yourself. A good rule of thumb would be to create a half-VGA (320 × 240) version of your video for sending to people who have a high-speed Internet connection, and a low-quality (176 × 120) version for people with slower 56 KBps connections.

Every IM program is different when it comes to sending files, but in general there are two ways of doing it: starting up a conversation with someone and then looking under the menu of that chat window for a "Send File" option or dragging a file into the chat window. In the case of Windows Messenger (MSN Messenger), it's simplest to start a conversation with them, ask if they'll be online long enough to receive a file, then drag the file into the window. As

Figure 9-25 shows, they're given an option about whether or not to accept the file transfer, and an estimate is given for how long it will take. Thankfully, few people are using 28.8 KBps modems today, so the file transfer will always take a lot less time than estimated. You can continue to chat while the file is transferring, but it's best to keep the file transfers to one at a time. Once the file is finished transferring, the person on the other end will be able to open and view the file.

Caution   Make sure to ask if the other person has the right kind of video player before initiating the file transfer. You don't want them to wait 20 minutes for a large file transfer only to discover they can't view it!

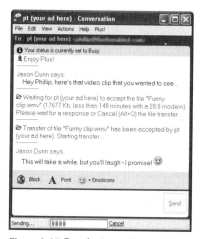

Figure 9-25 Transferring a video file using Windows Messenger is simple.

Tip   If you're having trouble initiating a file transfer, it may be due to a *firewall* blocking the *ports* at your end, their end, or both. By default, the ports needed for most IM clients won't be opened for security reasons. If you're using Windows Messenger, you'll need to open ports 3819 and 1863 in order for file transfers to occur. If you're using a software firewall, like Zone Alarm (*www.zonealarm.com*), it's probably easiest to simply shut it down temporarily while the file is transferring. If you're using another IM client, you'll have to do a Google search to find out what ports need to be opened. And if you're not using a firewall, you should be! Check out Zone Alarm— it's free and works quite well.

Lingo   A *firewall* is a virtual barrier that blocks and filters incoming and outgoing data for security purposes. It acts as a filter by looking at each request that comes to your computer, and it stops intruders from getting at your PC and the data on it. Firewalls come in both dedicated hardware forms (like the D-Link 714-P) and software (Zone Alarm), but both accomplish the same thing: They protect your computer from hostile intruders. They have the side effect of stopping file transfers over IM clients as well, unless you know how to open the correct ports.

Lingo   A *port* is an element on a firewall that can best be thought of as a door. If that door (port) is open, traffic can pass through it. For instance, if you have an FTP server on your computer, you'll need to open port 21 in order for people outside your firewall to access it. In the same way, in order for someone to send you a file over IM, you'll need to have the right ports open. I've found Google (*www.google.com*) to be a tremendous research tool in helping me to determine what ports need to be opened. Unfortunately, most IM clients (Windows Messenger included) have no means to automatically work with firewalls—they force you to get in and alter your firewall ports before they'll work properly.

Sending Your Video over E-mail

E-mail, considered one of the most popular Internet tools in use, is a good medium for distributing smaller video clips but one that is fraught with difficulties and frustrations if you're not careful. The most important thing to remember when e-mailing video is to determine the following:

- **Does the person wish to receive this video?**   There's nothing more frustrating than checking your e-mail and having it take five minutes, only to discover a "friend" sending you a video file you have no desire to see. Unless you're 100 percent sure someone wants to receive the video over e-mail, always send a preliminary e-mail asking them first. Better to be courteous than to cause someone frustration!

- **Does the person have a high-speed Internet connection?**   If they don't, my advice is to not send them video over e-mail, period. Even a small 2 MB video file would take over nine minutes to download when attached to an e-mail message, and while that video attachment is downloading, they can't get to any other e-mail on the server or effectively do anything else online (all their bandwidth is going toward downloading that big e-mail message).

- **How big can file attachments be with their Internet service provider (ISP)?**   ISPs all have different limits on file attachments—some limit file attachments to 2 MB, others will allow up to 10 MB. If you send a file that crosses over the limit set by the ISP, the e-mail will return to you undelivered. You've wasted your time uploading the e-mail message, and they won't even see it.

Tip   If you're using the Windows Media Encoder to transcode your video files, use the e-mail template. It will create a file suitable for e-mailing to others, but be sure to check the file size before attaching to an e-mail message.

Using the E-mail Function from Within a Video Editor

Although not all video editors on the market support this function, many allow you to directly send an e-mail from within the program. It's not quite as exciting as it sounds—the application simply opens a blank e-mail message from your default e-mail program and attaches the video file to it. Nothing flashy, but it does save you a step. Figure 9-26 shows you the Export options from Ulead VideoStudio 6—you'll notice that e-mail is one of the options listed.

Figure 9-26 Export options in Ulead VideoStudio 6 are shown above.

Clicking on the e-mail option generates a blank e-mail with the video file attached (see Figure 9-27). You fill in the recipient's e-mail address (or select it from your address book), give the e-mail a subject line and some descriptive text, and click Send. Remember that depending on the size of your attachment, sending the e-mail may take quite some time, even with a broadband connection.

> **Note**   If your video-editing client doesn't have an e-mail function, simply open a new e-mail message and drag and drop the video file into the message. It should attach itself to the message. Alternatively, there should be a button to click for attaching files. Check the Help files for your application if you're not sure.

> **Note**   If you want to secure your video attachment from prying eyes, Zip it with software like Winzip or Picozip (*www.picozip.com*) and apply a password to it. Don't put the password in the same e-mail message—send it under a different e-mail message, send it over IM, or even phone the person and give them the password.

Caution   If you use Web-based e-mail services like Hotmail, you'll likely have a limit on the attachment sizes that can be sent. For the free Hotmail e-mail accounts (not the enhanced option), the file size limit is 1 MB. If you run into this problem, consider using one of the online file storage services mentioned above, like Yahoo! Briefcase. If your video file is extremely close to the limit, try zipping it—although video files rarely compress very much, the 1 percent to 3 percent you'll typically get may be enough to let you squeak by the upload limit.

Figure 9-27 This is the e-mail generated with the attachment—fill in your text and hit send!

Key Points

■ Advantages to sharing video digitally include speed of distribution and no barriers of time and space.

■ Advantages to sharing video physically include higher quality and a finished product.

■ The 9 Series Windows Media Encoder is a powerful tool for compressing your videos for sending over e-mail or posting to a Web site.

■ Web-based communities will let you share video, but most have file size limits.

■ Web-based storage sites like Xdrive allow you to have dedicated storage space for storing and sharing your videos.

■ Before e-mailing someone a video, first make sure they want it and have a fast enough Internet connection to receive it.

Chapter 10

Sharing Your Video with Others—Using a Physical Medium

Talk about an awkward chapter title! I couldn't come up with a clever way to say "This chapter is about taking your video and burning it to a DVD or putting it on a Pocket PC or watching it on a portable VCD player." In the last chapter I talked about techniques and concepts dealing with sharing your video digitally, and this chapter is all about the cold, hard world of physical objects that make platforms for sharing digital video. I found some interesting devices that let you burn, copy, share, and view your digital videos. Before we get into the expensive tools, I want to give you an overview of the advantages and disadvantages of sharing video digitally.

The Advantages of Sharing Digital Video Using a Physical Medium

There are a lot of advantages to using a physical medium to share digital video. There's a time and place for e-mailing someone a video, but for long-term storage and use, there's something very appealing about burning a disc with your memories on it.

A Finished Product

If you're anything like me, when you buy a CD or DVD, you open up the packaging to examine what's inside. You look at the insert and the photos and read everything that's there. I love looking at the intricately printed images on the front of modern DVDs (I wish my printer could do that!). The point is, there's something very appealing about holding a finished product in your hands. Using simple software and a regular printer, it's possible to create professional-looking disc labels, inserts for the CD tray, and great-looking covers and inserts.

My wife, Ashley, created something special for her mother recently—during the party we threw for her 50th birthday, I took dozens of pictures with my Canon G2 digital camera (what a camera!). A few days after the party, Ashley took the digital pictures and, using a product from Ulead called DVD Picture-Show (*www.ulead.com*), created a VCD-based photo album complete with background music recorded the year her mother was born. Using some Avery software that came with the labels we bought, she created a CD label that had a picture from the party on it, an insert for the back, and a nice cover. The end result was a high-quality, personalized present that her mother will treasure for years. If Ashley had simply e-mailed her mother the photos, it just wouldn't have been the same. Having a finished product means it's something you can share, lend out, and show off.

Maximum Quality Video

In Chapter 9, "Sharing Your Video with Others—the Digital Way," I talked about the limitations of bandwidth, both as it related to e-mail and to putting video on a Web server—physical mediums don't have those limitations. The video you encode can be as high quality as you want it to be (within the format's limitations), and, unlike video on a Web server, when you've gone over your bandwidth limitations, it won't cost you anything when people watch it over and over.

Computer Independent

Unlike purely digital formats, physical mediums can be computer independent. If you have a childhood video you want to bring to your sibling's house, you can bring a DVD with you instead of your laptop. With the advent of digital video devices like portable DVD players and Pocket PCs (we'll cover these at the end of the chapter), you can easily carry both the playback mechanism and the playback content with you. Transmission of the video is less error prone— you just carry it with you instead of wondering if that e-mail you sent made it through to the recipient. Just tonight I e-mailed my friend a song I wanted him to hear, and the e-mail returned with an "undeliverable" error. E-mail works great most of the time, but it's not as reliable as carrying a VCD to your friend's house.

There's also the factor of whether or not everyone you want to share the video with even owns a computer. My grandmother doesn't own a computer, but she does have a VCR. Always consider your audience's resources!

Security

If you have video that you don't want people to share digitally, it's a no-brainer to burn it to a disc: just ask any of the major movie studios. This process isn't perfect, however—a handful of software products on the market will break the electronic security measures (encryption) on the DVD. In fact, when no one would make a software DVD player for the Linux market, a few clever coders took it upon themselves to crack the DVD encryption so they could watch movies on their computers. Surprisingly, it only took seven lines of code. Despite this, average users aren't going to spend any time trying to crack DVD encryption—they're just going to go buy a copy of the movie at a local store. In the same way, if you tie your video to a physical medium, odds are it will stay that way. I should note, however, that one of the things I've learned over the years in this industry is that if people want access to something on a computer, they'll find a way to make it happen.

The Disadvantages of Sharing Digital Video Using a Physical Medium

If you want to go down the road of putting your video projects on a disc, you should keep a few things in mind.

Time and Cost of Reproduction

Every physical copy of your video has to be created, burned, or copied. Unlike the purely digital version, if you want to have 20 copies of your video to share with your relatives across the country, you need to buy 20 DVD-R discs and 20 jewel cases and spend the time burning 20 discs. You can save time by taking your project to a professional media-duplication company, but then the cost may go up. Physical mediums are simply more costly to work in than digital ones.

Distribution Time and Cost

Now that you have your 20 DVDs, how do you get them to where they need to be? Unless there's a family reunion coming up, you're going to have to spend the time to mail each one, which is an added cost. It also takes time for the disc to get to the recipient, and mail can get lost. Digital distribution is easier to control because fewer elements can go wrong.

Duplication of VHS Tapes Will Be of Lower Quality

If your project is going to be put onto VHS tapes to save time or be more compatible with what your audience has, the quality will be lower than that of a digital duplication like an SVCD or DVD. If you're mass duplicating the VHS tapes yourself, there's the added factor of generational loss (every analog record is progressively a little worse in quality).

Vulnerable to Decay over Time

If you've ever looked at a VHS tape that's 10 years old, you'll understand what I'm talking about. Any physical medium (VHS, CD, DVD) is subject to decay over time. VHS tapes are the most vulnerable of the three to the ravages of time (average playable life of 10 years), but it's certain that CDs and DVDs won't last forever. Most peg the shelf life of a CD-R or DVD-R to be around 50 to 100 years, so although that's likely longer than you'll live, if you want to pass it down to your children's children, this is a consideration. Accidents and simple wear and tear can also lessen the life of your product—DVDs get scratches, and if the video is watched frequently, all those little scratches could add up to a disc that won't play.

Expense of Devices

Depending on the format you choose for your project, it might be expensive to get the devices to play it back on. VCRs are inexpensive and commonplace, and although the popularity of DVD players is exploding, they're not quite as common as VCRs yet. For a couple of years I had a DVD player in a computer hooked up to my TV set, and that's how I watched DVDs. Later on I got an Xbox and watched DVDs on it—but when I started experimenting with VCDs, I was frustrated to learn that the Xbox wouldn't play VCDs. That same night I went out in a snowstorm and bought a DVD player. If you don't have the right hardware to play back the things you're creating, it can be expensive buying it all!

Picking the Appropriate Format for Your Video

Each type of physical format for storing your video offers a tradeoff between features, quality, and cost. Here are the common formats for storing your video and what you should keep in mind when choosing them:

VHS

The oldest format of those listed here, VHS tapes are good from a compatibility standpoint, but not much else. In terms of cost, they're more expensive than a blank CD-R, but still quite inexpensive. Quality is average, and they don't have the durability of a disc-based medium. In the extremely rare case where your video is longer than a DVD can fit (roughly two hours at normal compression), a VHS tape can store extra-long projects. I believe 10-hour tapes are the longest-running VHS tapes on the market today. I should add, however, that if you have a 10-hour project, you should go back and read the chapter on editing a little closer. I consider VHS format to be a last-ditch option when the viewer can't use any other format. In three to five years, the penetration of DVD players and DVD recorders in the market will be so high that this format can finally start to fade away, but until then, be prepared to make a few VHS tapes.

VCD

Offering roughly the same quality as a VHS tape (slightly better, in my opinion), VCDs have two main advantages: They can be burned on inexpensive CD-R media, and they're compatible with most DVD players on the market (check the compatibility list at *www.vcdhelp.com* to be sure). With media costs of CD-R falling below 25 cents each, CD-R discs are a fraction of the cost of a VHS tape. CD-R discs are highly portable and durable and take up far less storage space than a VHS tape. VCD format discs can store up to 80 minutes of video (on a 700 MB CD-R), making them good choices for longer video pieces (compared to SVCD). Most software applications are capable of creating VCDs as well—the

MPEG1 encoding format is common in these applications, and several freeware VCD creation tools are on the market (like TMPGEnc). The VCD format has been around for several years, and with its genesis being in Asia, most of the Asian companies that make home electronics have full support for VCD playback.

Try This!   Have you ever wondered what those little 80-mm CD-R discs are for? People used to hand them out as "multimedia business cards," but thankfully that practice has been largely discontinued (it was a bit irritating to have to load a CD-ROM just to get some contact information). The little discs can hold 200 MB of storage, can be burned by most CD-R burners, and can be read by most DVD players. If you're distributing shorter video clips, these discs can be a novel way to do so. They can hold roughly 20 minutes of VCD video or 11 minutes of SVCD video, and their tiny size makes them even easier to carry than regular CD-R discs. It's also possible to purchase and print labels for them, so you can have a complete presentation.

SVCD

A much higher quality format than VCD, SVCD has many of the same advantages: low disc cost, portable, durable. At maximum quality, an SVCD holds roughly 35 minutes of video (700 MB CD-R), and if you push the quality down you can squeeze 60 minutes onto the disc. At maximum quality, an SVCD is very difficult to visually distinguish from a DVD—it uses the same MPEG2 file format, but at a lower bit rate. One of the key disadvantages of the SVCD format is that it's not as widely usable in DVD players as VCD is. It's a newer standard, and although I hope it will be supported more fully in the coming years, as DVD-burning adoption rates take off, that might not be the case. Another issue with SVCDs is that not all video-editing applications support creating the file format needed. Ulead products are particularly supportive of SVCD, but many applications I looked at didn't support SVCD creation and had no immediate plans to do so. All that said, if your home DVD player supports SVCD, and you have the right software tools to create them, SVCDs are a good choice for quality recordings without the cost of a DVD burner or DVD media. The excellent Main Concept MPEG Encoder is a good choice for creating SVCDs (*www.mainconcept.com*), and if you're looking for something less expensive, the TMPGEnc Plus encoder does a great job of encoding SVCDs (*www.pegasys-inc.com*).

Try This! If your DVD player doesn't support SVCDs but does support VCDs, there's a clever way to trick your DVD burner into thinking the SVCD is actually a VCD. It involves using TMPGEnc to change the header information (the index at the beginning of the disc) into a VCD header, while leaving the SVCD video alone. Since SVCD MPEG2 is similar to DVD MPEG2, it's usually the header that causes the problems, not the file itself. Complete details on this technique can be found here: *http://www.geocities.com/newestmoviesencode/dvdvcd.*

DVD-R and DVD+R

The DVD format is currently the reigning champ in quality and a close second in capacity. With a bit rate of up to 9800 Kbps, the quality of a DVD is incredible. Images are crisp, motion is fluid, audio is perfect—no other format can touch it. Capacity hovers around the two-hour mark (and you can get close to double that if you lower the quality), making it second only to VHS in terms of maximum capacity. The DVD-R format has a slight edge in compatibility with stand-alone DVD players, with VCDHelp.com estimating that roughly 85 percent of all DVD players on the market can read DVD-R format discs. That number falls to around 65 percent if you're using the rewritable format (DVD-RW). DVD+RW has slightly less compatibility, at around 80 percent, but slightly better rewritable compatibility, at roughly 70 percent. The downside to DVD-burning formats right now is twofold: The players are stuck at around 2x burn speeds (which isn't terribly fast), although a 4x Pioneer burner is coming soon. DVD media is also expensive. If you buy generic-brand media, the cost can get very low, but there are risks with compatibility. The reasons are complex, but they involve the type of dyes used on the discs and the overall reflectivity of the discs.

Tip   When you're just starting to experiment with burning DVDs, make sure to use the rewritable formats—it can get extremely expensive if you're burning normal –R or +R discs and having to redo the burns for whatever reason. The rewritable disc formats can be used and erased up to 1000 times, so one "experimenting" disc should be enough.

> **Tip**　Before buying a new DVD player, make sure to check the box for VCD, SVCD, DVD-R, and DVD+R compatibility. Most modern DVD players support all these formats, but you don't want to get home and find out the player doesn't support the type of disc you want to burn. If you'd like to do your research before stepping foot in the store, the VCDHelp DVD player compatibility list is a great help (*www.vcdhelp.com/dvdplayers.php*).

What Software Is Available for Video Burning Projects?

In a sluggish computer industry, DVD/VCD burning is a bright, shining light of hope for profits—because consumers are jumping all over the chance to make their own video discs. Because of this, many packages are available for burning VCDs, SVCDs, and DVDs. Some are strictly burners, some help you convert the files, and some are integrated into more full-featured editing applications. Pinnacle Studio 8, for example, has an integrated VCD/SVCD/DVD-burning application and includes full *DVD menu* creation tools. Here are a few of the more popular ones on the market today.

> **Lingo**　The *DVD Menu* is the interface that the viewer interacts with. A typical DVD menu offers choices such as starting the video, jumping to a specific chapter, and, in the case of advanced menus created with the more expensive tools I mention below, the ability to switch between language tracks, view subtitles, and select the audio type (like Dolby Digital).

Sonic MyDVD 4 Plus

One of the more full-featured burning products, Sonic (*www.sonic.com*) dramatically revamped the user interface (Figure 10-1) of this product with version 4.0 (version 3.0 was confusing to use). One of the more unique features is the "Direct To DVD" wizard—it allows you to connect a video source and immediately burn it to DVD with no interim steps. This is useful only if your video is already edited, of course, but it's a great innovation to make the process of going from videotape to DVD a little faster. MyDVD 4 includes professionally designed menu templates and the ability to create both traditional DVD videos and photo slideshows with digital stills. The addition of motion menus is a welcome surprise to an entry-level package like this: Motion menus allow you to have a video clip playing in the background of your menu or even have video playing inside the buttons for each scene. Very cool!

Figure 10-1 Sonic MyDVD 4 is a great entry-level package for video and photo burning.

One of Sonic's other inventions is the OpenDVD specification. OpenDVD allows users to go back and change elements on the DVD and reburn the disc (if it's an RW disc) or burn a new one. This is extremely useful because it means you can start creating a "family holidays" DVD and over the years keep adding to it—a big advantage over burning a disc every time. Currently, it can create VCD and DVD format discs, not SVCD. It's a good value, but check to see if your DVD burner came with a version of MyDVD—it's very commonly bundled with DVD burners.

Caution Although your DVD-R disc might have 4.7 GB written on the package, the reality is that you won't be able to fit more than 4.37 GB worth of video and audio on it. The reason? Technically, the term "kilobyte" means 1000 bytes. However, in the computer industry, one KB is actually 1024 bytes, so this means that one GB (which should be 1 billion bytes) is actually 1,024,000,000 bytes. The net result is that you always end up with less space than you think you should have (2.4 percent less per GB). So why do they mark 4.7 GB on the package? Because 4.7 GB looks better than 4.37 GB. This marketing sleight-of-hand is also present in any other sort of storage: CD-Rs, CompactFlash memory cards, Secure Digital memory cards, and all hard drives. Ultimately it's a marketing trick designed to fool consumers, but now that you know the secret, you won't be fooled again!

Ulead DVD MovieFactory

One of the heavy hitters in the multimedia world, Ulead has a huge array of products that address the video and photo worlds (curiously, they've stayed out of the audio arena). When the prices of DVD burners began to drop, Ulead was ready—they rapidly had several products on the market for consumers to burn their video projects with. DVD MovieFactory is an entry-level product made for basic projects. It offers some basic capture abilities, which is great if you don't need transitions or any special effects in your video. You can capture video directly from any video source (with the appropriate hardware, of course), trim the video, and the software automatically creates chapter thumbnails for each scene. I found the product very simple to use and the user interface easy to figure out (Figure 10-2), and the quality of the encoding was good enough for my uses. I should note, however, that I didn't check their site for patches when I first installed it, so my first burn attempt resulted in a locked-up computer. Always check for patches on the vendor Web site before first using a product!

Caution   Be sure to download the trial version before buying this software. Ulead software is fantastic and easy to use, but it has some curious issues with not always working with the hardware it's supposed to. Their tech support is poor, often dishing out responses like "Reinstall Windows" as a solution to the problem. Even if it says your CD-R or DVD-R is supported, download the trial and make sure it works with your gear.

Figure 10-2 Adding a new scene to your video is simple—a few clicks and you're done.

An electronic version is available from *www.ulead.com* (the trial version is available too), making this one of the least expensive applications I've seen that burns videos to disc. The support for VCD, SVCD, and DVD is a welcome addition, making this a package that I strongly recommend for beginners.

Tip If you're interested in creating photo slideshows in VCD format, check out Ulead DVD PictureShow (*http://www.ulead.com*). It's a fantastic application, and very inexpensive.

Nero Burning ROM 5.5

Created by Ahead Software (*www.nero.com*) and not simply a "video burning application," Nero Burning ROM 5.5 (Figure 10-3) brings some interesting things to the table. Long held to be the best CD burning application on the market by computer experts, Nero has added some useful wizards to make burning CDs and DVDs even easier. Nero burns CDs easily, quickly, and, most important of all, with rock-solid stability. Competing CD burning programs often have the nasty habit of causing general system instability. Primarily a CD burning program, if there's a CD format out there, Nero can burn it—audio CD, mixed-mode CD, VCD, SVCD, bootable CD, International Standards Organization (ISO), and more. Nero doesn't include MPEG2 support out of the box, however. The electronic version is quite affordable for all the power that it offers.

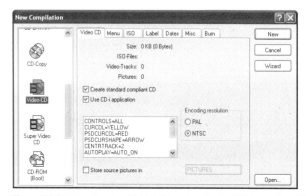

Figure 10-3 Nero Burning ROM 5.5 is a burning toolkit for audio, video, and data.

If you want to burn SVCDs, you can purchase an electronic version of their MPEG-2/SVCD plug-in. If DVDs are your goal, you'll need the MPEG-2/DVD encoder, which as of this writing hasn't been released (I assume the price will be similar to their SVCD plug-in). It seems a little strange for Ahead Software to break apart the encoder like that, but I suppose if you want only to encode SVCDs, it's a cheap add-on.

Ahead Software's newest product, NeroVision Express, looks like a strong contender. Targeted at people who want to burn VCDs, SVCDs, and DVDs, Nero-Vision Express offers simple trimming of video clips, automatic scene detection for chapters, and menu templates that can be customized, and the preview mode is handy for checking your product. A demo version will be available for evaluation when the product is released later this year.

> **Tip**   More than likely, your CD-R came with software called EZCD Creator Basic from Roxio. There's a "Platinum" upgrade from Roxio that adds the ability to create photo slideshows and VCDs, so if you're interested in enhancing the software you already own, go to *www.roxio.com* and look at the upgrade.

Ulead DVD Workshop

This is a professional tool and gives professional-quality results. Aimed at the Prosumer market, this is a flexible tool capable of generating some interesting DVD menus. It also supports VCD and SVCD formats, making it useful for generating projects onto the less expensive CD-R media. DVD Workshop has integrated video capture capabilities, and while you're capturing the video you can convert it directly to MPEG1 or MPEG2 as part of the capture—this saves hard drive space. The menu creation system supports motion menus (embedded video clips), text effects, and highlight color customization. Unlike its less expensive sibling, DVD MovieFactory, DVD Workshop supports still photos and lets you quickly create slideshows accompanied by audio tracks. The software package comes with templates and backgrounds, giving you professional results quickly (Figure 10-4).

Another strong feature is the built-in preview mode. Before burning your video project, you can use the preview interface and on-screen remote control to work your way through the DVD, making sure that everything is hyperlinked correctly. A free trial is available on the Ulead Web site, so take the software for a spin.

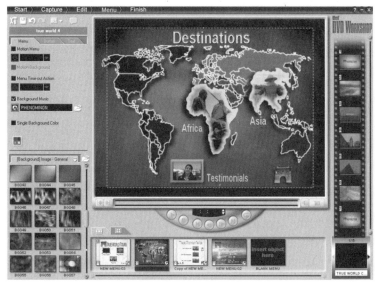

Figure 10-4 DVD Workshop is loaded with templates and backgrounds.

Sonic DVDit! PE 2.5

Sonic's mid-range product for DVD authoring is DVDit!. The "PE" stands for professional edition of the software. The SE version (Standard Edition) is half the price and differs from the PE version in that it can't work with Dolby Digital audio (either importing or encoding) and lacks widescreen 16:9 support. Both packages are offerings aimed squarely at the Prosumer or professional market, offering features that most average consumers won't be interested in. The user interface is quite intuitive (Figure 10-5), and the application is easy to use.

Figure 10-5 Despite being a high-end product, DVDit! is easy to use.

One of the strongest features of DVDit! is the ability to convert audio and video formats to DVD-compliant formats. Lower-end packages typically give you an "incompatible format" error, but DVDit! has the ability to transcode most files to the correct DVD format.

Sonic ReelDVD 3.0

Have you ever wondered what software the Hollywood studios use to create their DVDs? Well, about 80 percent of them use software created by Sonic. I didn't realize how significant a player Sonic was in the DVD realm until I started working on this book, but after a conference call with them, I grew to realize what a significant market presence they had. Sonic ReelDVD 3.0 (Figure 10-6) is a high-end product aimed at corporate and independent video professionals. This package isn't for the casual user—if you're buying this package, you're either going to be making money from your DVDs or you have a departmental budget to spend on it. Believe it or not, ReelDVD isn't their most high-end product: Sonic Scenarist is the industry standard application for creating most of the DVDs on the market today, but its "little brother," ReelDVD, can do a capable job at that task as well.

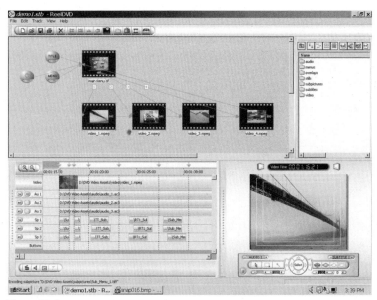

Figure 10-6 ReelDVD 3.0 is aimed at the professional market.

This product is ideal for professionals because it combines Sonic's Hollywood standard DVD formatting with a friendly, easy user interface. A unique feature of this product is the ability to internationalize your video by including multiple audio and subtitle tracks (up to three). So you can have an English film with French or German subtitles and have it be a hit all over Europe, as well as in North America! ReelDVD lets you record to DVD-R, DVD+R, DVD-RW, CD-R/RW, and DLT tapes. So if you have a preference, chances are you'll still be able to record using it. Finally, because you can internationalize your content and record it to so many different medias, you can distribute your videos on the most compatible DVDs to wherever you are, which can then be viewed on a wide range of set-top or PC-based DVD players.

Burning Your Project to Disc

If you've been working along with me throughout this book, as we're nearing the end you should have some video footage that you've recorded, captured to your computer, and edited to perfection. Now it's time to roll up your sleeves and burn your first video disc! For this example, I'm going to keep things simple and use Ulead MovieFactory—it's an easy package to install and start using within a few minutes. We're going to create a simple menu system as well. Most video burning packages are fairly standard in the way they work, so you should be able to follow along even if you don't have the exact software. You can download the free 30-day trial from *www.ulead.com* if you'd like to match my exact steps. You'll also need a blank CD in your CD-R and at least one video clip, preferably in DV AVI format, or two clips if you want to create the menu. This might seem a little daunting because it's so many steps, but the software is quite intuitive, and I'm confident you'll be able to follow along.

1   When you first start DVD MovieFactory, the splash screen appears (Figure 10-7). Because our video is in DV AVI format, we can't just burn it to the disc—we need to convert it first. To do so, click the Capture Video button. It really should say "Capture And Convert Video," because this is where the video gets transcoded from AVI to MPEG. Once you click Capture Video, the software automatically loads the next application.

Figure 10-7 We're starting up DVD MovieFactory for our first burn project.

2   The Capture interface now loads. It should put you in the Edit tab,
         unless you have a camera connected, in which case simply click the
         word Edit. Down in the bottom-left corner there's a small black file
         folder (Figure 10-8)—when you hover over it, it says Insert Video Files.
         Click it.

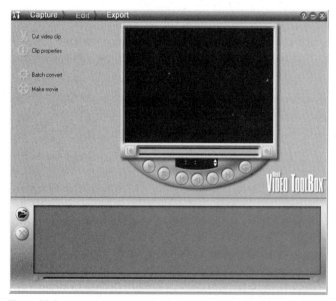

Figure 10-8 We load our video into the Capture application to convert it.

3   A new Open Video File window appears, giving us the option to pick from a huge variety of formats: AVI, Animated GIF files, Quicktime (MOV), MPEG, WMV, and ASF. I'm going to select an AVI file that I captured from a VHS tape using Pinnacle Studio Deluxe. The resolution is 720 x 480, the same as a DV AVI file. If you'd like to learn more about the video clip you've selected, such as how long it is and what codec was used for the video compression, you can click the Info button. Once you've selected the video you want, click Open (Figure 10-9).

Figure 10-9 You select your video clip to be transcoded.

4   The next screen shows your clip as a thumbnail down at the bottom of the screen, and it also appears in the large preview window (it's not in Figure 10-10 due to Microsoft Windows "security" regarding video files). If we were using one video file, we'd click the Export tab in the upper right. Since we have multiple clips, in order to create our menu, we'll import them using this same interface, and finally Export when all the clips are in place.

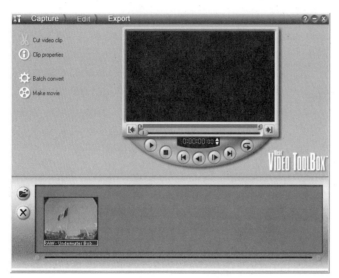

Figure 10-10 Your video clip appears as a thumbnail at the bottom of this screen.

5 Now that we're in the Export tab (Figure 10-11), you'll see some buttons on the left side. The three top buttons (Create DVD Title, Create SVCD Title, and Create VCD Title) are the ones you'll most commonly use. Since my video clips are fairly short (3 to 5 minutes) and I want the maximum quality on a CD-R, I'm going to click the Create SVCD Title button.

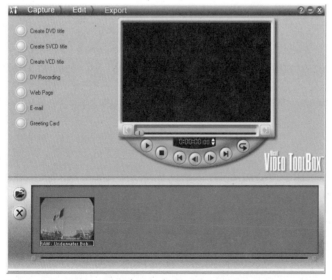

Figure 10-11 In the Export tab, you choose the type of project you want to create.

6   A warning window appears, looking very much like Figure 10-12.
Essentially this message says that the file we selected isn't in the right
format for an SVCD, so the file will have to be transcoded to a new format. Click OK.

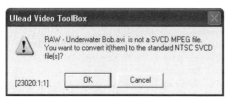

Figure 10-12 A warning message tells you that the file isn't in the right format.

7   Figure 10-13 shows the Save As window that appears. Simply select the
location where you want to save the file, type in the name you want it
to have, and then click Save.

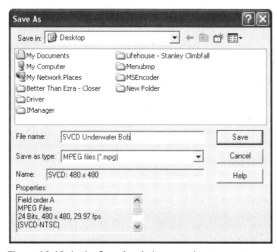

Figure 10-13 In the Save As window, you give a name to your soon to be transcoded file.

8   Once you've clicked Save, the transcoding process of converting the
AVI file to an MPEG2 SVCD file begins. How long this takes depends
heavily on your computer's overall power and the length of the clip.
Even on the speedy Intel Pentium 4 2.53 GHz processor–based system
I'm using, it took around 15 minutes to convert the files. Figure 10-14
shows the progress bar—there's not much you can do other than sit
back and wait at this point. Multiple clips are converted in order.

Figure 10-14 When you see the Converting progress indicator, it's time to take a break and let it work!

9 Once the file(s) has been converted, DVD MovieFactory automatically takes you to the next step, which is to build the menu for the DVD. In the DVD I'm building I have two video clips, so a simple menu will work best. Since both clips are fairly short, I'm not going to create chapter markers. Figure 10-15 shows the menu-building interface. If you see only one of your clips there, click Add MPEG File and add your other files—remember that they have to be SVCD-compliant for this example. You can click each clip to see the file details, including the clip's format. Once the thumbnails and video selection are to your liking, click Next.

Tip   You'll notice that the thumbnail of my clip on the left is black. The thumbnail preview, by default, shows the first frame in the video file. Since my video starts out with a black frame, this makes for a boring thumbnail. Changing it is easy: right-click the thumbnail, select Change Thumbnail, and select a new frame.

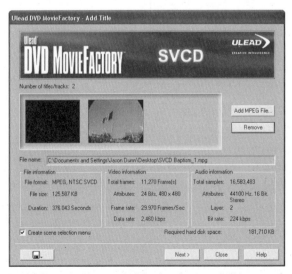

Figure 10-15 In the menu-building interface, you build a menu for your SVCD.

10 This is the interface where we add scenes (Figure 10-16). By default, each of our two video clips will be part of the menu we're creating. The Select Title/Track drop-down menu at the top allows us to switch between each clip. On the left side (the Scene List) we have the thumbnail of the video currently in our menu. As above, you can right-click the thumbnail to change the default image. If my video clips were longer, I would use this interface to create chapter markers by using the VCR controls to find the scene I wanted to mark and clicking the Add button. Each of these scenes would then be a chapter that you could select after selecting the main video. It's a little confusing, I know, but since we don't want to go down that path right now, the default thumbnails are just fine. We have two video clips, which means we'll have two choices on our menu. Perfect! Click Next to continue.

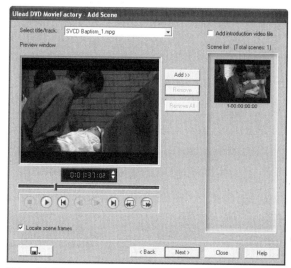

Figure 10-16 You use the Add Scene interface to add scenes to your video menu.

11 Here's where we really get creative: The Select Menu Template is where we pick the elements for our menu (Figure 10-17). You'll see thumbnail images of your two video clips, and the default template will have loaded. In the upper-left corner there's a drop-down menu where you're able to select from several categories of menu templates: Business, Classic, Cool, Cute, and Romance. Each category has half a dozen or so choices. Double-clicking each template applies the template. Figure 10-17 shows the default template—let's pick another one.

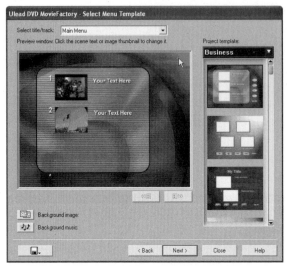

Figure 10-17 In the Select Menu Template, you select the elements for your menu.

12 The template I've chosen is under the Classic section: palm trees and a sandy beach (Figure 10-18). You'll notice that there's text on the menu: one headline and one line under each thumbnail. There are also buttons at the bottom of the menu for changing the background image and adding background music. Let's customize our menu a little more.

Figure 10-18 We've chosen a template showing palm trees and a beach.

13 The text is simple to change—just click the text element, and a window pops up where you can change it. Depending on your background, you can also change the text color. If you wanted to change the background to something completely custom, you can click the Background Image button and select any BMP, JPEG, or TIFF image on your hard drive. With one DVD I made of my own wedding, I selected a nice photo of Ashley and myself walking down some stairs—it made a beautiful background. I like the palm tree scene for this video, so I'm going to leave it. I've changed all my text items (Figure 10-19), so now it's time to customize the menu with some music. When you click the Background Music button, a simple Load Audio window opens where you can select from any MP3 or WAV files on your computer. If you have multiple menus (like chapter menus) you can select unique music for each menu. Figure 10-19 shows my customized menu so far. It's done! Click Next to advance to the next screen.

Figure 10-19 You can customize the menu with text and music.

Tip   If you're worried about losing your work so far, in the bottom-left corner of every screen in DVD MovieFactory there's a small disk icon. Click this icon and select Save Project. Alternatively, you can press Control+S at any point to save it.

14 Now we come to the critical stage: Playback Simulation. This interface allows you to preview your video disc exactly as your DVD player will see it (Figure 10-20). Click the Play button, and the DVD goes to the menu we just created above and the music starts playing. Each video thumbnail has a small number beside it—clicking the corresponding number on the virtual remote starts that video playing. This is the stage where you check for any sort of errors, so spend a few minutes making sure everything looks correct. If it does, click Next.

Figure 10-20 In this stage, you preview the video disc and check for errors.

15 Now that we've finished our SVCD project, it's time to burn it to a CD. The window shown in Figure 10-21 is where you configure the output options. The default settings should be sufficient, although if you have multiple burners (CD and DVD) you'll want to specify the correct drive in the CD/DVD Recorder drop-down list. It tells you how much space is on the disc you have in the drive and how much space the project will take up. Click Next if all the settings are correct.

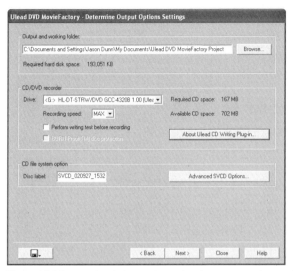

Figure 10-21 Use this window to determine the output options and settings for the CD burn.

16 The final stage is where the SVCD is actually burned. The Record To CD box should be checked by default. The Create SVCD button starts the recording (it says Create VCD or Create DVD, as appropriate). Click it. The burn process will now begin (Figure 10-22).

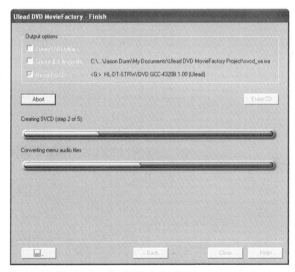

Figure 10-22 Burning the SVCD is the final step.

17 The CD goes through a few steps—it has to convert the MP3 to an SVCD-compliant audio format and then burn the data to the CD. Depending on the speed of your CD burner and the length of the files you're burning, this step can take as little as one minute or as much as an hour (or more). When the SVCD is completed, the disc ejects and you're finished!

Note   Before deleting your source footage, make sure that you test the video disc in a DVD player. It's quite possible that the software will report a successful burn, but when you test the disc it will be full of glitches. This happened to me with Pinnacle Studio 8–it reported a successful burn, but the resulting disc had audio and video that skipped.

Burning a Video Using a Stand-Alone Recorder

One of the more interesting home electronics developments over the past couple of years has been the emergence of the "digital VCR"—devices that use discs like CD-R and DVD-R instead of VHS tapes. It's a logical step—VHS tapes break down over time, have poor recording quality, and finding that one show on a six hour tape can be a frustrating task. The Panasonic DMR-E30 (*www.panasonic.com*) is one such device, and after using it for a few days, I had a hard time shipping it back to Panasonic. The DMR-E30 (Figure 10-23) records to DVD-R discs or DVD-RAM discs. DVD-RAM is the preferred format, because it can be erased and written to 100,000 times. For archival purposes and sharing with others who have DVD players, the single-use DVD-R discs are a good choice. Boasting up to 12 hours of recording on a DVD-RAM disc in EP mode, it's easy to see how devices like this will eclipse VCRs over the next decade. The DMR-E30 has all the features you've come to expect from a normal VCR like VCRPlus+ for easier recording, one touch recording and playback, and even has the ability to record a TV show and play back another at the same time—impressive!

Figure 10-23 The Panasonic DMR-E30 allows you to record video straight to DVD.

I performed a little experiment with the DMR-E30: I took the Canon GL2 DV camera, connected it to the front input panel on the DMR-E30, and connected the DVD recorder to my TV set. Panasonic keenly understood that in order for this technology to be successful, it would need to be as simple to record as using a VCR. It was exactly that—I pressed the Record button, watched the video coming from the Canon GL2, and when I pressed Stop it finalized the disc (making it playable on other DVD players) and then ejected it. The entire process was incredibly easy, and if you're looking for a very simple way to get your projects on to DVD, this may be a good solution. It doesn't give you as much control as a DVD-R in your PC, but in terms of sheer simplicity, it works nicely. The DMR-E30 is a fairly pricey component, but if you're looking for a new DVD player that will record as well as it plays back video, this is a very nice solution.

Tip If you're looking for a DVD recorder that combines the elements of a PVR with a DVD recorder, Panasonic's DMR-HS2 includes the features of the DMR-E30 but adds a 40 GB hard drive into the mix. This allows you to store up to 52 hours of video (EP mode). More information is available at *www.panasonic.com*.

Putting Your Video Back onto Tape

If the people you want to share the video with don't have a DVD player, you'll have to use good old VHS. Depending on the quality of the VCR doing the recording, quality can range anywhere from good to downright awful. There's no way to know what kind of results you're going to get until you give it a try. Always use a fresh, blank tape, and, if possible, use a *head cleaner* for the VCR to make sure it's in good shape.

Lingo A *head cleaner* is typically a special VHS tape that is designed to clean off the gunk that might have built up on the VCR's read/write heads. You can usually purchase head cleaners any-place blank VHS tapes are sold.

When going from digital to analog, there are two basic ways: an analog break-out box attached to your computer or using the DV camera as a transfer mechanism. The former requires you to have special hardware and can be fairly tricky to configure and get working properly. The latter, using the DV camera as a transfer mechanism, is your best bet for both simplicity and quality, so that's what I recommend you do.

You'll need to take a few basic steps to accomplish this, and I'm going to keep them generic in nature so you can apply them to whatever software you're using. Before beginning, you'll want to have your DV camera ready with a fully charged battery, the DV AVI file edited, rendered, and ready to go on your computer, and your VCR with a blank tape (and a TV set connected to that VCR). Let's go!

1   The first step is to get the digital file on your computer onto the DV
camera. I suggest having a fresh tape in the DV camera for maximum
quality. The method of getting the DV AVI involves using your software to record that signal back onto the camera. Whatever program
you used to capture the video should also have the option to record it
back again—both muvee autoProducer Cobalt and Pinnacle Studio 8
can record DV AVI back down to the camcorder. Connect the DV camera to your computer through FireWire, and record the DV AVI onto it.

2   Once the video is on the DV camera, give it a quick preview to make
sure it transferred okay.

3   Connect your DV camera to your VCR. DV cameras always come with
a cable to connect to other video components—one end connects to
the camera, and the other end should be RCA cables (one for video,
two for audio). Connect these cables using the same procedure
described in Chapter 6, "Capturing Your Video," but you'll want to connect them to the IN ports on the VCR. The signal will be coming out of
the DV camera and into the VCR.

4   Once you have everything connected, test the signal by pressing Play
on the DV camera and seeing if the signal shows up on the TV set connected to the VCR (don't hit Record yet). If you connected the RCA
cables to ports on the front of the VCR, this means it's usually an auxiliary input (the main inputs are on the back of the VCR). You might
need to switch the channel to below two—with most VCRs and TV
sets, in order to view what's coming on an auxiliary input, the VCR
needs to be on the "auxiliary channel." It should be one or two channels below channel two.

5   Once you verify that the signal from the DV camera is coming through
without any problems (audio and video), press Stop on the DV camera
and rewind the tape.

6   Press Record on the VCR, wait three seconds, and then press Play on
the DV camera. If everything is configured correctly, the VCR will
record that signal. There's no automated way to stop the VCR when the
DV camera is finished, so you'll want to be standing by to hit Stop at
the right time. It's best to hit Stop on the VCR before hitting Stop on the
DV camera.

7 You're done! You should now have an analog version of your digital video. The quality won't be quite as high as it could be if you went with a digital format, but now your VCR-based friends and family can watch your masterpiece.

The Finishing Touches

Once you've finished your disc, it's time to add a little personal flair to it. Sure, you could just take a black Sharpie marker and write "Family Vacation" on it, but what fun is that? Using some simple software, you can create a great-looking label and jewel case insert. Here are a few pointers to get you going in the right direction.

Disc Labels

Adding a customized disc label adds a nice touch of class to any project. The good news is that they're very simple to make. Go to a local office supply store (Office Depot, Office Max) and look for CD labels. They're typically sold in kits, and inside the kit you'll get blank labels, some sort of tool to apply the labels, and software to create them. Avery is the king of this industry, and I've been quite pleased with the quality of their labels. Their software leaves something to be desired, but it's fairly straightforward to use—you can add text and pictures and change fonts on the disc label. There are third-party software tools, like Ulead Photo Express 4.0, that allow you to create more advanced disc labels if you want to move beyond the Avery software (Ulead PhotoImpact 8 also supports label printing). The labels today come in a wide variety of colors and textures—basic white, high-gloss white, clear, and even metallic tones! Most are designed for inkjet printers—if you only have a laser printer, you'll want to make sure you get the right kind of labels. Inkjet labels can melt inside a laser printer if you're not careful!

Caution   I don't recommend that you put labels on your DVDs unless those labels are designed specifically for DVDs. I've seen several discussions spring up on the Web about problems with labels coming off inside the DVD player. It's difficult to nail down why it happens more often with DVDs than CDs, but I think it relates to the fact that DVDs are slightly thicker than CDs (so the label might catch on something inside the DVD player) and that DVDs are watched longer than a VCD or SVCD. The longer a video disc spins, the more pressure is placed on the label, and the more heat is generated. In my experience it seems safe to use labels on VCDs and SVCDs as long as they're high-quality labels.

Note   If you're interested in printing on your DVDs, you have two choices. You can send your DVDs to a commercial printing agency that specializes in printing on DVDs (*www.digidocsystems.com*) or you can purchase a special type of printer designed to print on CDs and DVDs. One of the few I could find was the Primera Signature IV, sold by CD Printers (*www.cd-printers.net*), and priced for the professional.

VHS Labels

VHS labels are a little more difficult to create, if only because in all my online searches I was unable to find a quick source of VHS labels for consumers. Many companies sold VHS labels, but all were sold in huge quantities. Label king Avery doesn't seem to carry VHS labels (I couldn't find them on *www.avery.com*), so your best bet is to pick Avery shipping labels that are close in size to VHS labels. The bigger label on the face of the VHS tape should be 3.1" wide and 1.75" tall. The long, skinny label for the side should be around 5.75" long and 0.8" wide. You should have no trouble finding the taller labels, but you'll have to settle for something "close" with the side label. The nice thing about Avery labels is that even if the labels don't include the Avery software, Microsoft Word XP has templates for every Avery label on the market. There's also a piece of software from Broderbund called The Print Shop CD Label Creator that has templates for VHS labels.

Jewel Case Inserts and Cover

This is where you can really have some fun! If you don't mind doing a little manual trimming, you can use high-gloss paper and templates in Microsoft Publisher to create high-quality CD covers with photos and text. The Avery software I mentioned above includes the ability to print basic jewel case inserts (the back insert that has flip-up sides), and Avery makes some high-quality jewel case inserts as part of their After Burner label series. Available in white matte and glossy, both enable a quality inkjet printer like the Epson C80 to create stunning covers and inserts.

Video on Portable Devices

What happens if you want to take your video with you? There's the obvious solution, such as a laptop that would play your video files off the hard drive or the CD/DVD drive, but what if you want something even more portable? Even the smallest laptops are fairly large when used strictly for video playback, and battery life is always a real challenge. Luckily for you, some very clever companies are doing some innovative things out there. There are two main categories of devices that I looked at: devices that played video off a disc (CD-R or DVD-R) and devices that played files digitally off of internal memory or a storage card. One of my favorite devices for digital media is the Pocket PC—I carry one with me all the time (and run a Web site at *www.pocketpcthoughts.com* all about Pocket PCs), so it's easy to load it up with movies, music, and photos to show others. When I travel, I don't bring a CD player or DVD player with me—only the Pocket PC. There's a special way you'll need to optimize your video for the Pocket PC, so I'm going to give you a quick step-by-step procedure to optimize your video for this device.

The Pocket PC

Pocket PCs are made by a wide variety of manufacturers (Toshiba, hp, Asus, Casio, and others) and run an operating system called Windows CE. Created by Microsoft specifically for small devices, Windows CE is quite different from your desktop operating system: It can be installed in as little as 500 KB of storage space, and only applications designed for Windows CE can run on a device using that operating system. Pocket PCs range in price from as low as $249 (Toshiba e310) up to nearly $750 (the iPAQ 3970 shown in Figure 10-24).

Figure 10-24 The iPAQ Pocket PC is made by Compaq.

You can use Pocket PCs, much like most PDAs, to keep track of your contacts, calendar, tasks, and notes—they synchronize with Microsoft Outlook, giving you access to your data on the go. But unlike most other PDAs on the
market today, Pocket PCs are powerful multimedia devices—with CPUs running
at up to 400 MHz, 64 MB of RAM, and storage card expansion reaching 1 GB,
carrying one of these little devices really is like carrying a PC in your pocket.
They come with a built-in version of Windows Media Player (Figure 10-25), so
they're capable of playing WMV (video) and WMA (audio) out of the box. If you
already own a Pocket PC, but would like to put some video on it, here's how.

Figure 10-25 Pocket PCs come with a built-in version of Windows Media Player.

Caution   At the time of this writing, Microsoft didn't supply me with the beta of the Windows
Media Player 8.5, the version that has support for 9 Series multimedia. Until that player comes out
(hopefully by the time you're reading this book), the file created in this step-by-step procedure
won't be playable on a Pocket PC. But rather than give you a step-by-step for the old encoder that
won't be available in a few months, I wanted to give you a method that would work with the powerful 9 Series Encoder.

---

1   When you start the 9 Series Encoder, the New Session wizard appears
(Figure 10-26). Select Convert File and click OK.

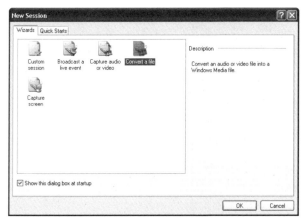

Figure 10-26 We want to convert a file for use on a Pocket PC.

2   The next screen brings us to the File Selection, where we simply browse to the file we want to convert (Figure 10-27). The 9 Series Encoder can accept a variety of files, including AVI, MPEG, ASF, and others. Because this file will be quite small in size, you can leave the Output File location alone.

Figure 10-27 In the File Selection window, you select the file you want to encode and the location in which it should be saved.

3   The Content Distribution step is where we select how the file will be used. Pocket PC is on the list (Figure 10-28), so select it and click Next.

Figure 10-28 In the Content Distribution window, you select the Pocket PC preset for content distribution type.

4   The encoding options are fairly limited for the Pocket PC profile. There are two choices under the Video drop-down menu (Figure 10-29): Pocket PC Standard Skin (which is a video file 208 x 160 in resolution) and Pocket PC Widescreen. The widescreen mode seems to be the most appealing—by turning the Pocket PC sideways, you get an aspect ratio very similar to a movie theaters. The widescreen output resolution is 320 x 240, which means it will play full screen on the Pocket PC. The frame rate of 20 is sufficient, the CD quality audio is our only choice for audio, and with a total bit rate of 259.03 Kbps we should be able to store quite a bit of video on a storage card (a one hour movie would take up around 116 MB).

Figure 10-29 Use the drop-down menu to select the encoding options for your Pocket PC file.

5   Next we have the Display Information screen. This is the information that will be included in your file. On the Pocket PC you can examine the properties of a file and see the author and the date it was created. Figure 10-30 shows me using my favorite clip yet again—Underwater Bob!

Figure 10-30   We enter display information so we can remember what our clip was about if amnesia strikes.

6   The Settings Review shown in Figure 10-31 is simply a review of all the settings we've entered so far. If it all looks good, click Finish by default, and the encoder starts working.

Figure 10-31   The Settings Review screen gives us one final look at our choices.

7   Once the encoder starts, it's time to get up and stretch—it might take a while. Thankfully, because the resolution is quite low on the Pocket PC, it won't take as long as a more high-resolution clip. Figure 10-32 shows the encoder in action—you can monitor the bit rate as it encodes if you wish.

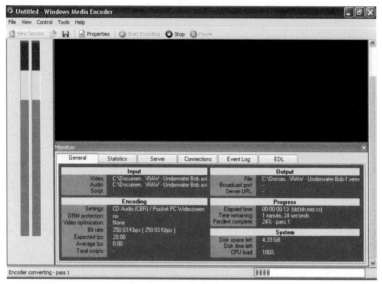

Figure 10-32 The encoder is crunching away at our file.

8   The Encoding Results window (Figure 10-33) appears when the encoding is complete. It tells you several things, the most important of which is the file size. My 607 MB AVI file has become a svelte 5.79 MB file that will fit easily on any Pocket PC.

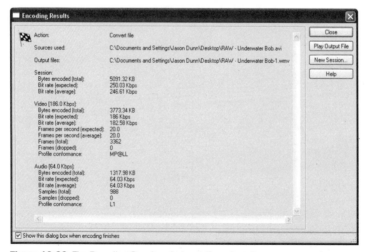

Figure 10-33 The Encoding Results window tells us how the process went.

9   That's it! You can perform this procedure with any video file you want to optimize for your Pocket PC. Don't worry too much about converting from the source material—you can convert from an MPEG or other compressed format because the degradation that might be visible on a large TV won't be noticeable on the small Pocket PC screen.

The PoGo Products Flipster

As digital media becomes more popular, there's a demand for new ways to carry and share that media. The PoGo Flipster (Figure 10-34) addresses this demand in a few interesting ways. Although it looks like a cell phone, the Flipster doesn't have any built-in communication abilities. The Flipster could best be described as a mobile multimedia device—it allows you to take audio, video, and photos with you. As a video player, it supports video files in ASF and WMV formats. Audio file formats supported include MP3, WMA, and AAC. If you want to carry pictures on the device, they can be in JPG, BMP, or GIF format.

The Flipster has a 2.5" LCD screen, but I found the resolution of the screen to be fairly poors—on-screen text looked quite jagged. Overall I liked the size and weight of the Flipster, and it had simple controls. The biggest hurdle I had was with the software. Despite installing the software on two different computers, I wasn't able to get it to works—it crashed when I tried to load it on each machine.

Figure 10-34 The Flipster is a clever little multimedia playback device.

The operating system on the Flipster is Windows CE, the same base OS that the Pocket PC has. Unlike the Pocket PC, there doesn't seem to be any third-party software. That's not a significant limitation, however, as the Flipster comes with everything you need out of the box. I found the Flipster to be a very interesting device in theory, but the big obstacle is the price: The 128 MB version is more expensive than a Pocket PC that would enable you to do even more. If they were able to cut the price in half and improve their software, the Flipster would be a truly compelling device. It has all the right pieces needed to easily carry and share your videos with other people, but a few too many rough edges for my taste.

Panasonic DVD-LV50 Portable DVD Player

Once you've created a video masterpiece, burned it to DVD or CD, you'll want to share it with others. But what if they don't have a DVD player, or you don't have a laptop? The solution is a portable DVD player. Popular with both business travelers and kids in the back seat of a car on a long trip, portable DVD players only do one thing, but they do it well.

The DVD-LV50 from Panasonic is a portable DVD player that plays normal DVDs, DVD-Rs and DVD-RAMs, as well as CDs containing VCD and SVCD video formats. I had no problem playing back an SVCD disc I created myself, and it worked well with the DVDs and VCDs I used for testing. It also supports MP3 playback, so you can use it as an oversized portable music player. Speaking of size, the DVD-LV50 is quite small (Figure 10-35)—it sits easily in the palm of your hand, and the 5" LCD screen has several positions for easy viewing. With a battery life of only 2.5 hours, and no option for an extended battery, you'll want to make sure the unit is fully charged before using it, and be sure to bring the AC adaptor with you.

Figure 10-35 Great for taking videos with you, the DVD-LV50 is small and light.

The DVD-LV50 is a good deal, especially if you're looking for a DVD player to hook up to your TV set. With a remote control, the DVD-LV50 performs every bit as well as a full-sized DVD player when connected to your home theater system. If you're keen to share your videos with others on DVD or VCD, the ability to connect the DVD-LV50 to a TV set for viewing makes this really easy.

Key Points

- Sharing your video on discs gives you a lasting, durable format for keeping your memories safe for years.

- Burning a video disc is easy with an application like Ulead DVD MovieFactory.

- Transferring your edited video to a VHS tape is best accomplished using your DV camera as a transfer mechanism.

- Avery produces the best-quality labels and covers for creating a polished package.

- Pocket PCs are powerful multimedia devices, and you can use the 9 Series Windows Media Encoder to prepare your video files for these devices.

- Portable DVD players and portable media players are a great way to carry your videos with you.

Appendix
Digital Video Resources

The resources listed in this appendix are designed to give you starting places for further learning. There are some fantastic Web sites worth book-marking for further reading, newsgroups great for community sharing, and magazines that will keep you up to date. If you love learning like I do, you'll find these resources invaluable. It's not a bad idea to do a Google search for "digital video" every few months to see what new sites pop up.

Web Resources

- **Faster Smarter**   A companion site (*www.fastersmarter.com*) launched to serve as an online resource for this book, my goal with this site is to make it a daily visiting spot for anyone interested in digital video, digital audio, or digital photography. My passions run deep in all three of these areas, so creating a Web site and online community around them was a natural fit. By the time you're reading this, the site should be in full swing. Stop by!

- **Adam Wilt.com**   For advanced digital video enthusiasts, or for intermediate users wanting to deepen their knowledge, this site (*www.adamwilt.com*) is a gem. From the information-packed FAQ, to the bits of valuable information in the Video Tidbits section, this is one of the best sites for raw knowledge. It's not much to look at, but if you want to deepen your knowledge of digital video, this is one site you should bookmark. I looked to this site for information when researching certain concepts, so I give it my highest recommendation.

- **Digital Video Editing**   A frequently updated site, Digital Video Editing (*www.digitalvideoediting.com*) covers all the bases for those of us who call digital video a personal passion. The editorials by Charlie White are fantastic, and the product reviews are top notch. This site combines a professional edge with the personality of an independent site. This is a great resource.

■ **Digital Video.com** Only one guess what this site (*www.dv.com*) is about! News, columns, and in-depth features are available on this site. You'll need to register in order to access most of the content, but it's free and simple. A CMP Media site, it has more of a professional flair than most other sites I found. A good, quality site.

■ **DivX.com** If you're looking to encode your video to DivX format, there's no better source on doing so than this site (*www.divx.com*). The forums are particularly active, so there's some great peer-to-peer knowledge being exchanged on everything DivX.

■ **Pinnacle Video Vignettes** Home to the dynamic duo of Scott and Eric, Pinnacle Video Vignettes (*www.pinnaclesys.com/ads/vin/index.html*) are short video clips that introduce users to basic concepts using a dash of flair and humor.

■ **Adobe Digital Video Primer** Available in PDF format, this document from Adobe is a 50-page primer on digital video (*www.adobe.com/motion/primers.html*). It's a good resource that complements this book because it goes into more technical information than I do in some sections. I wouldn't recommend this primer for beginners, but if you're an intermediate user, give this a go—Adobe did a great job with this document.

■ **Camcorderinfo.com** A solid blend of daily news bits, reviews, and useful tutorials, this site (*www.camcorderinfo.com*) is run by a team of people who clearly know what they're doing. It's a good resource to bookmark for keeping up to date on the world of digital video.

■ **Consumer DV Reviews.com** One of the things I enjoy most about this site (*www.consumerdvreviews.com*) is the way they've collected together the most popular DV cameras and their specs, including information on the lowest prices for each camera. Frequent news updates make this site one worth frequent visits.

■ **Luke's Video Guide** Although it's mostly aimed at the topic of how to capture, compress, and encode cartoons, this site (*www.lukesvideo.com*)

has some good resources for understanding concepts like interlacing, comparing codec quality, and encoding video.

- **Doom9.net**   Created for those who wish to back up their DVDs, this site (*www.doom9.net*) is no stranger to controversy. Does "fair use" include making a backup copy of a DVD in case the original is lost or stolen? Doom9.net says yes, but the Digital Millennium Copyright Act (DMCA) says no. Backing up your DVDs is a multi-step process not for the faint of heart, but the methods covered by this site will help you do just that, as well as create versions of the movies in VCD and SVCD formats.

- **Mike Shaw's Pages**   Mike Shaw is a big fan of Pinnacle Studio video-editing software, and he's created a whole Web site (*http://www.mikeshaw.co.uk*) devoted to helping people understand Studio and what it can do. He also sells a CD-ROM full of tips and tutorials for Hollywood FX, so if you're interested in learning more about this tool, check the site out.

- **PapaJohn's Video Encoding Page**   A regular in many video newsgroups, "PapaJohn" has created a useful page (*http://pws.chartermi.net/~papajohn/WindowsMedia.html*) with samples from various video encoders. This allows you to compare his video source file with different encoders on the market, including the 9 Series Windows Media Encoder, Adobe Premier, TMPGEnc, and others.

USENET (Newsgroup) Resources

- **alt.video**   A general catchall for all manner of video topics, this newsgroup includes some discussion on digital video, but a great deal of the messages focus on other aspects of video—equipment (both analog and digital), professionals swapping tips, and the like.

- **alt.video.dvd.authoring and alt.video.dvd.software**   Primarily for the discussion of DVD creation, these groups focus on DVD-burning software, hardware and best practices.

- **comp.graphics.apps.ulead**   Although it says "graphics," this newsgroup is the only USENET newsgroup specific to Ulead products, so quite a bit of discussion goes on here about Media Studio Pro and Ulead's other video products.

■ **rec.video and rec.video.desktop**   By far my two favorite news-groups for peer-to-peer video discussion, these groups contain some fantastic knowledge. I learned a lot by asking questions, and it's a good exercise of your knowledge to help others with their problems. *rec.video* focuses more on issues for professionals, while *rec.video.desktop* handles most of the consumer-level hardware and software levels. Both groups are frequented by highly experienced people willing to share their knowledge with others.

Magazines

■ *Computer Videomaker*   A professional publication from beginning to end, Computer Videomaker is a full-color magazine that is aimed at intermediate-level users. Beginners will find it a little complex, but if you made it this far in the book I think you can handle the magazine without trouble. I really like this publication—a nice combination of reviews, columns, and practical "how to" guides make it a good resource for keeping up to speed on the world of digital video. Although some people predicted the death of print media when the Web became popular, the depth of coverage in this magazine can't be matched by most of the Web sites I found. The ads were almost as fun to look at as the articles!

■ *Camcorder & Computer Video*   Another great magazine, Cam-corder & Computer Video magazine is aimed more at the beginner. With articles such as "Shooting like a Pro," the magazine covers things that a beginner would need to know. More experienced readers will still find the magazine highly useful though—the hardware and soft-ware reviews were quite strong. I found it a little distracting that the magazine was partially in color and partially in greyscale, but the con-tent was solid—check your local newsstand and pick up a copy.

Index

Jason R. Dunn

Jason R. Dunn is an avid digital media enthusiast whose interests run deep into digital video, graphic design, and user interface design. He is an experienced classroom instructor, he's written several technology books, and he publishes a popular news and views Web site for the Pocket PC.

The manuscript for this book was prepared and submitted to Microsoft Press in electronic form. Pages were composed by nSight, Inc., using Adobe FrameMaker+SGML for Windows, with text in Garamond and display type in ITC Franklin Gothic Condensed. Composed pages were delivered to the printer as electronic pre-press files.

Cover designer:	Tim Girvin Design
Interior Graphic Designer:	James D. Kramer
Principal Compositor:	Beth McDermott
Project Manager:	Carmen Corral-Reid
Copy Editor:	Joe Gustaitis
Technical Editor:	Jana Sweeney, Don Lesser
Proofreaders:	Asa Tomash, Robert Saley
Indexer:	Jack Lewis

Learn how to get the job done every day—
faster, smarter, and easier!

Faster Smarter Digital Photography	**Faster Smarter Microsoft® Office XP**	**Faster Smarter Microsoft Windows® XP**	**Faster Smarter Home Networking**
ISBN: 0-7356-1872-0	ISBN: 0-7356-1862-3	ISBN: 0-7356-1857-7	ISBN: 0-7356-1869-0
U.S.A. $19.99	U.S.A. $19.99	U.S.A. $19.99	U.S.A. $19.99
Canada $28.99	Canada $28.99	Canada $28.99	Canada $28.99

cover how to do exactly what you do with computers and technology—faster, smarter, and easier—with FASTER SMARTER
ks from Microsoft Press! They're your everyday guides for learning the practicalities of how to make technology work
way you want—fast. Their language is friendly and down-to-earth, with no jargon or silly chatter, and with accurate how-
nformation that's easy to absorb and apply. Use the concise explanations, easy numbered steps, and visual examples
understand exactly what you need to do to get the job done—whether you're using a PC at home or in business,
turing and sharing digital still images, getting a home network running, or finishing other tasks.

Microsoft Press has other FASTER SMARTER titles to help you get the job done every day:

Faster Smarter PCs
ISBN: 0-7356-1780-5

Faster Smarter Microsoft Windows 98
ISBN: 0-7356-1858-5

Faster Smarter Beginning Programming
ISBN: 0-7356-1780-5

Faster Smarter Digital Video
ISBN: 0-7356-1873-9

Faster Smarter Web Page Creation
ISBN: 0-7356-1860-7

Faster Smarter HTML & XML
ISBN: 0-7356-1861-5

Faster Smarter Internet
ISBN: 0-7356-1859-3

Faster Smarter Money 2003
ISBN: 0-7356-1864-X

To learn more about the full line of Microsoft Press® products, please visit us at:

microsoft.com/mspress

Work smarter—
conquer your software *from the inside out!*

Hey, you know your way around a desktop. Now dig into Office XP applications and the Windows XP operating system and *really* put your PC to work! These supremely organized software reference titles pack hundreds of timesaving solutions, troubleshooting tips and tricks, and handy workarounds in a concise, fast-answer format. They're all muscle and no fluff. All this comprehensive information goes deep into the nooks and crannies of each Office application and Windows XP feature. INSIDE OUT titles also include a CD-ROM full of handy tools and utilities, sample files, an eBook links to related sites, and other help. Discover the best and fastest ways to perform everyday tasks, and challenge yourself to new levels of software mastery!

MICROSOFT® WINDOWS® XP INSIDE OUT
ISBN 0-7356-1382-6

**MICROSOFT WINDOWS SECURITY INSIDE OUT
FOR WINDOWS XP AND WINDOWS 2000**
ISBN 0-7356-1632-9

MICROSOFT OFFICE XP INSIDE OUT
ISBN 0-7356-1277-3

MICROSOFT OFFICE V. X FOR MAC INSIDE OUT
ISBN 0-7356-1628-0

MICROSOFT WORD VERSION 2002 INSIDE OUT
ISBN 0-7356-1278-1

MICROSOFT EXCEL VERSION 2002 INSIDE OUT
ISBN 0-7356-1281-1

MICROSOFT OUTLOOK® VERSION 2002 INSIDE OUT
ISBN 0-7356-1282-X

MICROSOFT ACCESS VERSION 2002 INSIDE OUT
ISBN 0-7356-1283-8

MICROSOFT FRONTPAGE® VERSION 2002 INSIDE OUT
ISBN 0-7356-1284-6

MICROSOFT VISIO® VERSION 2002 INSIDE OUT
ISBN 0-7356-1285-4

MICROSOFT PROJECT VERSION 2002 INSIDE OUT
ISBN 0-7356-1124-6

Microsoft
microsoft.com/mspress

Self-paced
training that works
as hard as you do!

Information-packed STEP BY STEP courses are the most effective way to teach yourself how to complete tasks with the Microsoft Windows operating system and Microsoft Office applications. Numbered steps and scenario-based lessons with practice files on CD-ROM make it easy to find your way while learning tasks and procedures. Work through every lesson or choose your own starting point—with STEP BY STEP'S modular design and straightforward writing style, *you* drive the instruction. And the books are constructed with lay-flat binding so you can follow the text with both hands at the keyboard. Select STEP BY STEP titles also prepare you for the Microsoft Office User Specialist (MOUS) credential. It's an excellent way for you or your organization to take a giant step toward workplace productivity.

Microsoft Press also has STEP BY STEP titles to help you use earlier versions of Microsoft software.

- **Home Networking with Microsoft® Windows® XP Step by Step**
  ISBN 0-7356-1435-0

- **Microsoft Windows XP Step by Step**
  ISBN 0-7356-1383-4

- **Microsoft Office XP Step by Step**
  ISBN 0-7356-1294-3

- **Microsoft Word Version 2002 Step by Step**
  ISBN 0-7356-1295-1

- **Microsoft Project Version 2002 Step by Step**
  ISBN 0-7356-1301-X

- **Microsoft Excel Version 2002 Step by Step**
  ISBN 0-7356-1296-X

- **Microsoft PowerPoint® Version 2002 Step by Step**
  ISBN 0-7356-1297-8

- **Microsoft Outlook® Version 2002 Step by Step**
  ISBN 0-7356-1298-6

- **Microsoft FrontPage® Version 2002 Step by Step**
  ISBN 0-7356-1300-1

- **Microsoft Access Version 2002 Step by Step**
  ISBN 0-7356-1299-4

- **Microsoft Visio® Version 2002 Step by Step**
  ISBN 0-7356-1302-8

microsoft.com/mspress

Get a **Free**
*e-mail newsletter, updates,
special offers, links to related books,
and more when you*
register on line!

Register your Microsoft Press® title on our Web site and you'll get a FREE subscription to our e-mail newsletter, *Microsoft Press Book Connections.* You'll find out about newly released and upcoming books and learning tools, online events, software downloads, special offers and coupons for Microsoft Press customers, and information about major Microsoft® product releases. You can also read useful additional information about all the titles we publish, such as detailed book descriptions, tables of contents and indexes, sample chapters, links to related books and book series, author biographies, and reviews by other customers.

Registration is easy. Just visit this Web page and fill in your information:

http://www.microsoft.com/mspress/register

Microsoft

Proof of Purchase

Use this page as proof of purchase if participating in a promotion or rebate offer on this title. Proof of purchase must be used in conjunction with other proof(s) of payment such as your dated sales receipt—see offer details.

Faster Smarter Digital Video

0-7356-1873-9

CUSTOMER NAME

Microsoft Press, PO Box 97017, Redmond, WA 98073-9830